CERES
Celestial Legend
Volume 3: Suzumi
Shôjo Edition (2nd Edition)

This volume contains the CERES: CELESTIAL LEGEND installments
from Part 3, issue 1, through Part 3, issue 4, in their entirety.

STORY & ART BY YUU WATASE

English Adaptation/Gary Leach
Translation/Lillian Olsen
Touch-up Art & Lettering/Bill Schuch
Cover Design & Layout/Hidemi Sahara
Editor — 1st Edition/Andy Nakatani
Shôjo Edition Editors/Elizabeth Kawasaki and Andy Nakatani

Editor in Chief, Books/Alvin Lu
Editor in Chief, Magazines/Marc Weidenbaum
VP of Publishing Licensing/Rika Inouye
VP of Sales/Gonzalo Ferreyra
Sr. VP of Marketing/Liza Coppola
Publisher/Hyoe Narita

© 1997 Yuu WATASE/Shogakukan Inc. First published by Shogakukan Inc. in Japan as "Ayashi no Ceres."
New and adapted artwork and text © 2004 VIZ Media, LLC. All rights reserved.

The rights of the author(s) of the work(s) in this publication to be so identified have been asserted
in accordance with the Copyright, Designs and Patents Act 1988. A CIP catalogue record for this book
is available from the British Library.

Printed in the U.S.A.

Published by VIZ Media, LLC
P.O. Box 77010
San Francisco CA 94107

Shôjo Edition

10 9 8 7 6 5 4

First printing, April 2004
First English edition, January 2003
Fourth printing, December 2007

www.viz.com
store.viz.com

VIZ GRAPHIC NOVEL

CERES
Celestial Legend
Vol. 3: SUZUMI

Story and Art by
Yuu Watase

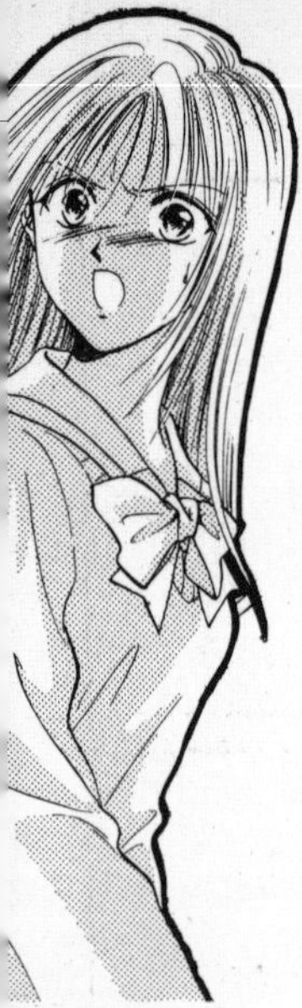

Aya Mikage is a boisterous, modern 16-year-old whose mind and body are being taken over by Ceres, a heavenly maiden with celestial powers who is obsessed with revenge against the Mikage family. In order to stop Ceres, Aya's own family tries to kill her. Amid the chaos, Aya falls for Tôya, a man hired by the Mikages to keep an eye on her.

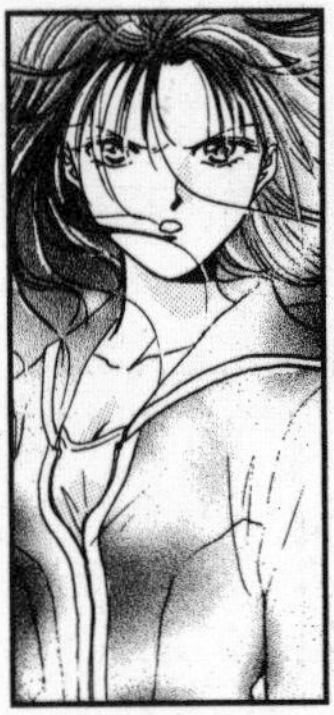

Ceres is a legendary tennyo, a celestial maiden, who inhabits Aya's mind and body. She vows to use her celestial powers against the descendants of the Mikage man who stole her hagoromo (celestial robe) ages ago, preventing her from returning to the heavens.

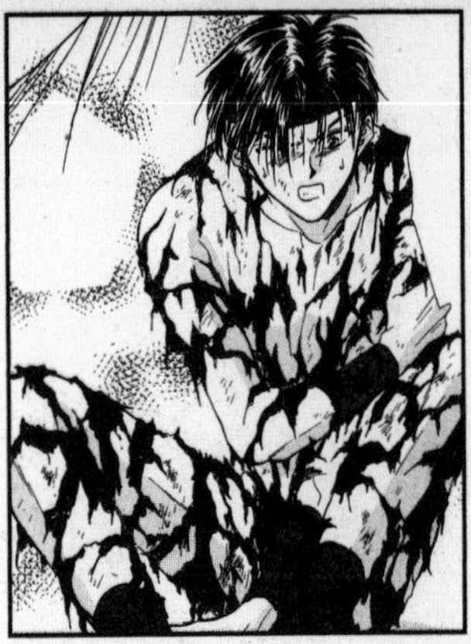

Yûhi Aogiri is Suzumi's brother-in-law, an aspiring chef and a proficient martial artist whom Suzumi has ordered to guard Aya. When he and Aya discover a classmate passed out on the street and take her to the infirmary, they discover Tôya has been planted as the school doctor to spy on Aya.

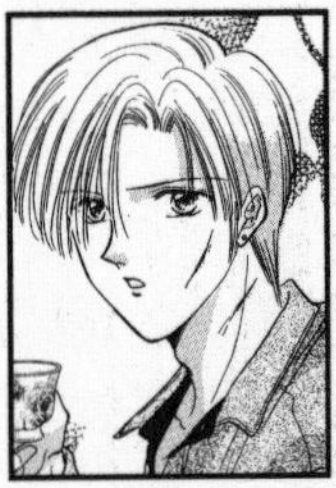

Aki Mikage is Aya's nice-guy twin brother who is taken into protective seclusion by his family to separate him from Aya. Aki is one of the subjects in the C-Project—a nefarious plan to use the power of the descendants of tennyo for the greater glory of the Mikage—because his cousin Kagami believes he bears the consciousness of the founder of the Mikage family (the man who stole Ceres' robes).

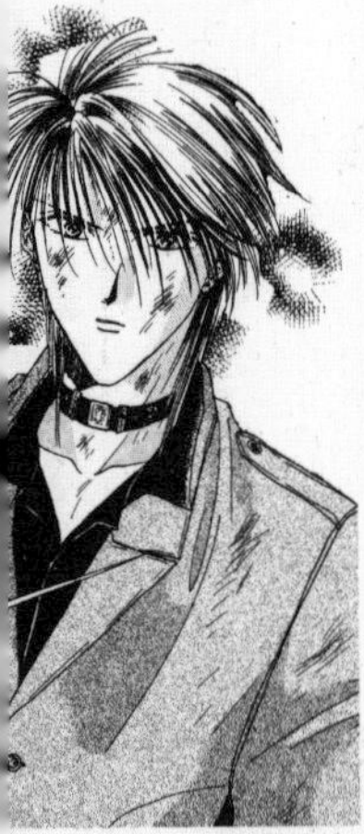

Tôya, a handsome but mysterious stranger who has amnesia, works for the Mikages with the hope that their advanced technology can help him regain his memory. However, he always feels compelled to help Aya escape dangerous situations.

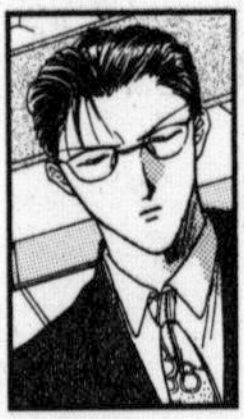

Kagami Mikage, Aya's cousin, has plans for Aya, Aki and Tôya. The Mikage family wants to kill Ceres through Aya, but as the head of Mikage International's research and development team, Kagami masterminds the C-Project, a plan to further his own agenda through the descendants of tennyo.

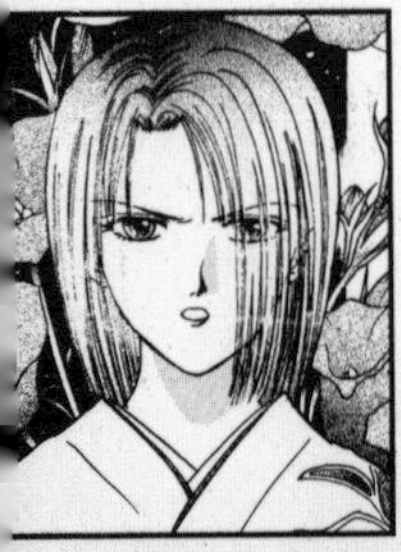

Suzumi Aogiri is a Japanese dance teacher and a descendant of a tennyo. She takes Aya into her home and tries to support and protect her, along with her brother-in-law Yûhi and faithful servant Mrs. Q.

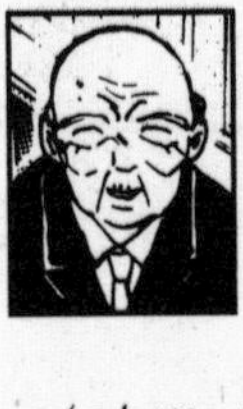

Grandpa Mikage is the head of the Mikage household and chairman of Mikage International, a vast corporation.

Mrs. Q (Oda Kyu) is the bizarre but faithful servant of Suzumi's household who occasionally provides comic relief.

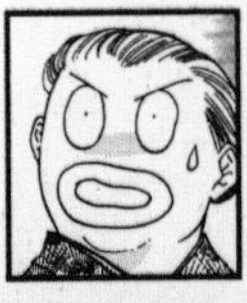

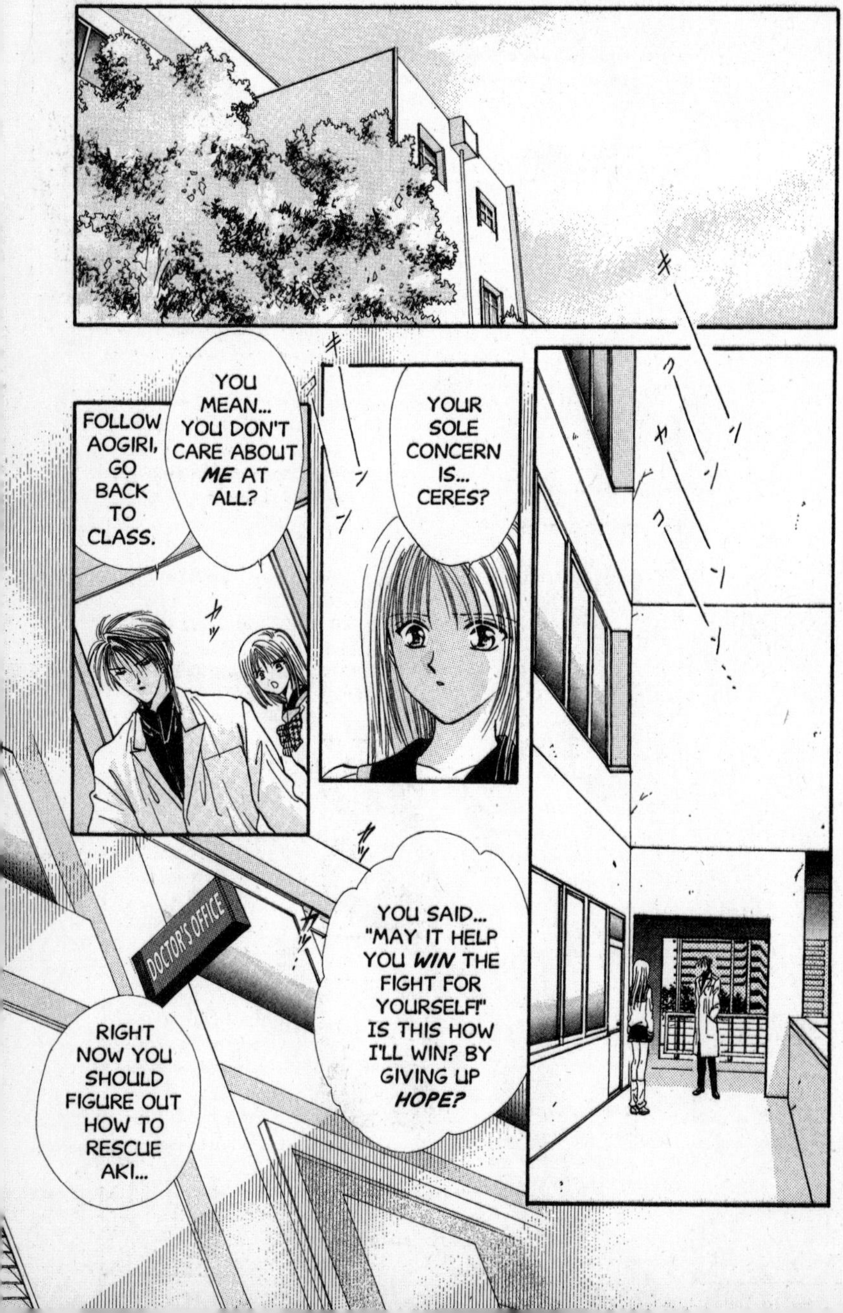
YOUR SOLE CONCERN IS... CERES?
YOU MEAN... YOU DON'T CARE ABOUT *ME* AT ALL?
FOLLOW AOGIRI, GO BACK TO CLASS.
YOU SAID... "MAY IT HELP YOU *WIN* THE FIGHT FOR YOURSELF!" IS THIS HOW I'LL WIN? BY GIVING UP *HOPE?*
DOCTOR'S OFFICE
RIGHT NOW YOU SHOULD FIGURE OUT HOW TO RESCUE AKI...

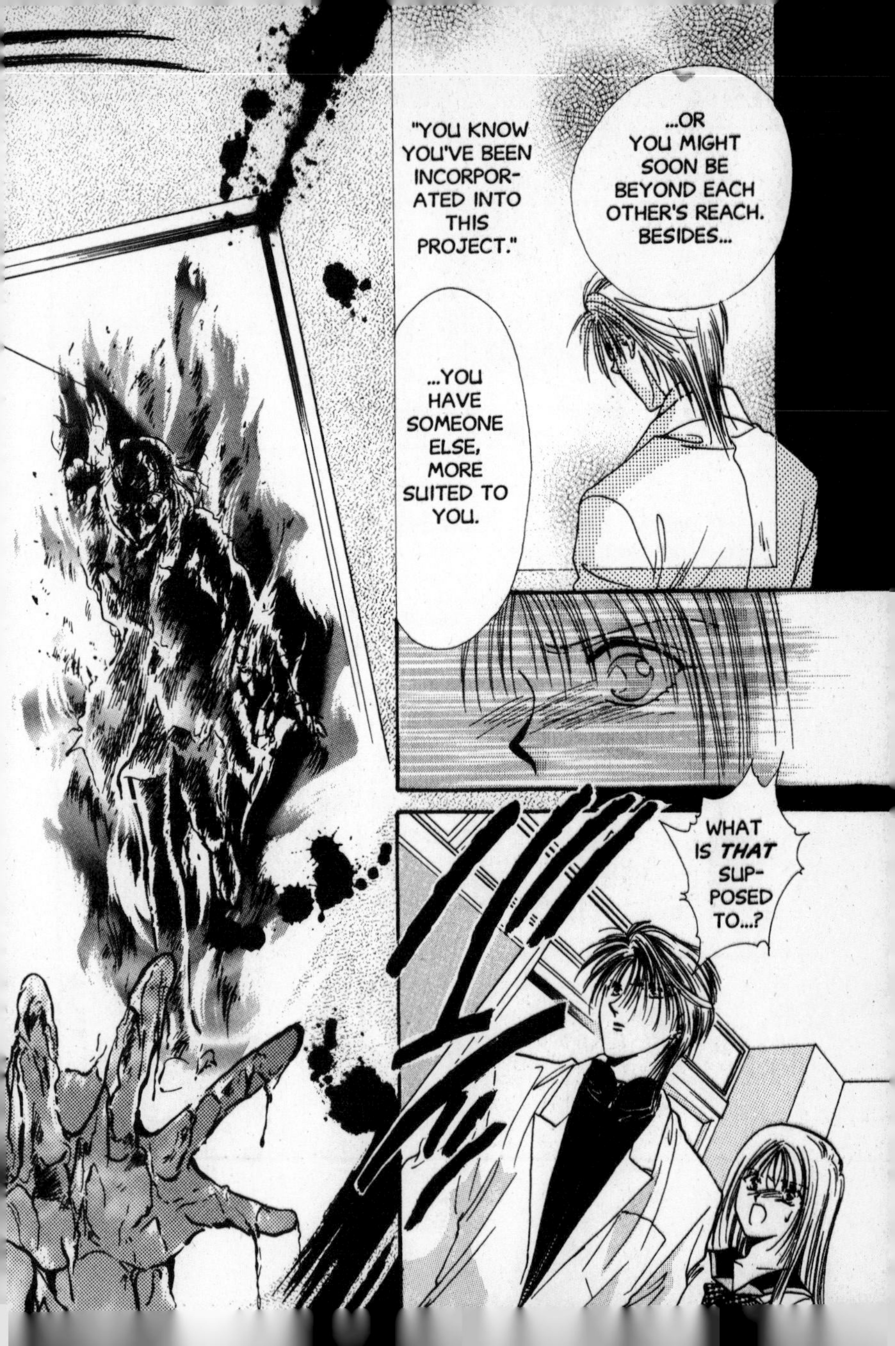
...OR YOU MIGHT SOON BE BEYOND EACH OTHER'S REACH. BESIDES...
"YOU KNOW YOU'VE BEEN INCORPOR-ATED INTO THIS PROJECT."
...YOU HAVE SOMEONE ELSE, MORE SUITED TO YOU.
WHAT IS *THAT* SUP-POSED TO...?

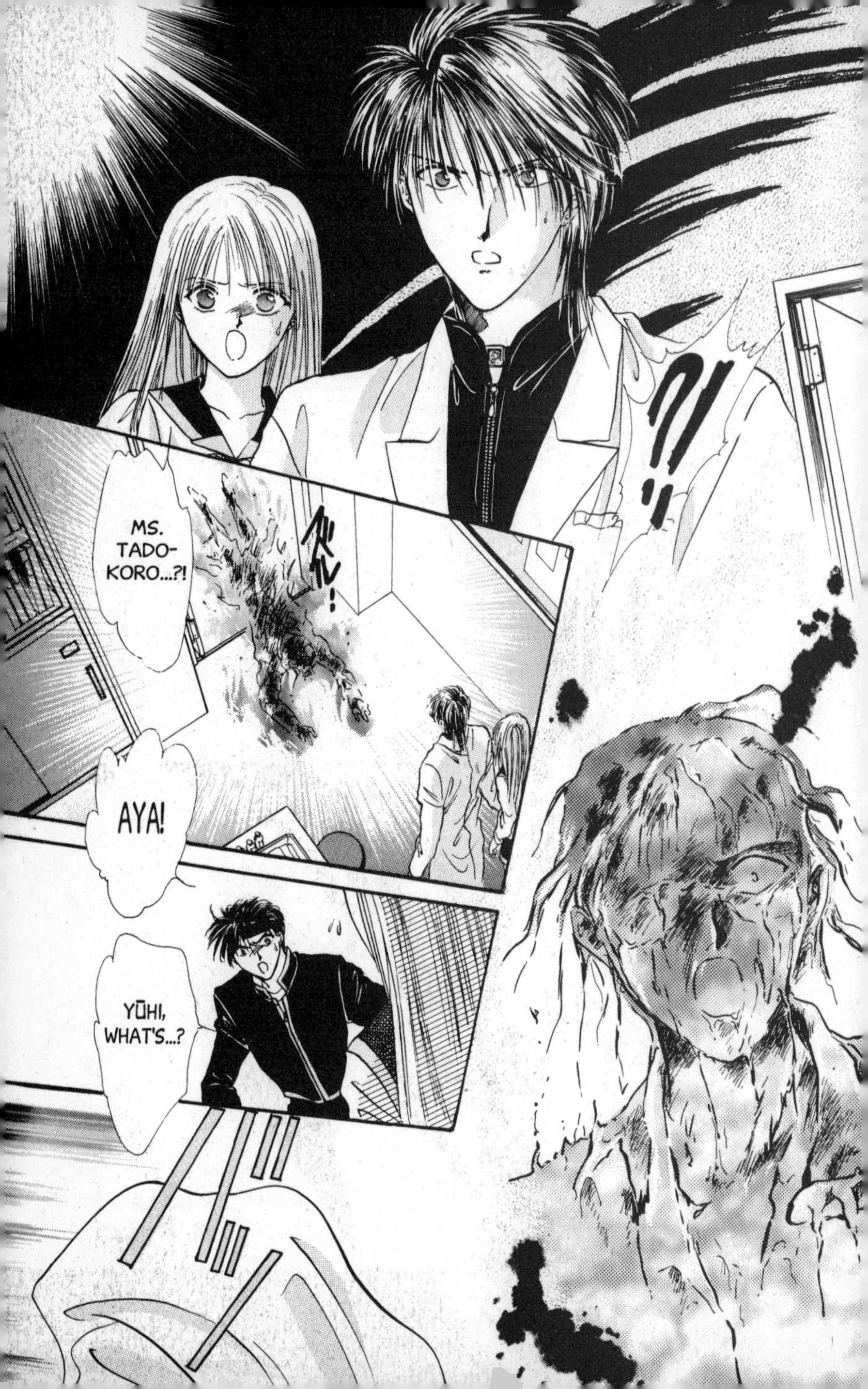
?!!
MS. TADO-KORO...?!
AYA!
YŪHI, WHAT'S...?

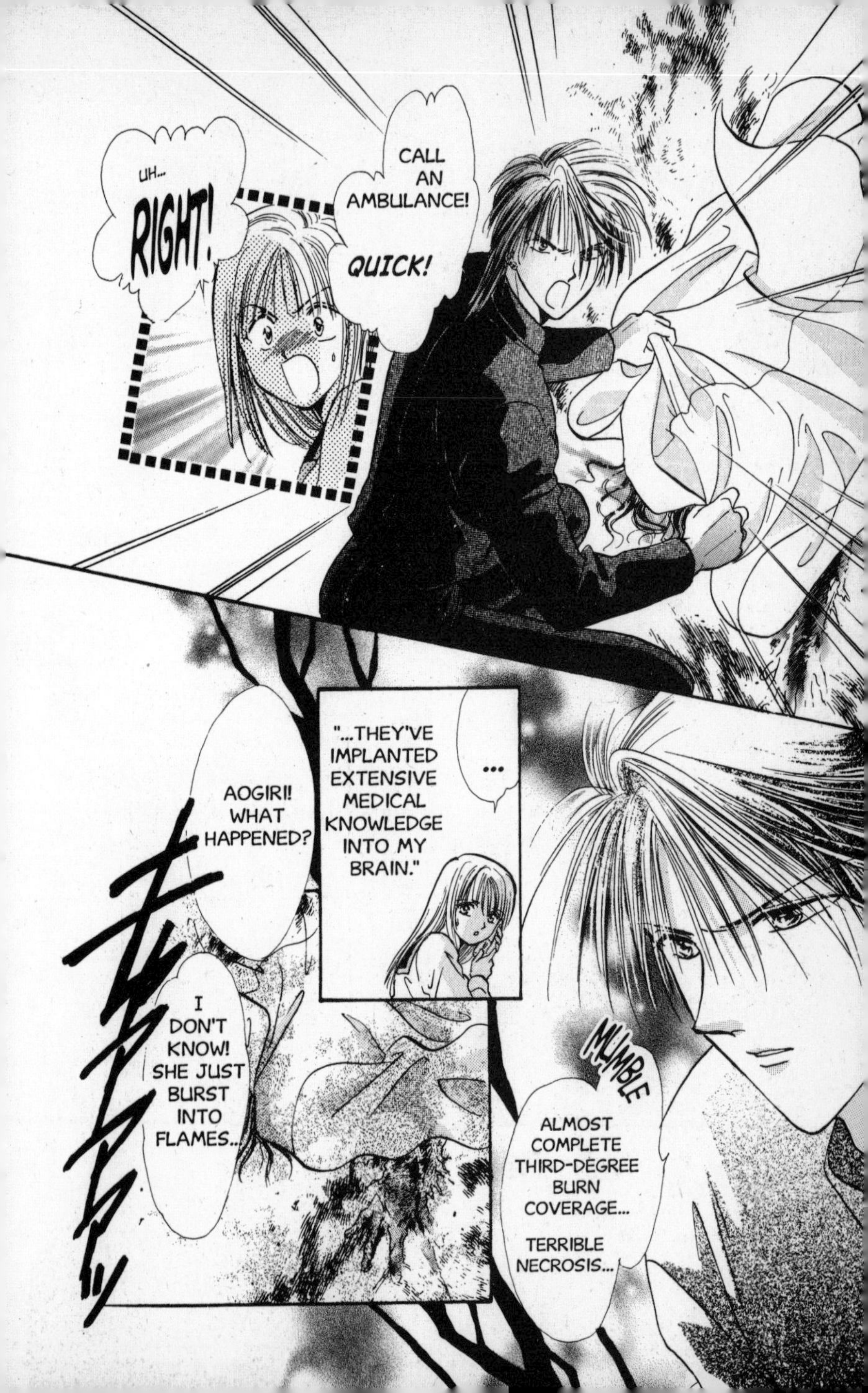
CALL AN AMBULANCE!
QUICK!
UH... RIGHT!
MUMBLE
ALMOST COMPLETE THIRD-DEGREE BURN COVERAGE...
TERRIBLE NECROSIS...
...
"...THEY'VE IMPLANTED EXTENSIVE MEDICAL KNOWLEDGE INTO MY BRAIN."
AOGIRI! WHAT HAPPENED?
I DON'T KNOW! SHE JUST BURST INTO FLAMES...

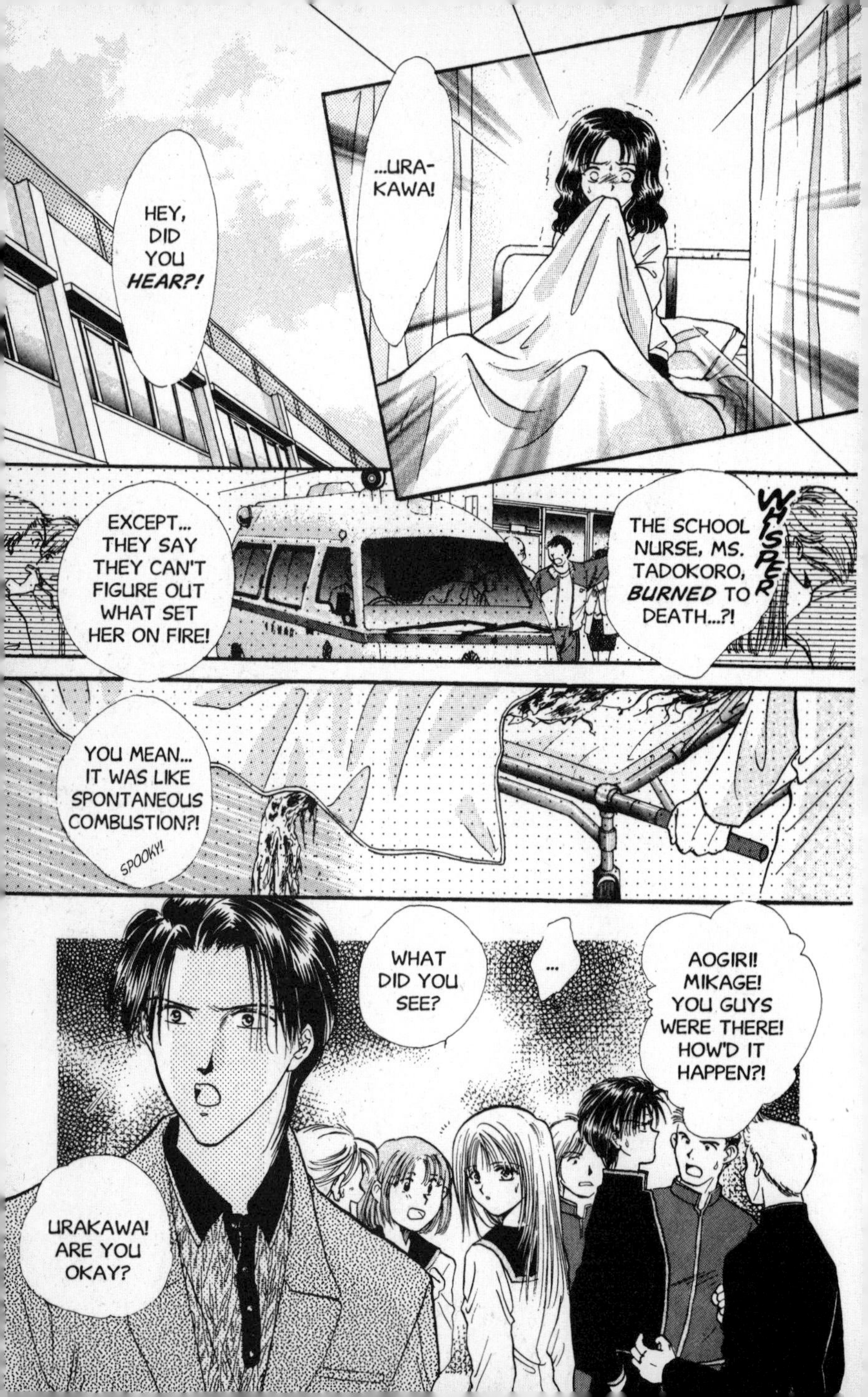
...URA-KAWA!
HEY, DID YOU HEAR?!
WHISPER
THE SCHOOL NURSE, MS. TADOKORO, BURNED TO DEATH...?!
EXCEPT... THEY SAY THEY CAN'T FIGURE OUT WHAT SET HER ON FIRE!
YOU MEAN... IT WAS LIKE SPONTANEOUS COMBUSTION?!
SPOOKY!
AOGIRI! MIKAGE! YOU GUYS WERE THERE! HOW'D IT HAPPEN?!
...
WHAT DID YOU SEE?
URAKAWA! ARE YOU OKAY?

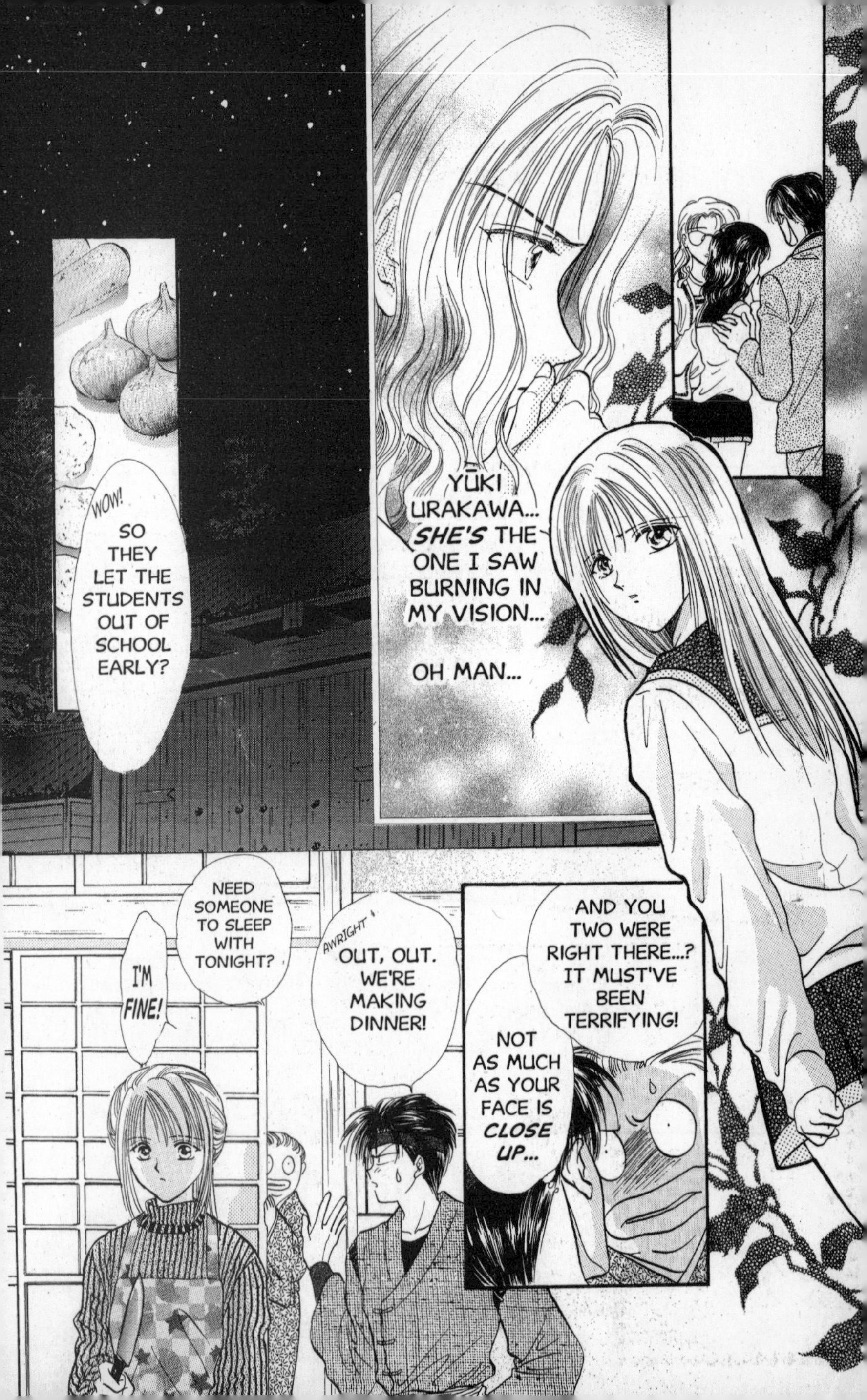
YŪKI URAKAWA... *SHE'S* THE ONE I SAW BURNING IN MY VISION...
OH MAN...
WOW!
SO THEY LET THE STUDENTS OUT OF SCHOOL EARLY?
AND YOU TWO WERE RIGHT THERE...? IT MUST'VE BEEN TERRIFYING!
NOT AS MUCH AS YOUR FACE IS *CLOSE UP*...
AWRIGHT
OUT, OUT. WE'RE MAKING DINNER!
NEED SOMEONE TO SLEEP WITH TONIGHT?
I'M *FINE!*

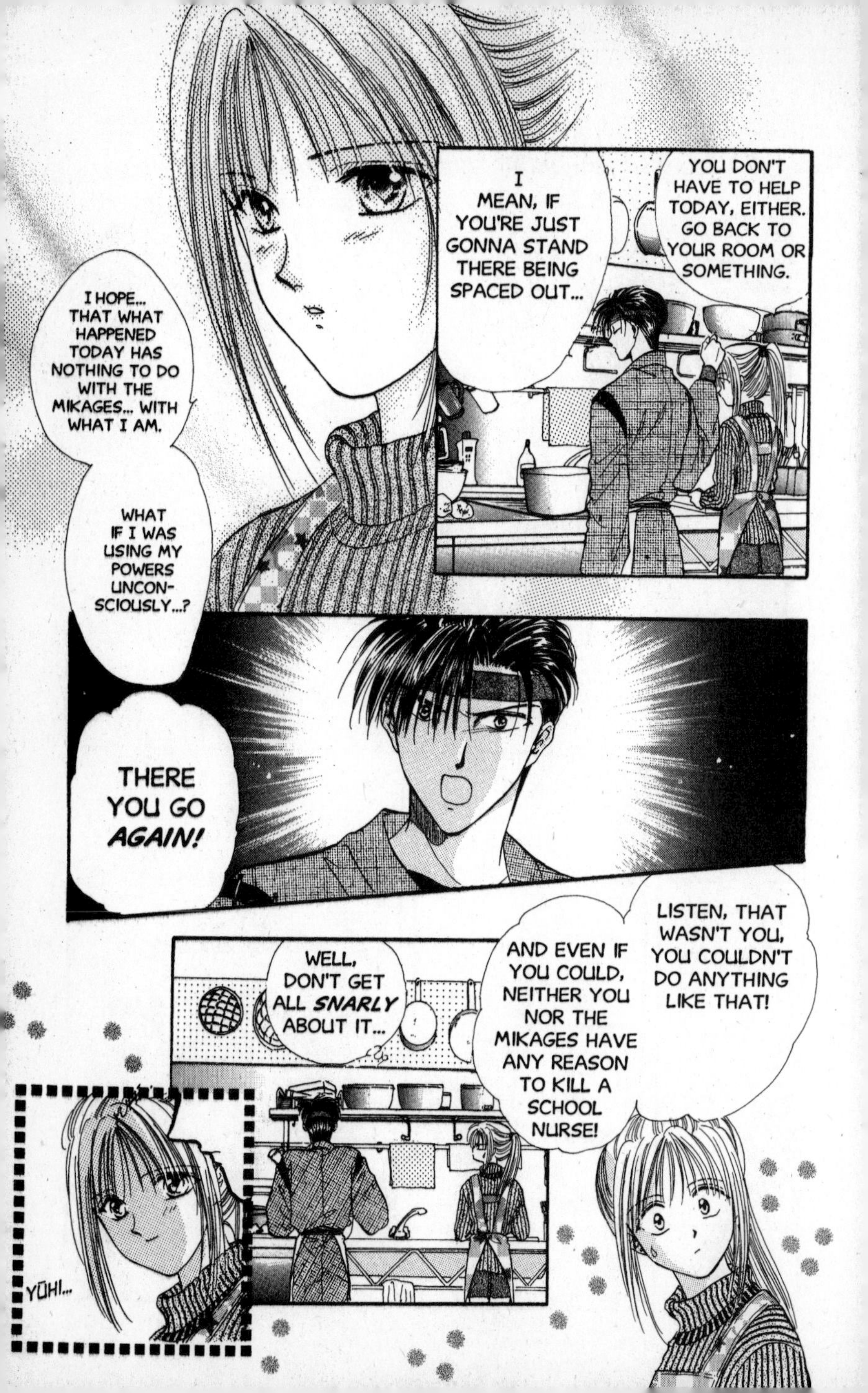
YOU DON'T HAVE TO HELP TODAY, EITHER. GO BACK TO YOUR ROOM OR SOMETHING.
I MEAN, IF YOU'RE JUST GONNA STAND THERE BEING SPACED OUT...
I HOPE... THAT WHAT HAPPENED TODAY HAS NOTHING TO DO WITH THE MIKAGES... WITH WHAT I AM.
WHAT IF I WAS USING MY POWERS UNCONSCIOUSLY...?
THERE YOU GO *AGAIN!*
LISTEN, THAT WASN'T YOU, YOU COULDN'T DO ANYTHING LIKE THAT!
AND EVEN IF YOU COULD, NEITHER YOU NOR THE MIKAGES HAVE ANY REASON TO KILL A SCHOOL NURSE!
WELL, DON'T GET ALL *SNARLY* ABOUT IT...
YŪHI...

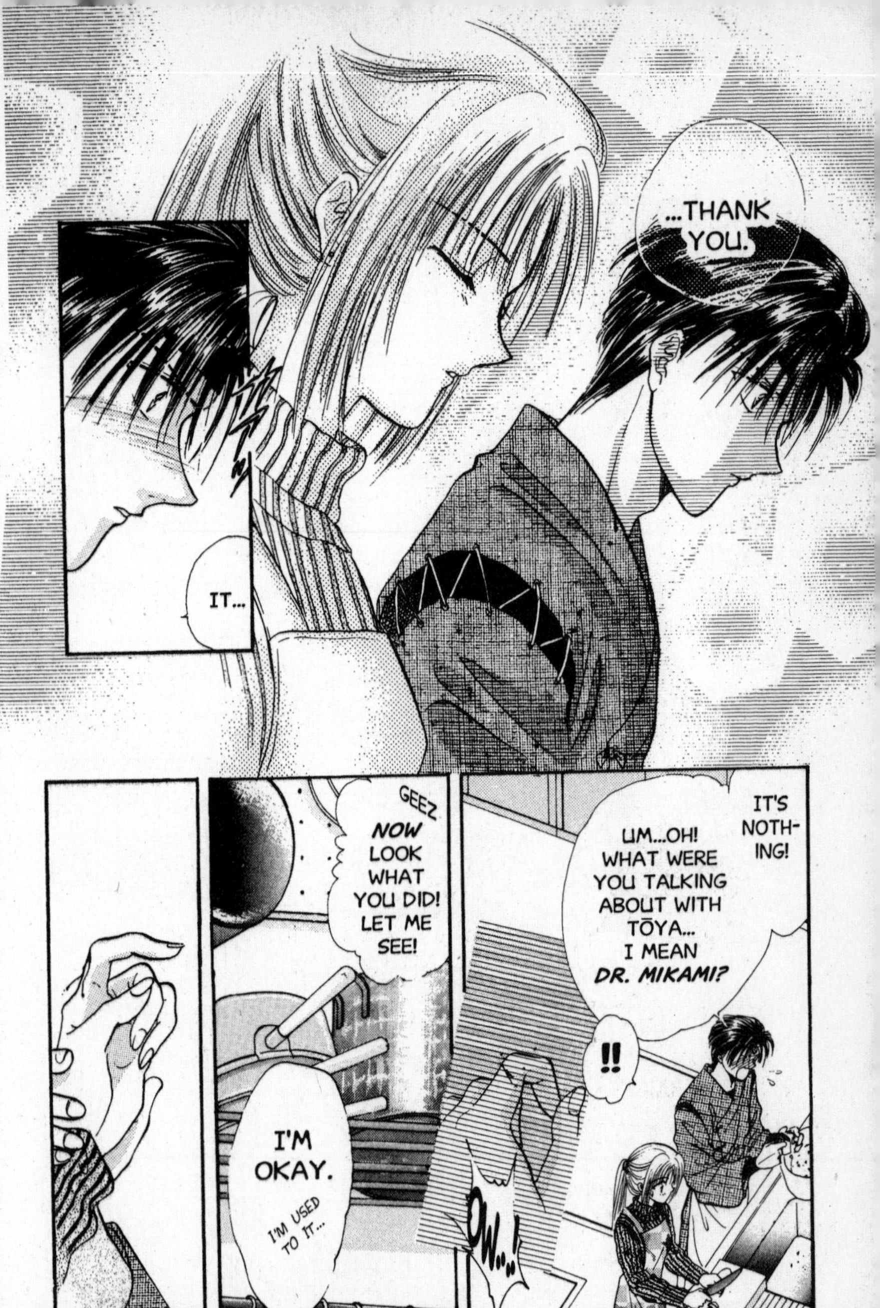
...THANK YOU.
IT...
IT'S NOTHING!
UM...OH! WHAT WERE YOU TALKING ABOUT WITH TŌYA... I MEAN *DR. MIKAMI?*
!!
OW...!
GEEZ
NOW LOOK WHAT YOU DID! LET ME SEE!
I'M OKAY.
I'M USED TO IT...

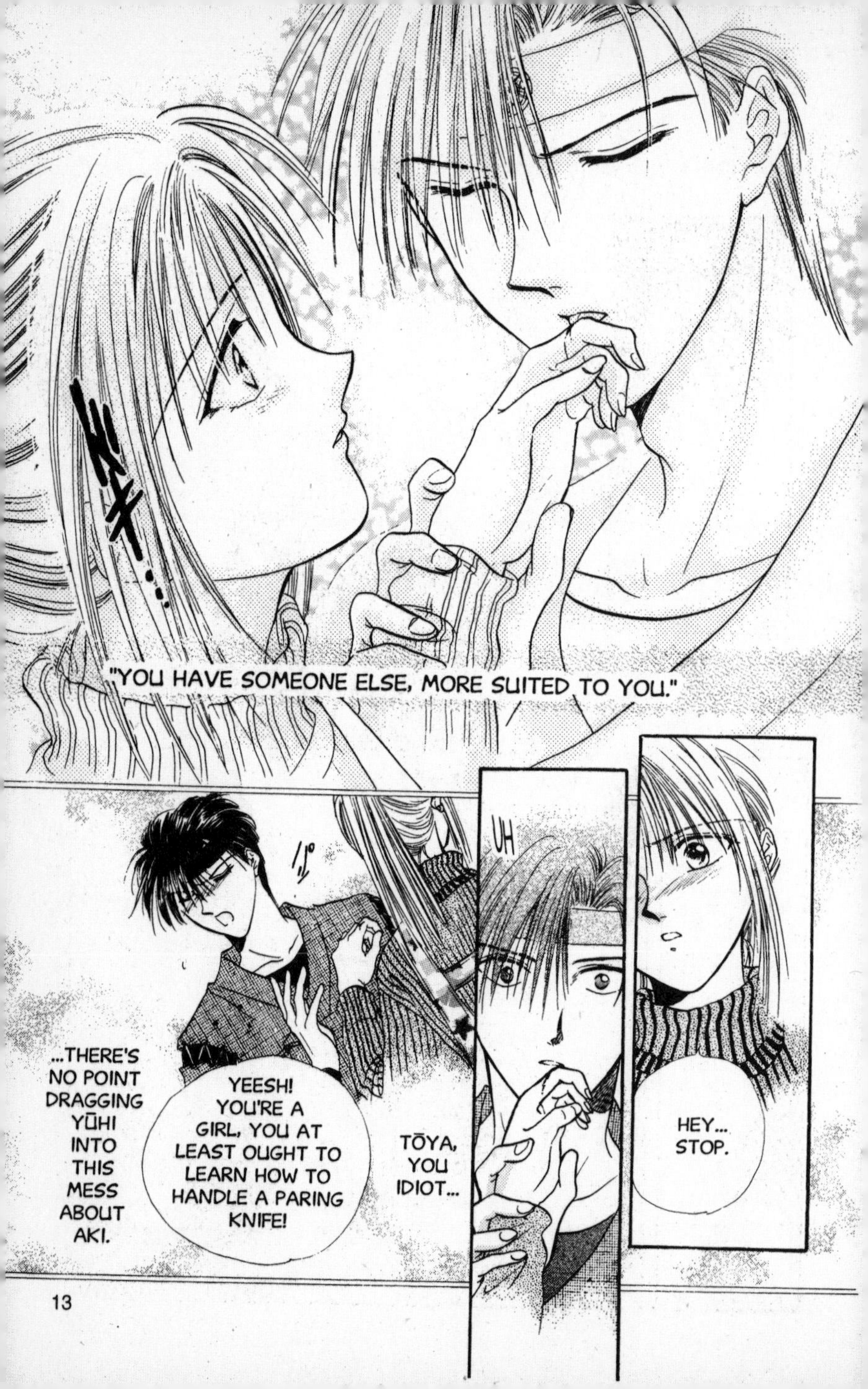
"YOU HAVE SOMEONE ELSE, MORE SUITED TO YOU."
HEY... STOP.
UH
TŌYA, YOU IDIOT...
YEESH! YOU'RE A GIRL, YOU AT LEAST OUGHT TO LEARN HOW TO HANDLE A PARING KNIFE!
...THERE'S NO POINT DRAGGING YŪHI INTO THIS MESS ABOUT AKI.

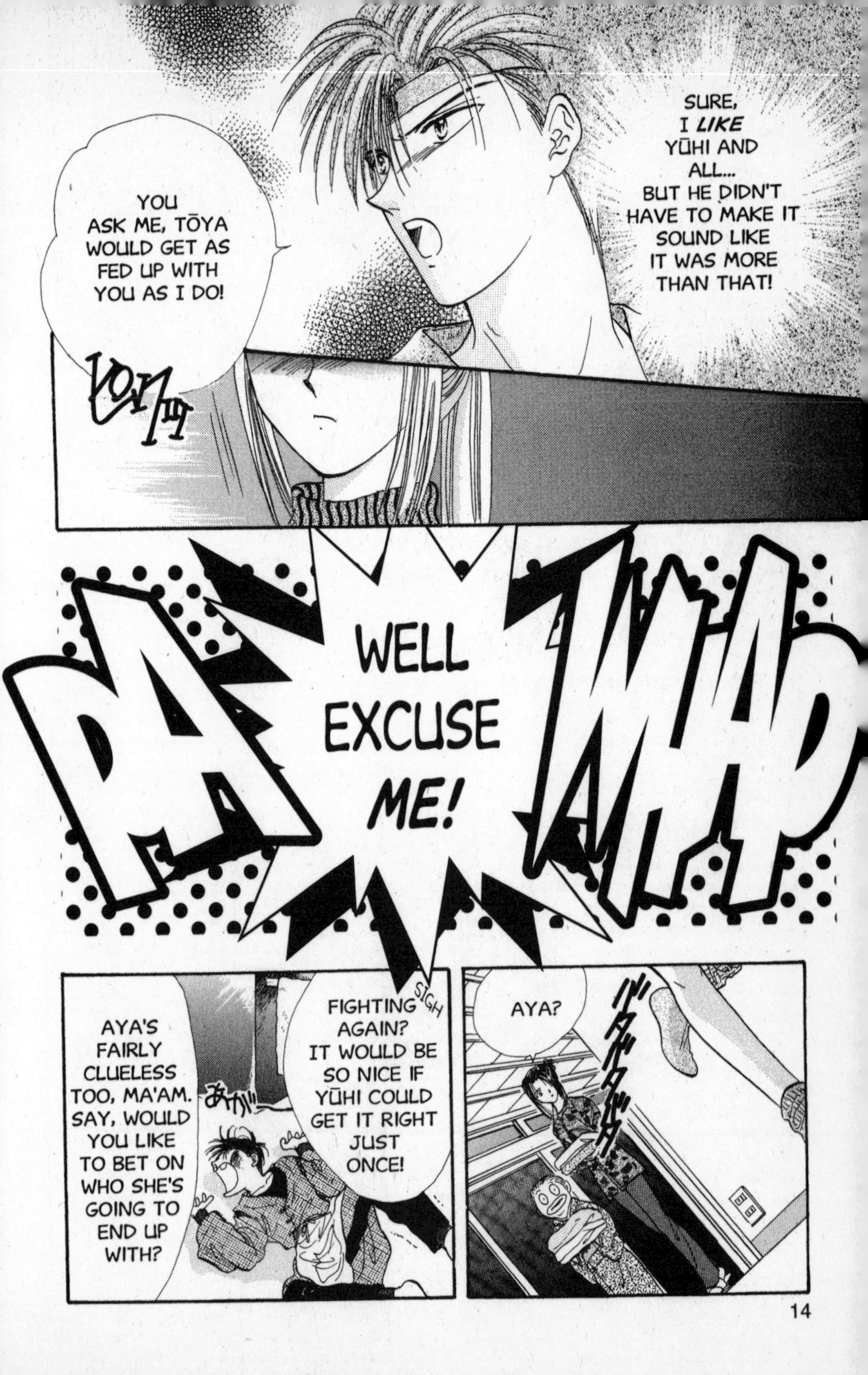
SURE, I *LIKE* YŪHI AND ALL... BUT HE DIDN'T HAVE TO MAKE IT SOUND LIKE IT WAS MORE THAN THAT!
YOU ASK ME, TŌYA WOULD GET AS FED UP WITH YOU AS I DO!
WELL EXCUSE *ME!*
PA WHAP
AYA?
FIGHTING AGAIN? IT WOULD BE SO NICE IF YŪHI COULD GET IT RIGHT JUST ONCE!
SIGH
AYA'S FAIRLY CLUELESS TOO, MA'AM. SAY, WOULD YOU LIKE TO BET ON WHO SHE'S GOING TO END UP WITH?

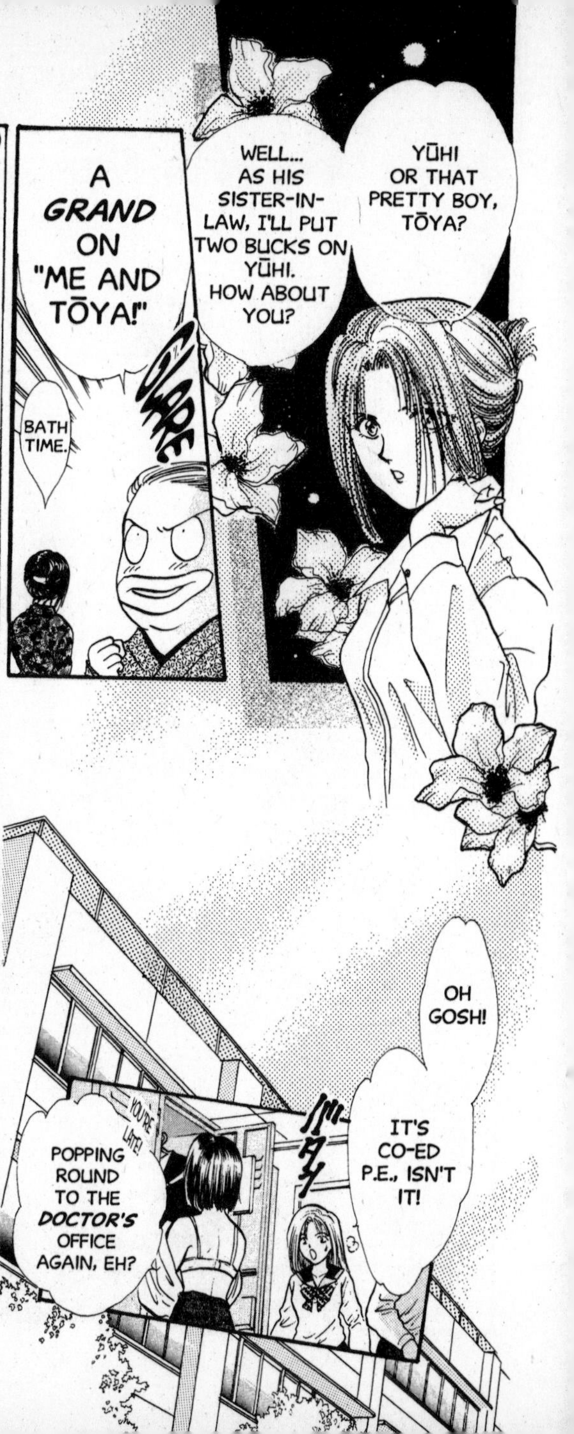
YŪHI OR THAT PRETTY BOY, TŌYA?
WELL... AS HIS SISTER-IN-LAW, I'LL PUT TWO BUCKS ON YŪHI. HOW ABOUT YOU?
A GRAND ON "ME AND TŌYA!"
GLARE
BATH TIME.
OH GOSH!
IT'S CO-ED P.E., ISN'T IT!
YOU'RE LATE!
POPPING ROUND TO THE DOCTOR'S OFFICE AGAIN, EH?

◆ SUZUMI ◆

Phew... (I'm starving already)
We're in the third volume already. Time flies! Thank you all for keeping up with the story. Somebody please think up the rest of the storyline.

No really, I **am** putting a lot of thought into it.

Manga that's based on someone else's story sounds so easy to do. Somebody else has already created the story for you. But I guess when it comes down to it I might not like doing it, precisely **because** it's not really mine. And it might be tough to put someone else's idea's down on paper. (I wouldn't know since I've never done it.) There really is no such thing as an easy job.

...Hmm, we're off to a whiny start; or rather, my fatigue is showing through. Why? Because I only got 3 hours of sleep! I'm sooo sleepy!

Wake up. I have no time. Right now, all you aspiring manga artists out there might be saying "All-nighters don't bother me," but that's only because you don't know how it really is! Yes... Before **I** went pro, I knew that it was going to be tough, but I hadn't actually experienced it yet; and I naively thought, "Once I turn pro, I'm going to draw this and that, and do whatever story I want!" Boy, was I wrong!

There is no job where you can do whatever you want. Your ego gets ripped to shreds, and you'll be humbled before you can ever feel proud of yourself; but then after a few years, some people will be flying high in the sky. ...
What the heck am I talking about?

Looks like I'm too hungry and sleepy...

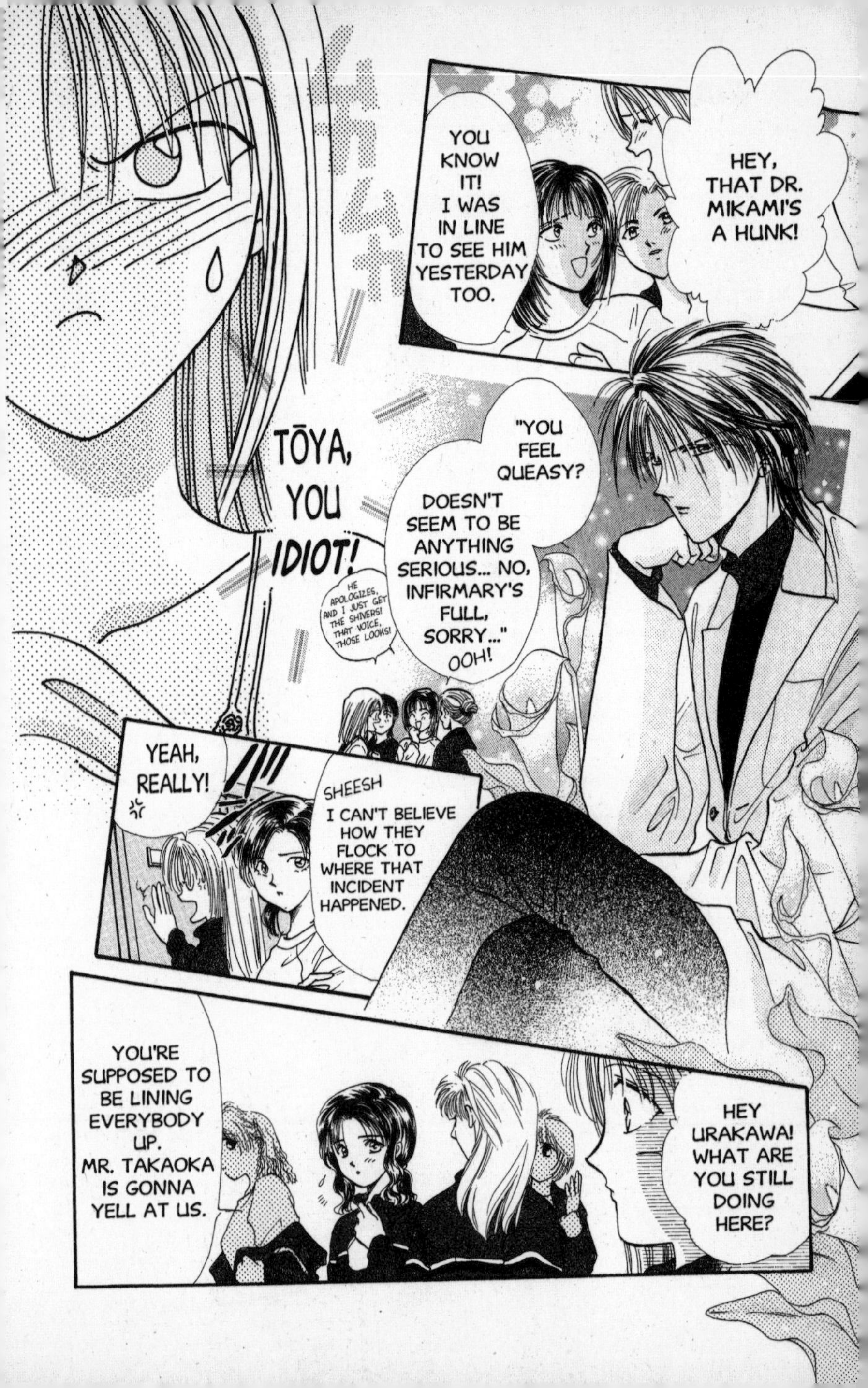
HEY, THAT DR. MIKAMI'S A HUNK!
YOU KNOW IT! I WAS IN LINE TO SEE HIM YESTERDAY TOO.
"YOU FEEL QUEASY? DOESN'T SEEM TO BE ANYTHING SERIOUS... NO, INFIRMARY'S FULL, SORRY..." OOH!
HE APOLOGIZES, AND I JUST GET THE SHIVERS! THAT VOICE, THOSE LOOKS!
TŌYA, YOU IDIOT!
SHEESH
I CAN'T BELIEVE HOW THEY FLOCK TO WHERE THAT INCIDENT HAPPENED.
YEAH, REALLY!
HEY URAKAWA! WHAT ARE YOU STILL DOING HERE?
YOU'RE SUPPOSED TO BE LINING EVERYBODY UP. MR. TAKAOKA IS GONNA YELL AT US.

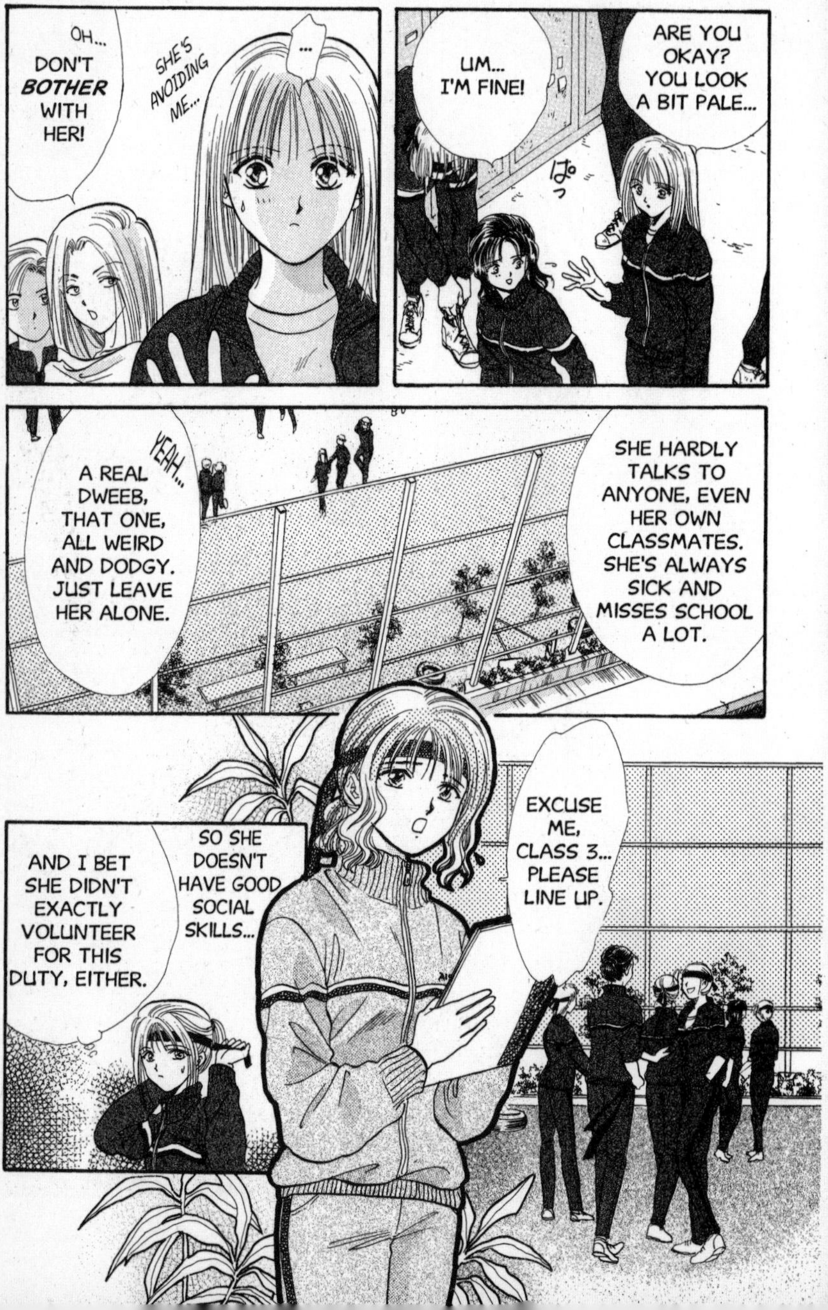
ARE YOU OKAY? YOU LOOK A BIT PALE...
UM... I'M FINE!
ぱっ
...
SHE'S AVOIDING ME...
OH... DON'T **BOTHER** WITH HER!
SHE HARDLY TALKS TO ANYONE, EVEN HER OWN CLASSMATES. SHE'S ALWAYS SICK AND MISSES SCHOOL A LOT.
YEAH...
A REAL DWEEB, THAT ONE, ALL WEIRD AND DODGY. JUST LEAVE HER ALONE.
EXCUSE ME, CLASS 3... PLEASE LINE UP.
SO SHE DOESN'T HAVE GOOD SOCIAL SKILLS...
AND I BET SHE DIDN'T EXACTLY VOLUNTEER FOR THIS DUTY, EITHER.

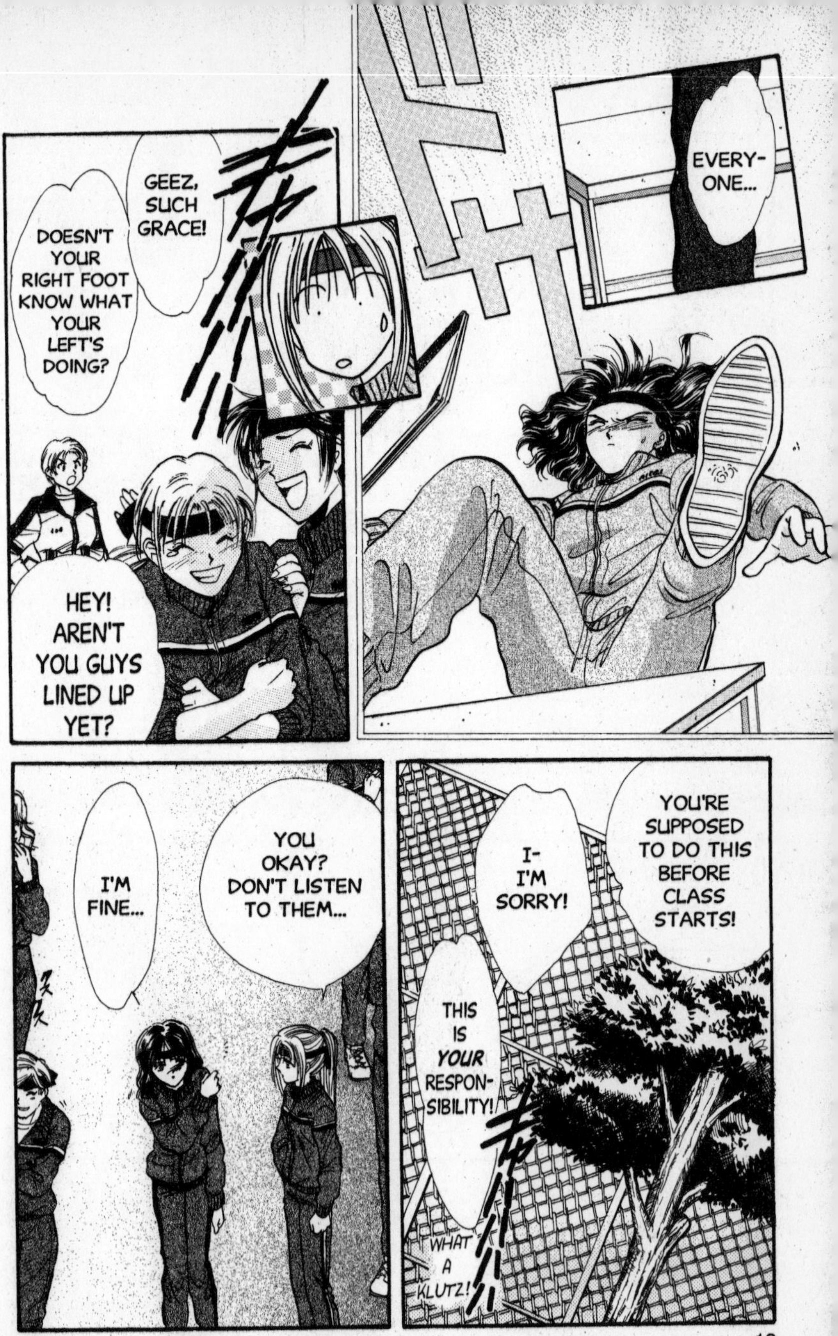
EVERY-ONE...
GEEZ, SUCH GRACE!
DOESN'T YOUR RIGHT FOOT KNOW WHAT YOUR LEFT'S DOING?
HEY! AREN'T YOU GUYS LINED UP YET?
YOU'RE SUPPOSED TO DO THIS BEFORE CLASS STARTS!
I- I'M SORRY!
THIS IS *YOUR* RESPONSIBILITY!
WHAT A KLUTZ!
YOU OKAY? DON'T LISTEN TO THEM...
I'M FINE...

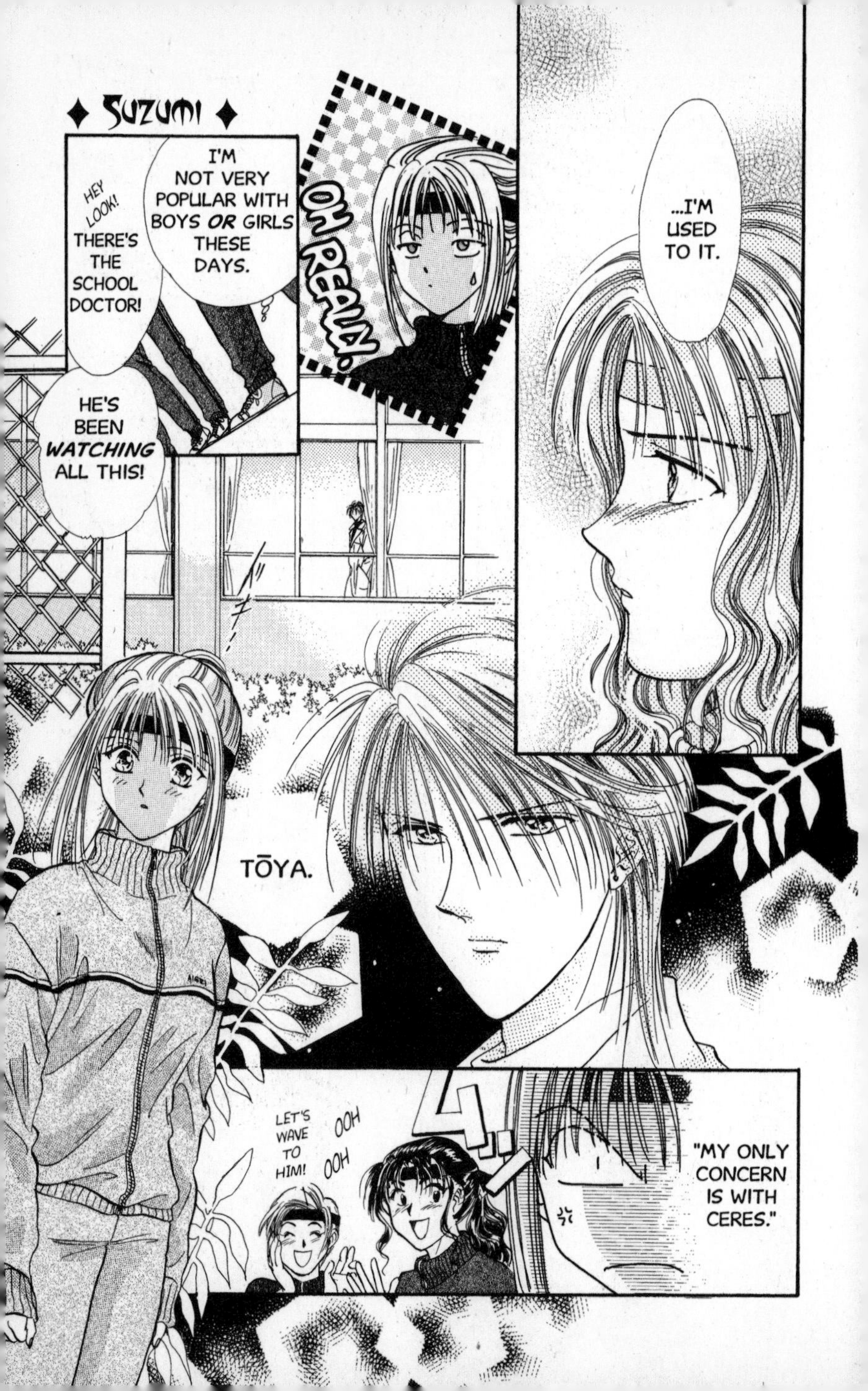
...I'M USED TO IT.
OH REALLY.
I'M NOT VERY POPULAR WITH BOYS *OR* GIRLS THESE DAYS.
HEY LOOK!
THERE'S THE SCHOOL DOCTOR!
HE'S BEEN *WATCHING* ALL THIS!
TŌYA.
"MY ONLY CONCERN IS WITH CERES."
OOH OOH
LET'S WAVE TO HIM!

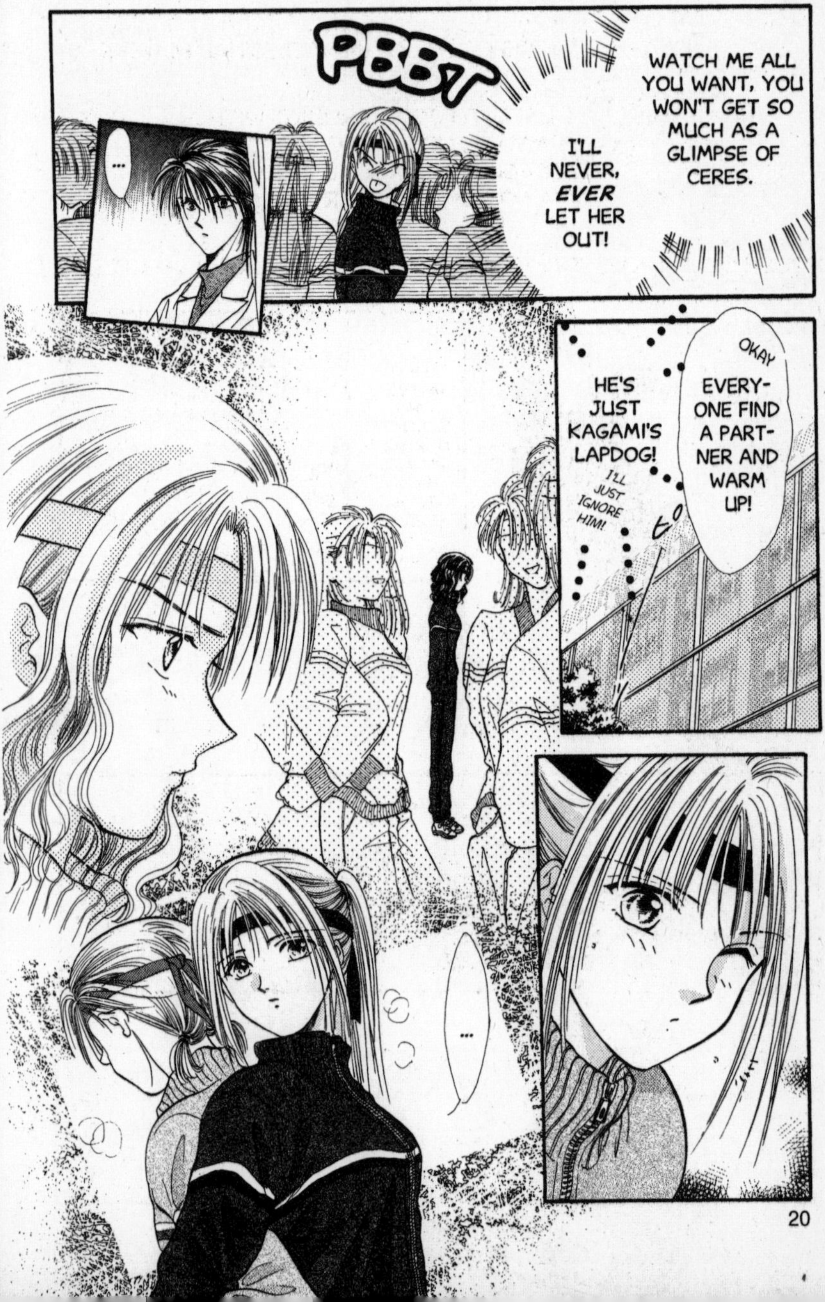
WATCH ME ALL YOU WANT, YOU WON'T GET SO MUCH AS A GLIMPSE OF CERES.
I'LL NEVER, *EVER* LET HER OUT!
PBBT
...
OKAY
EVERYONE FIND A PARTNER AND WARM UP!
HE'S JUST KAGAMI'S LAPDOG!
I'LL JUST IGNORE HIM!
...

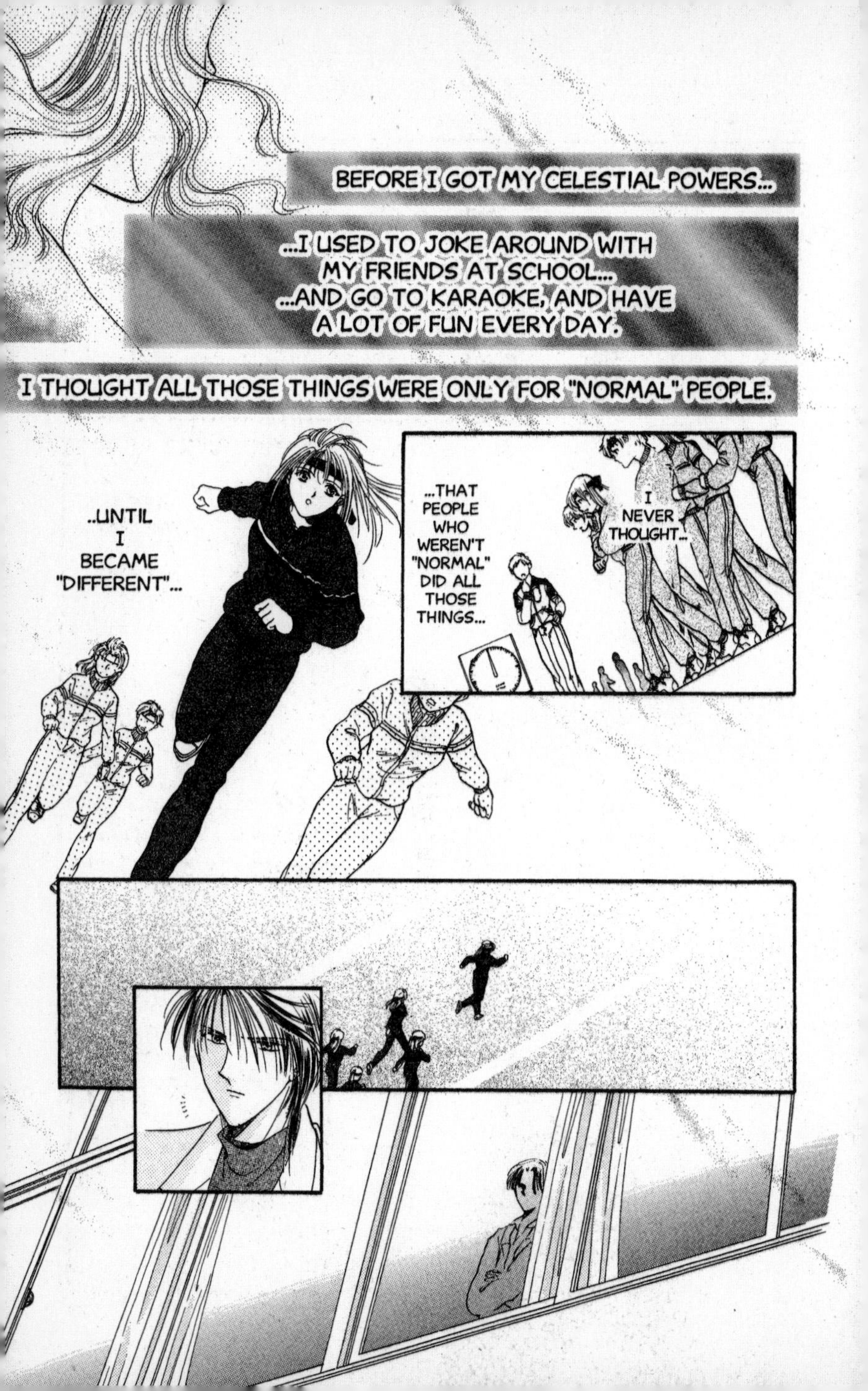
BEFORE I GOT MY CELESTIAL POWERS...
...I USED TO JOKE AROUND WITH MY FRIENDS AT SCHOOL... ...AND GO TO KARAOKE, AND HAVE A LOT OF FUN EVERY DAY.
I THOUGHT ALL THOSE THINGS WERE ONLY FOR "NORMAL" PEOPLE.
I NEVER THOUGHT...
...THAT PEOPLE WHO WEREN'T "NORMAL" DID ALL THOSE THINGS...
..UNTIL I BECAME "DIFFERENT"...

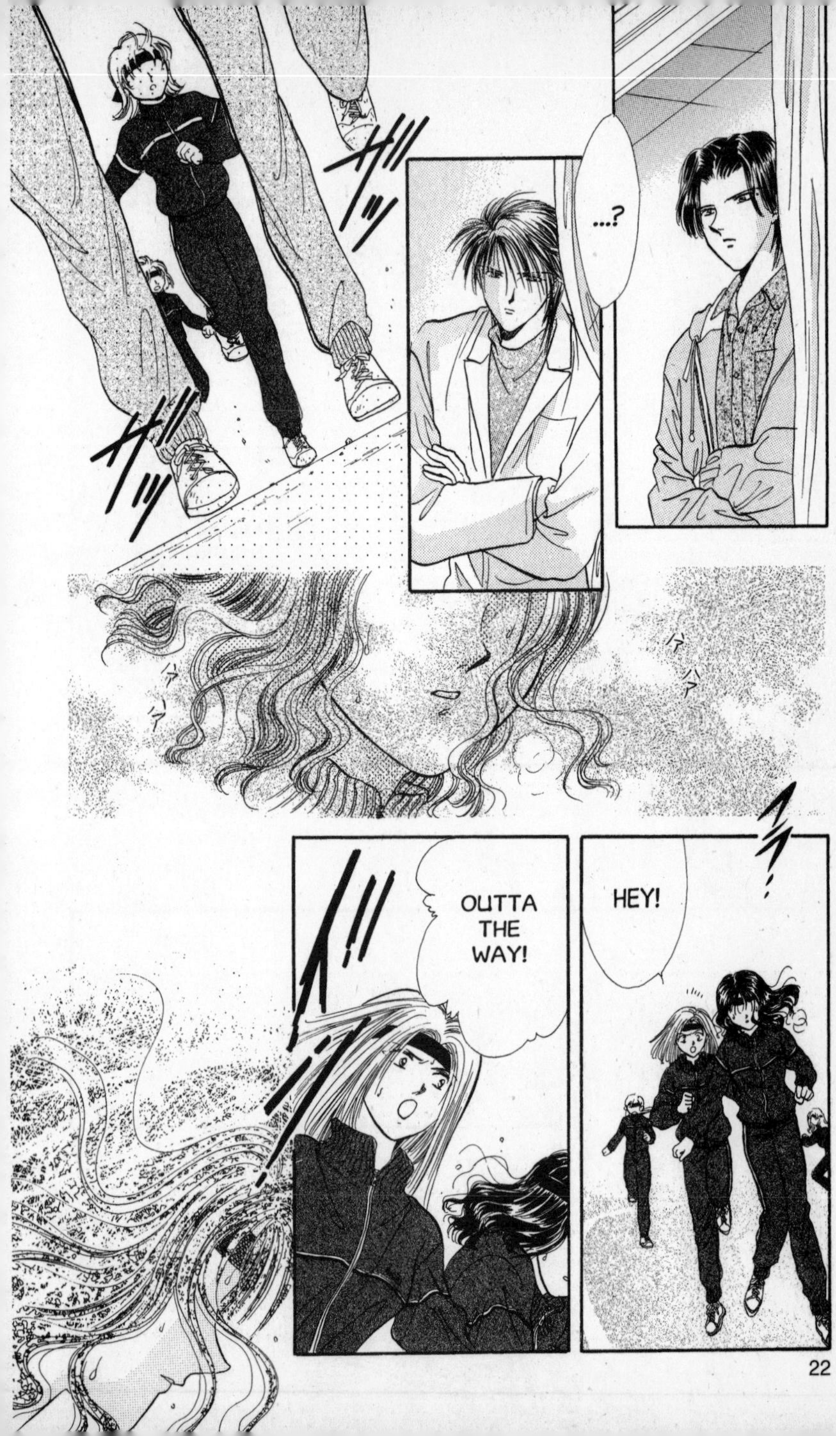
...?
HEY!
OUTTA THE WAY!

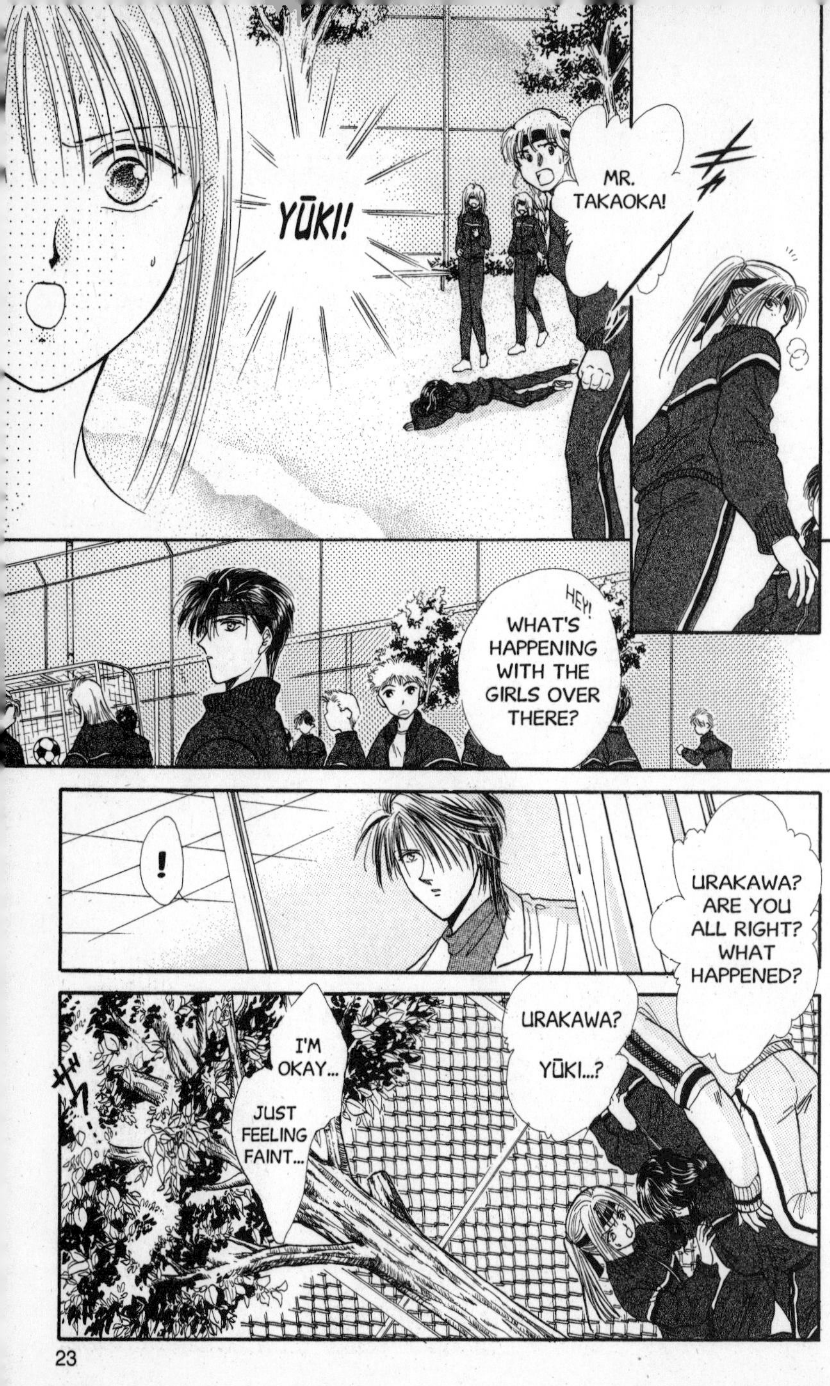
MR. TAKAOKA!
YŪKI!
HEY!
WHAT'S HAPPENING WITH THE GIRLS OVER THERE?
!
URAKAWA? ARE YOU ALL RIGHT? WHAT HAPPENED?
URAKAWA?
YŪKI...?
I'M OKAY...
JUST FEELING FAINT...

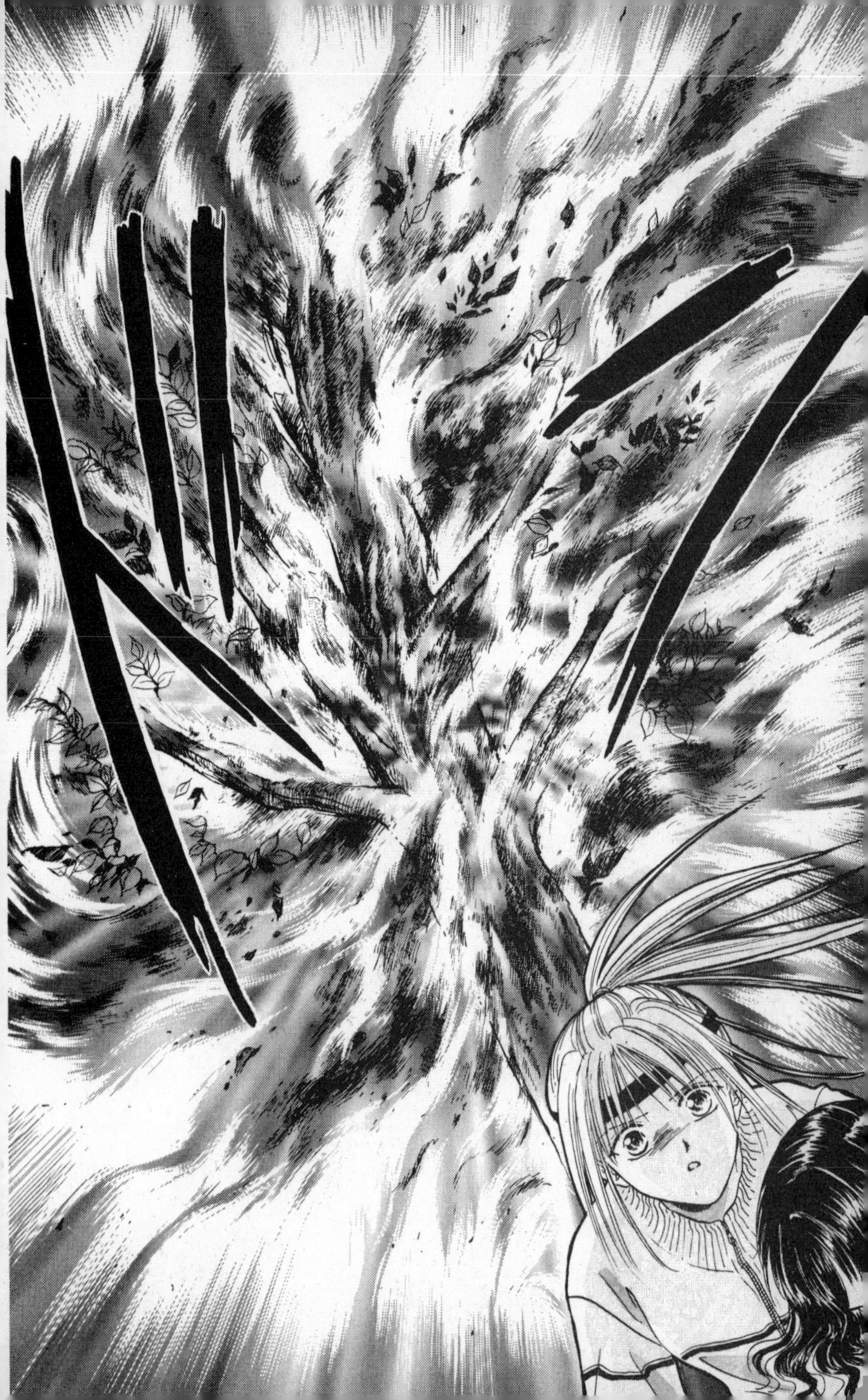

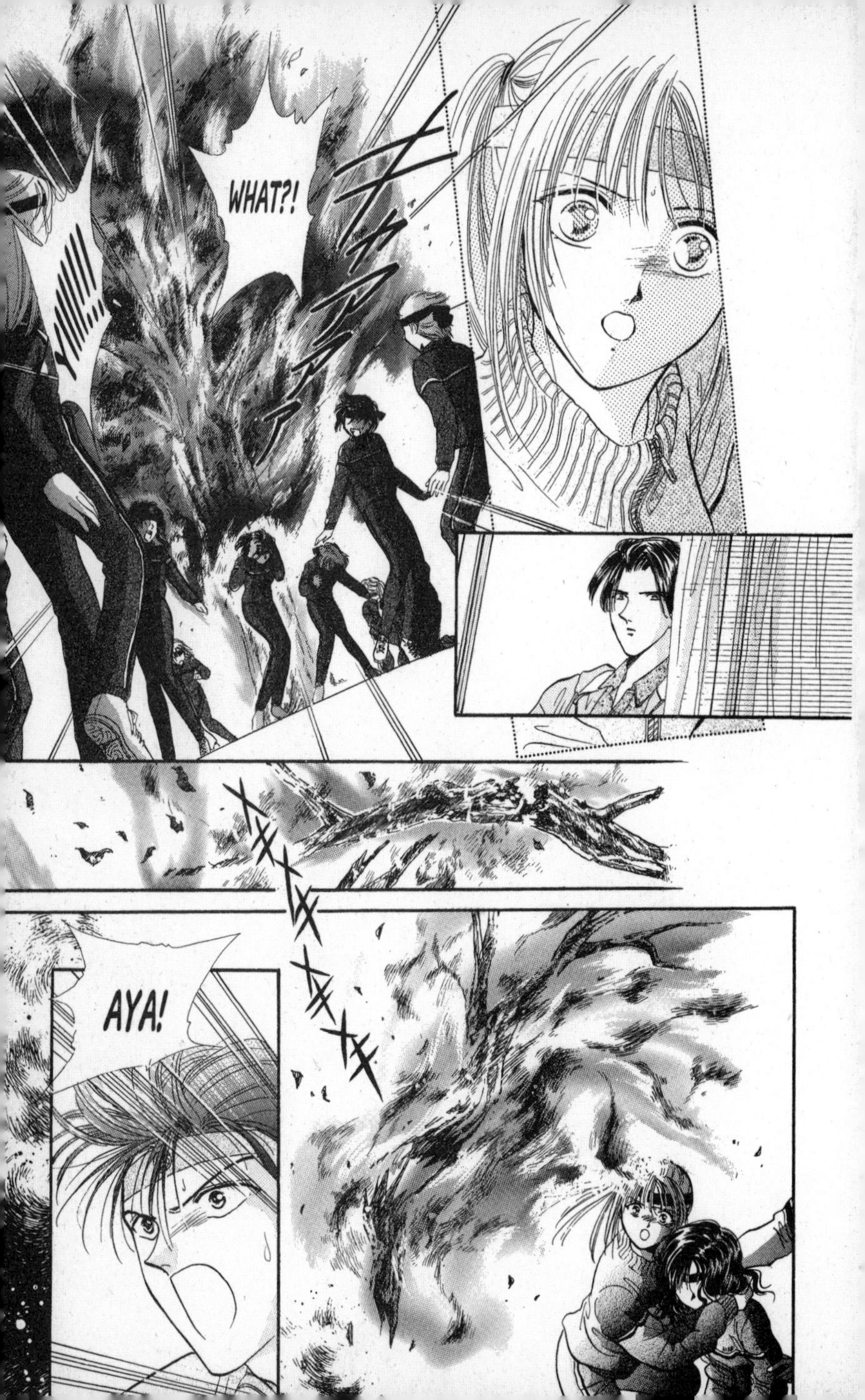
WHAT?!
YIIII!!!
AYA!

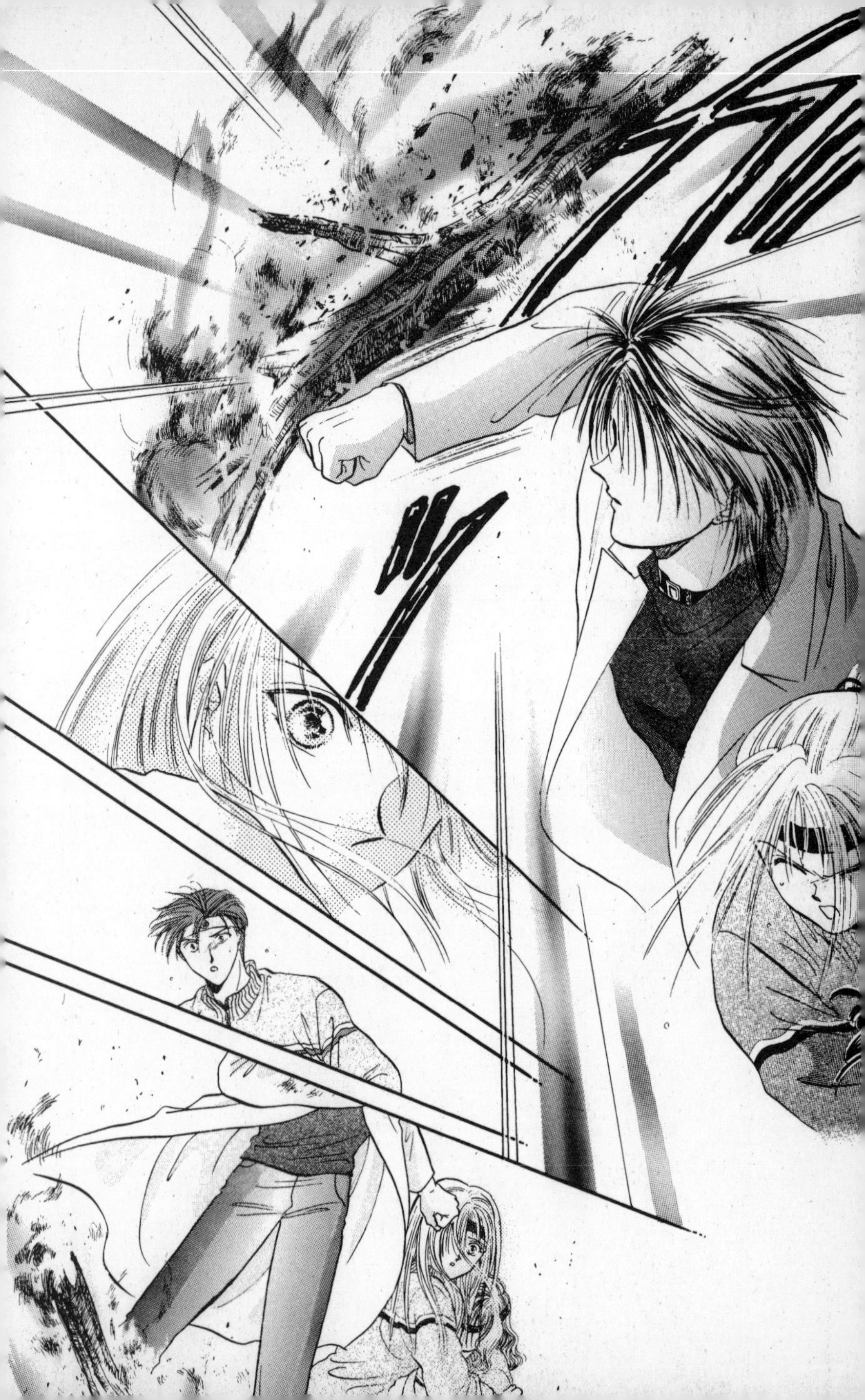

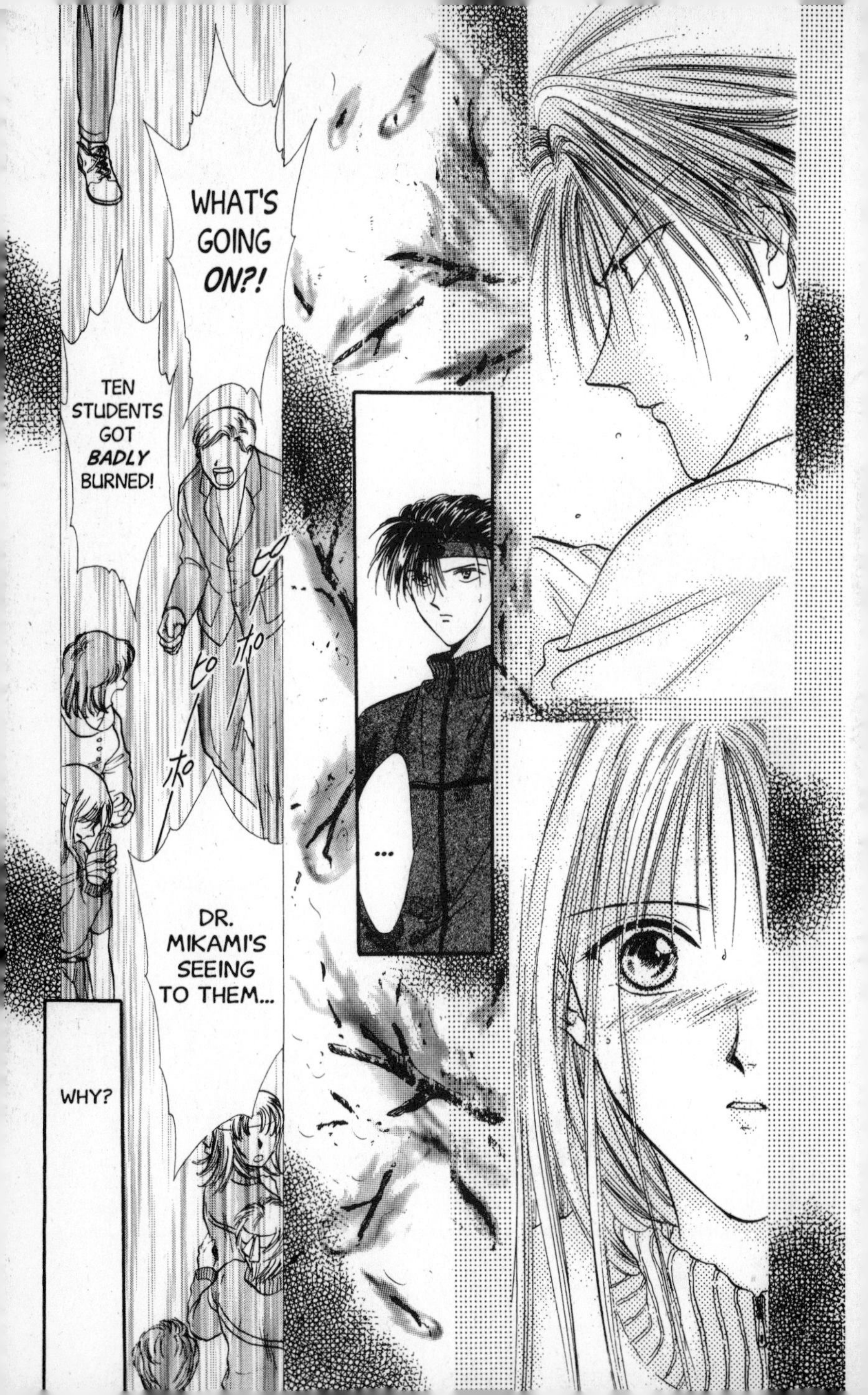
...
WHAT'S GOING ON?!
TEN STUDENTS GOT BADLY BURNED!
ピーポー ピーポー
DR. MIKAMI'S SEEING TO THEM...
WHY?

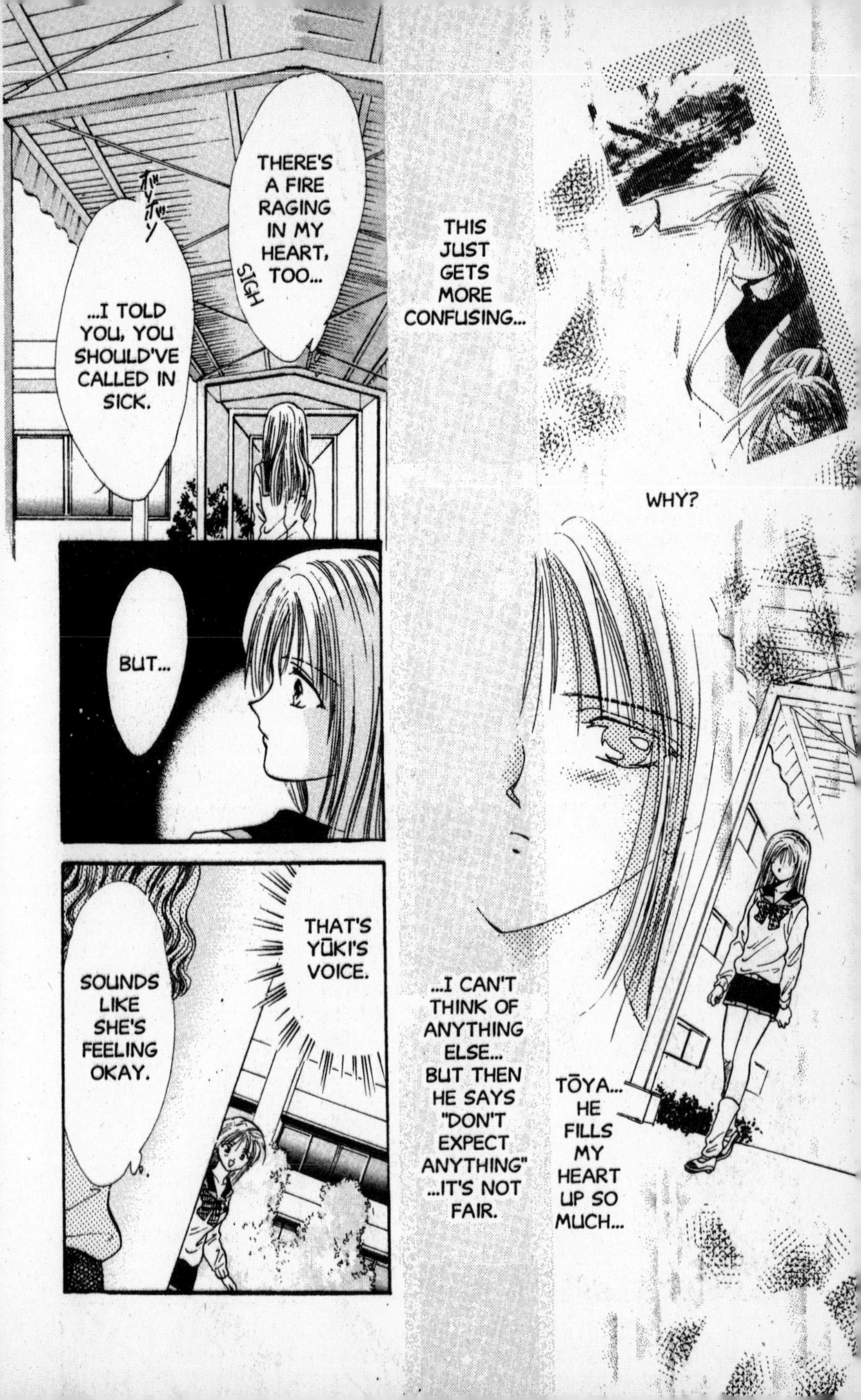
THIS JUST GETS MORE CONFUSING...
WHY?
TŌYA... HE FILLS MY HEART UP SO MUCH...
...I CAN'T THINK OF ANYTHING ELSE... BUT THEN HE SAYS "DON'T EXPECT ANYTHING" ...IT'S NOT FAIR.
THERE'S A FIRE RAGING IN MY HEART, TOO...
SIGH
...I TOLD YOU, YOU SHOULD'VE CALLED IN SICK.
BUT...
THAT'S YŪKI'S VOICE.
SOUNDS LIKE SHE'S FEELING OKAY.

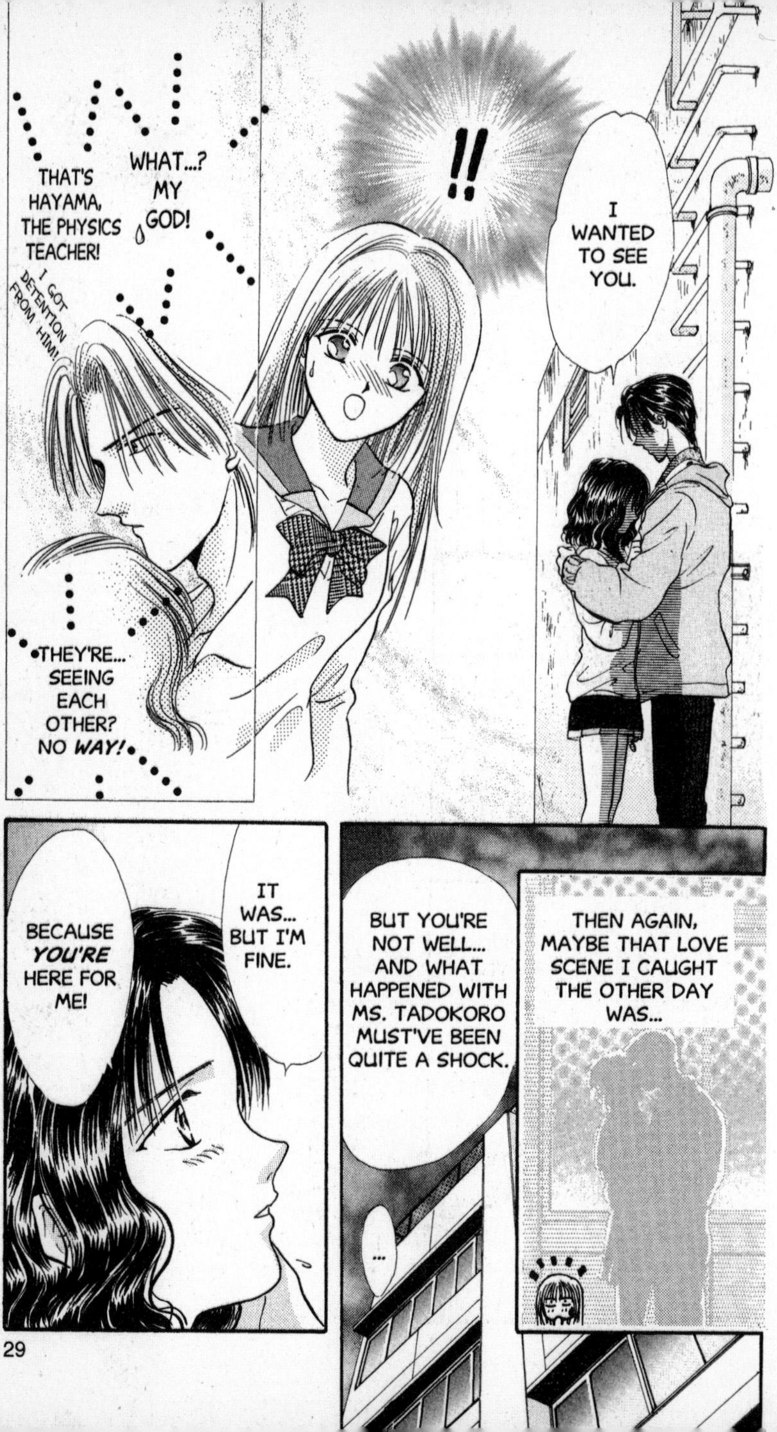
I WANTED TO SEE YOU.
!!
WHAT...? MY GOD!
THAT'S HAYAMA, THE PHYSICS TEACHER!
I GOT DETENTION FROM HIM!
THEY'RE... SEEING EACH OTHER? NO *WAY!*
THEN AGAIN, MAYBE THAT LOVE SCENE I CAUGHT THE OTHER DAY WAS...
BUT YOU'RE NOT WELL... AND WHAT HAPPENED WITH MS. TADOKORO MUST'VE BEEN QUITE A SHOCK.
...
IT WAS... BUT I'M FINE.
BECAUSE *YOU'RE* HERE FOR ME!

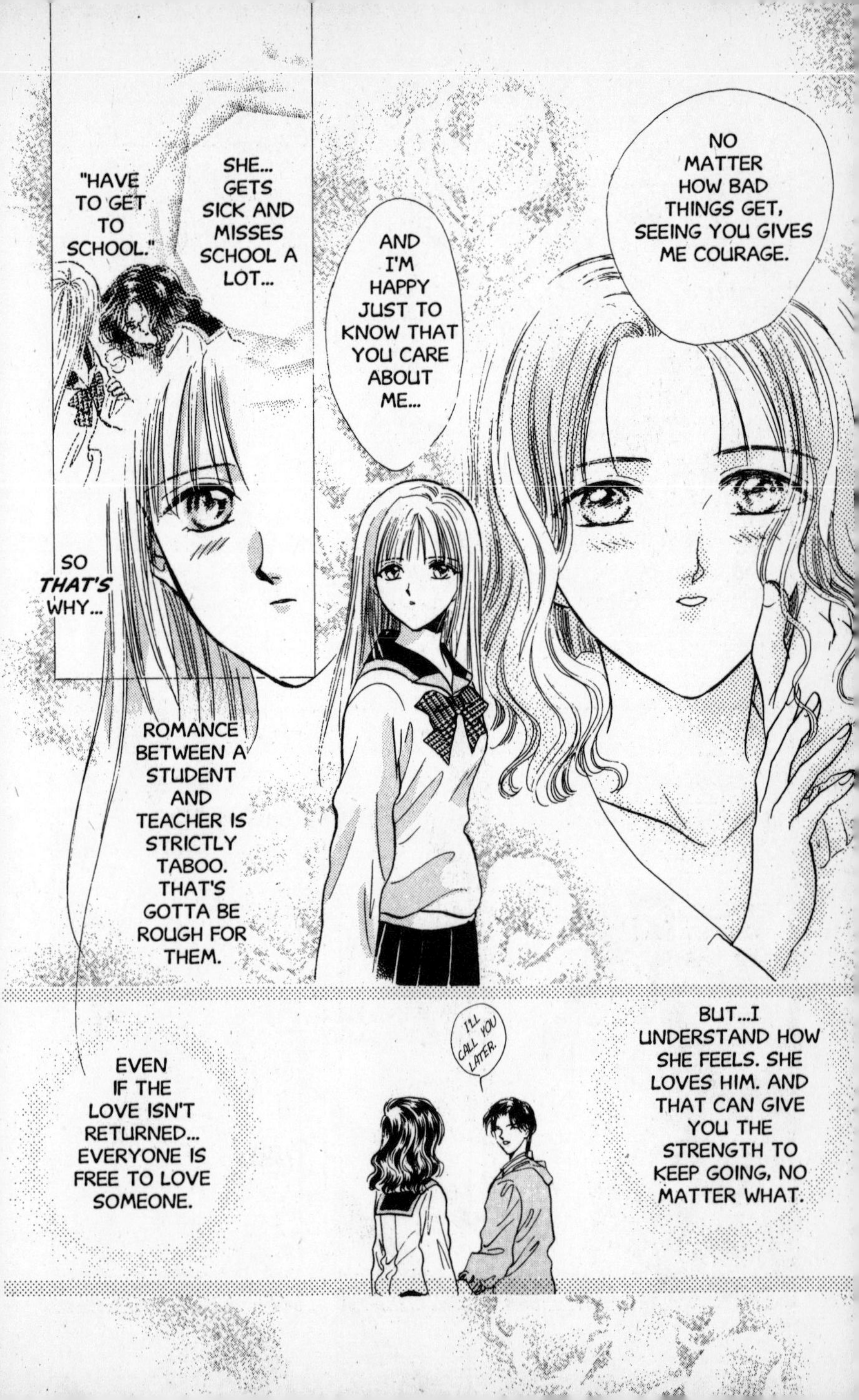
NO MATTER HOW BAD THINGS GET, SEEING YOU GIVES ME COURAGE.
AND I'M HAPPY JUST TO KNOW THAT YOU CARE ABOUT ME...
SHE... GETS SICK AND MISSES SCHOOL A LOT...
"HAVE TO GET TO SCHOOL."
SO *THAT'S* WHY...
ROMANCE BETWEEN A STUDENT AND TEACHER IS STRICTLY TABOO. THAT'S GOTTA BE ROUGH FOR THEM.
BUT...I UNDERSTAND HOW SHE FEELS. SHE LOVES HIM. AND THAT CAN GIVE YOU THE STRENGTH TO KEEP GOING, NO MATTER WHAT.
I'LL CALL YOU LATER.
EVEN IF THE LOVE ISN'T RETURNED... EVERYONE IS FREE TO LOVE SOMEONE.

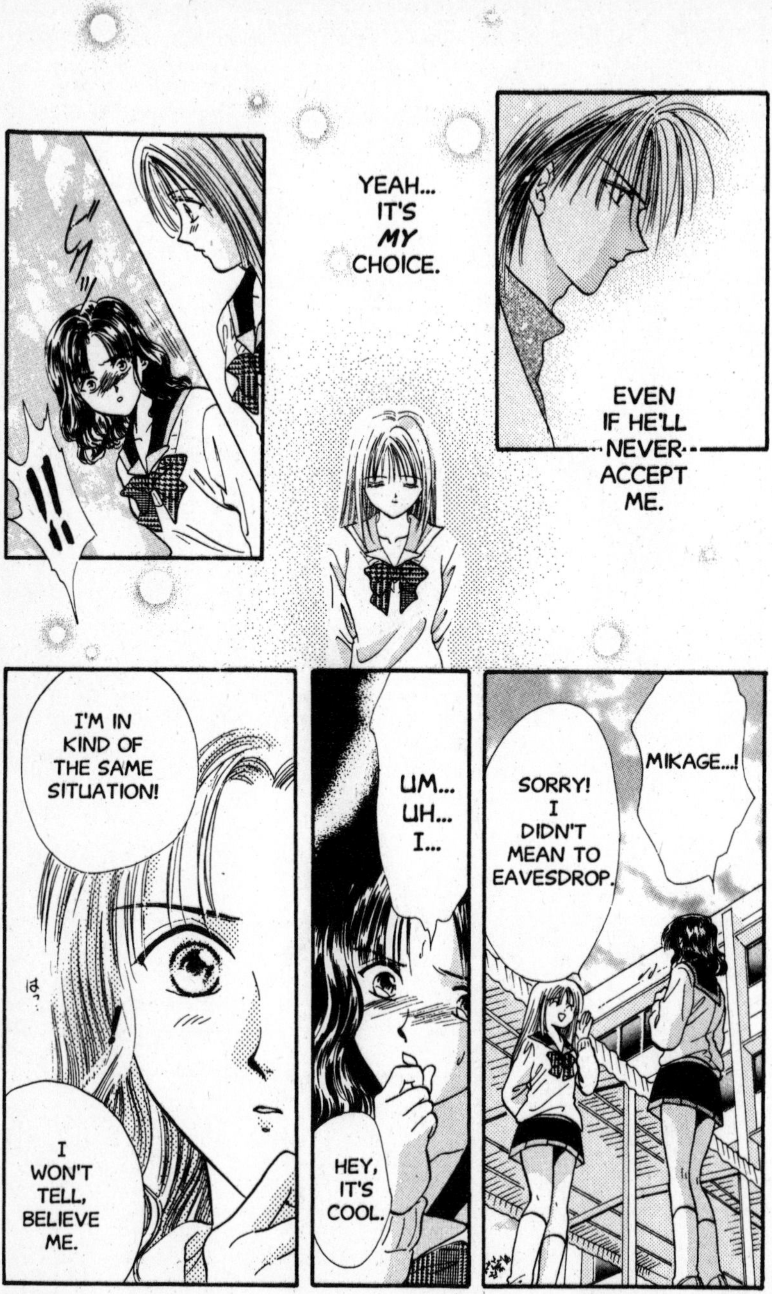
YEAH... IT'S *MY* CHOICE.
EVEN IF HE'LL NEVER ACCEPT ME.
MIKAGE...!
SORRY! I DIDN'T MEAN TO EAVESDROP.
UM... UH... I...
HEY, IT'S COOL.
I'M IN KIND OF THE SAME SITUATION!
I WON'T TELL, BELIEVE ME.

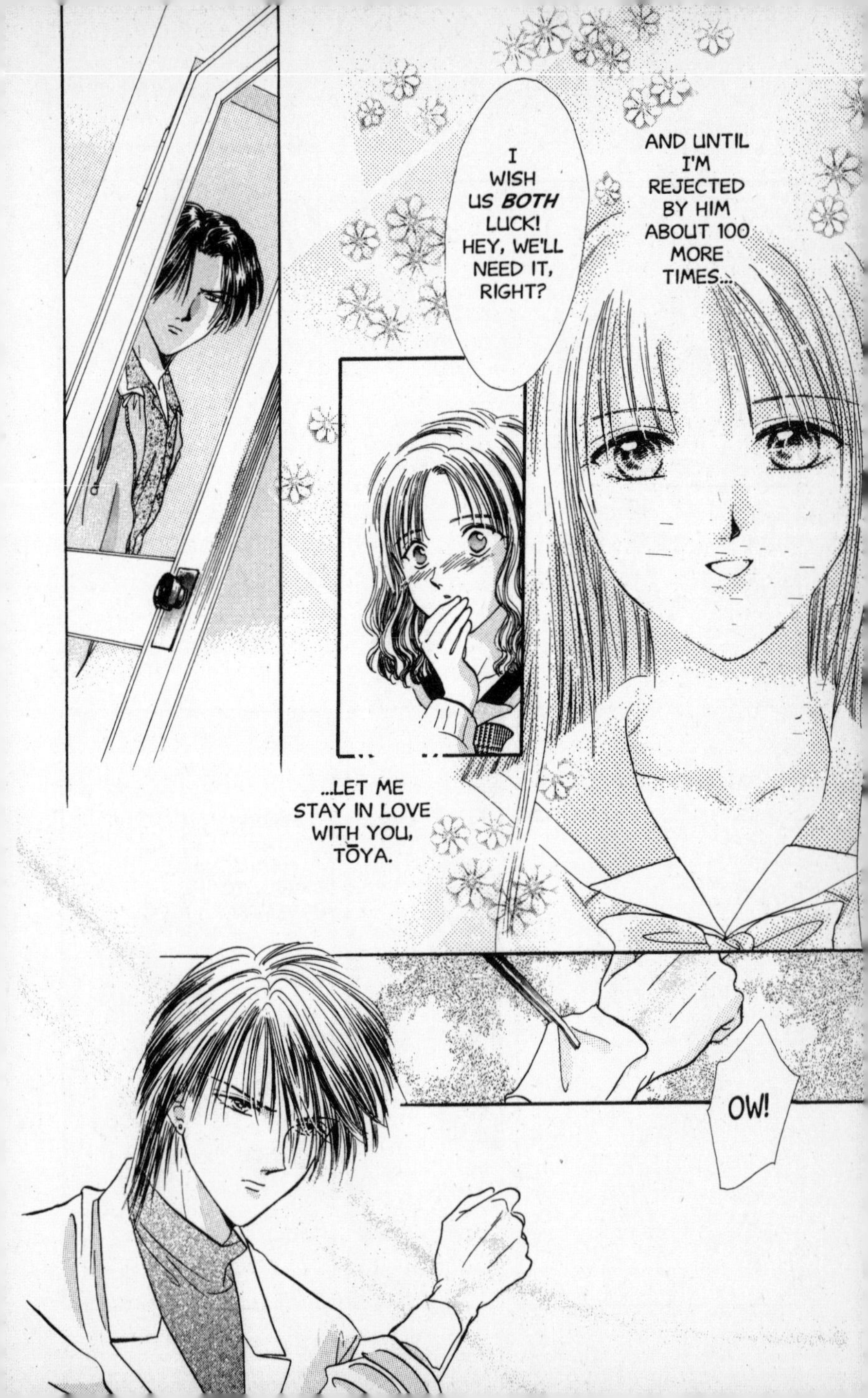
AND UNTIL I'M REJECTED BY HIM ABOUT 100 MORE TIMES...
I WISH US *BOTH* LUCK! HEY, WE'LL NEED IT, RIGHT?
...LET ME STAY IN LOVE WITH YOU, TŌYA.
OW!

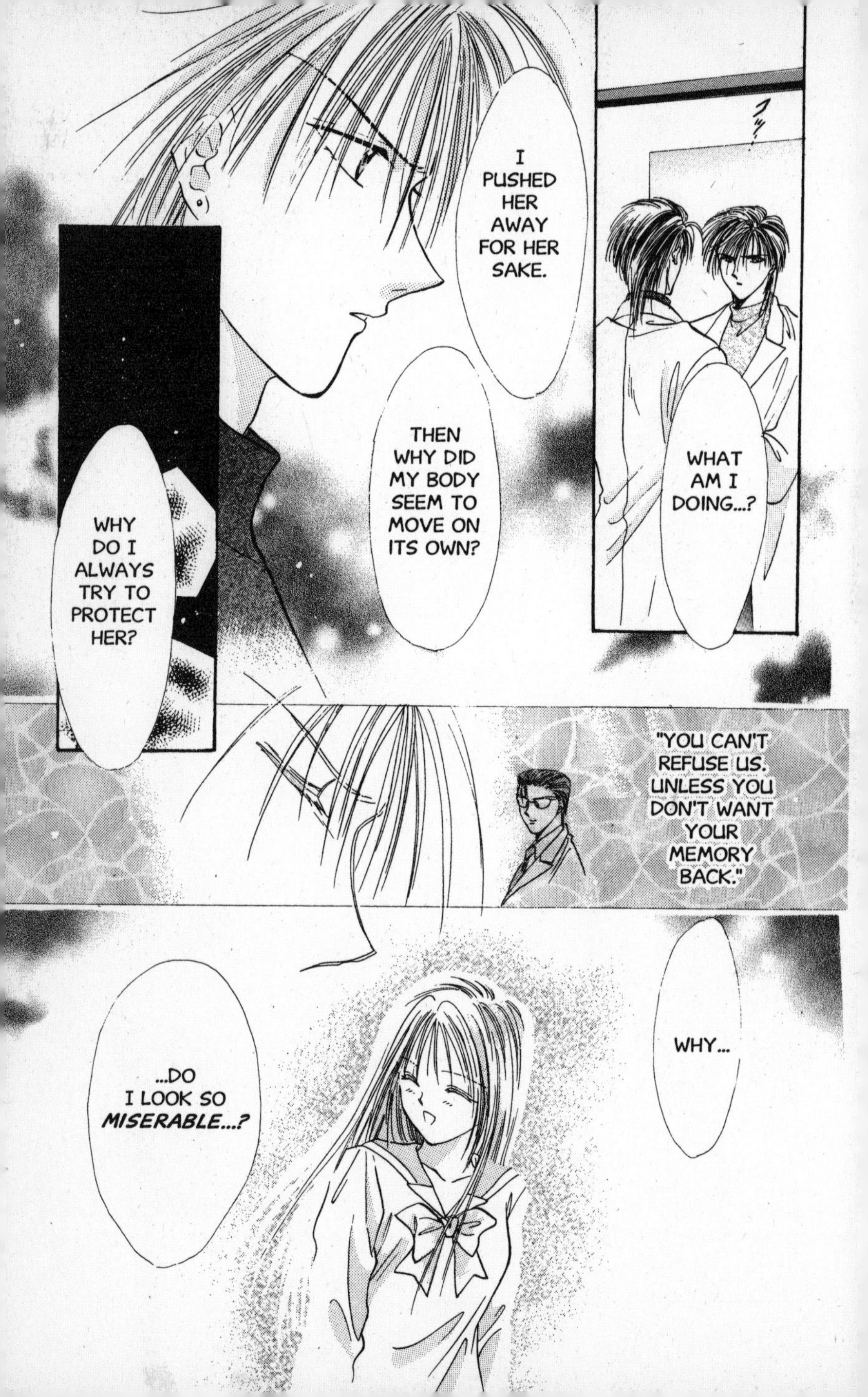

WHAT AM I DOING...?
I PUSHED HER AWAY FOR HER SAKE.
THEN WHY DID MY BODY SEEM TO MOVE ON ITS OWN?
WHY DO I ALWAYS TRY TO PROTECT HER?
"YOU CAN'T REFUSE US. UNLESS YOU DON'T WANT YOUR MEMORY BACK."
WHY...
...DO I LOOK SO *MISERABLE*...?

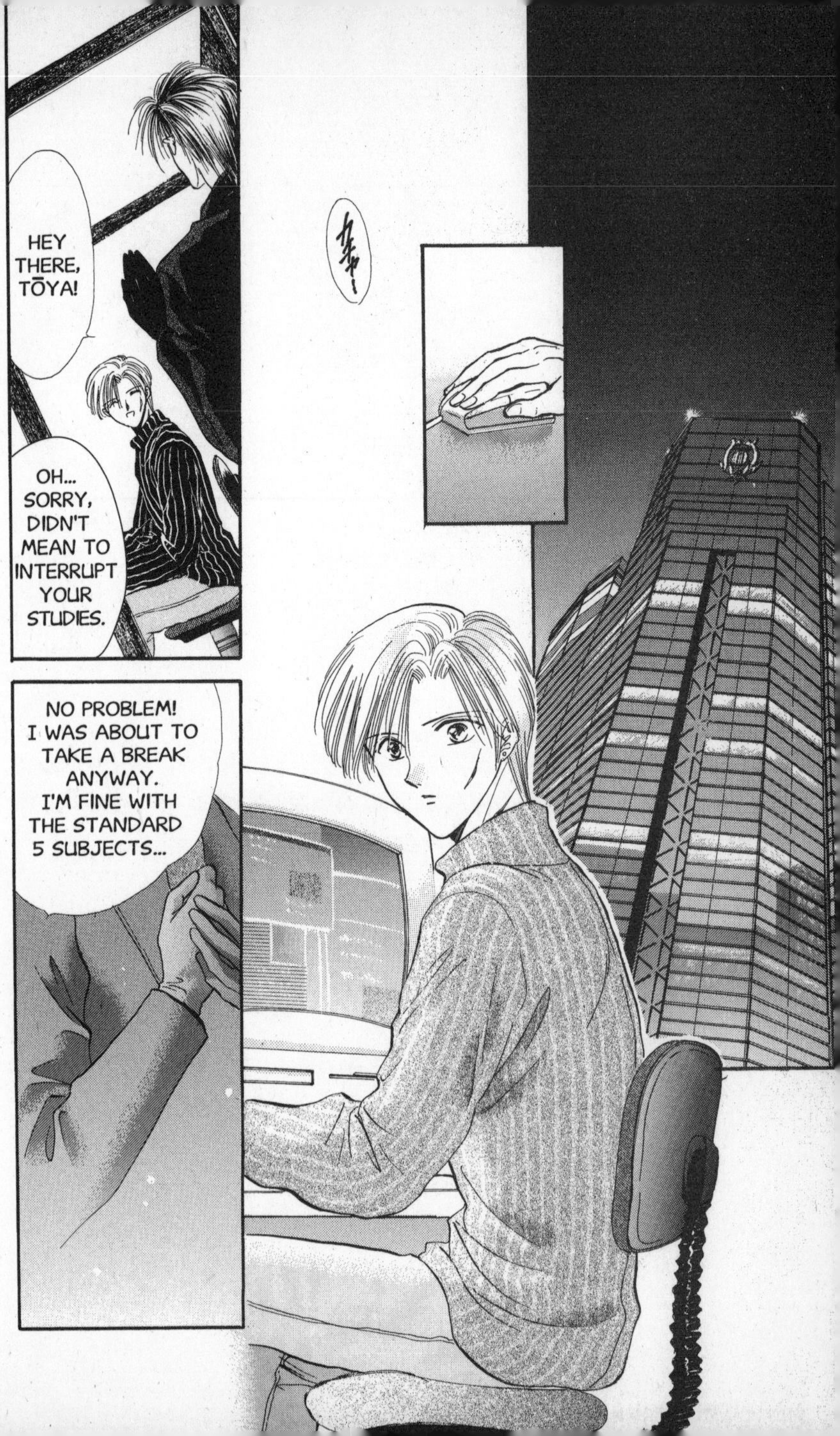
HEY THERE, TŌYA!
OH... SORRY, DIDN'T MEAN TO INTERRUPT YOUR STUDIES.
NO PROBLEM! I WAS ABOUT TO TAKE A BREAK ANYWAY. I'M FINE WITH THE STANDARD 5 SUBJECTS...

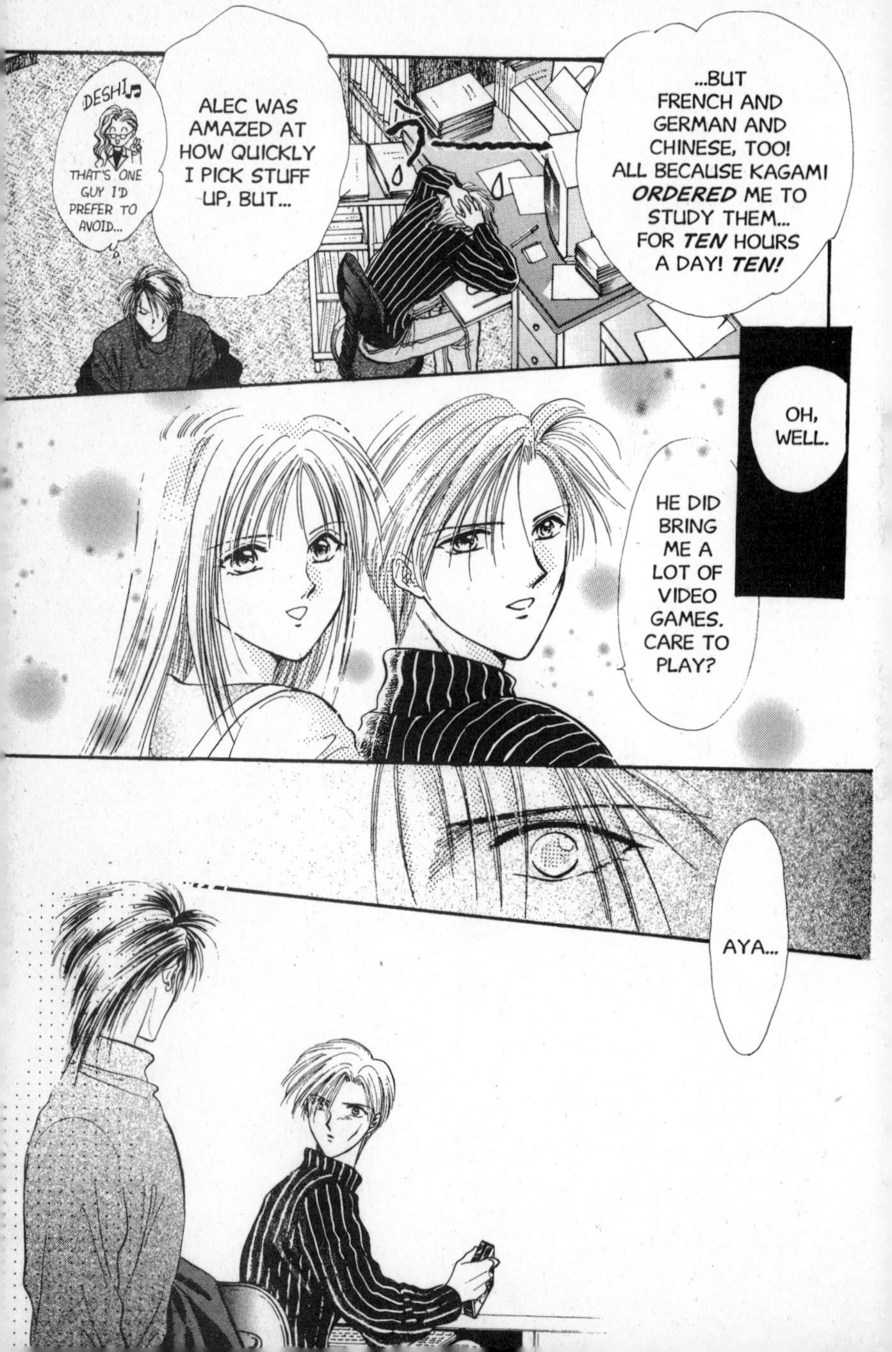
ALEC WAS AMAZED AT HOW QUICKLY I PICK STUFF UP, BUT...
...BUT FRENCH AND GERMAN AND CHINESE, TOO! ALL BECAUSE KAGAMI *ORDERED* ME TO STUDY THEM... FOR *TEN* HOURS A DAY! *TEN!*
DESHI♪
THAT'S ONE GUY I'D PREFER TO AVOID...
OH, WELL.
HE DID BRING ME A LOT OF VIDEO GAMES. CARE TO PLAY?
AYA...

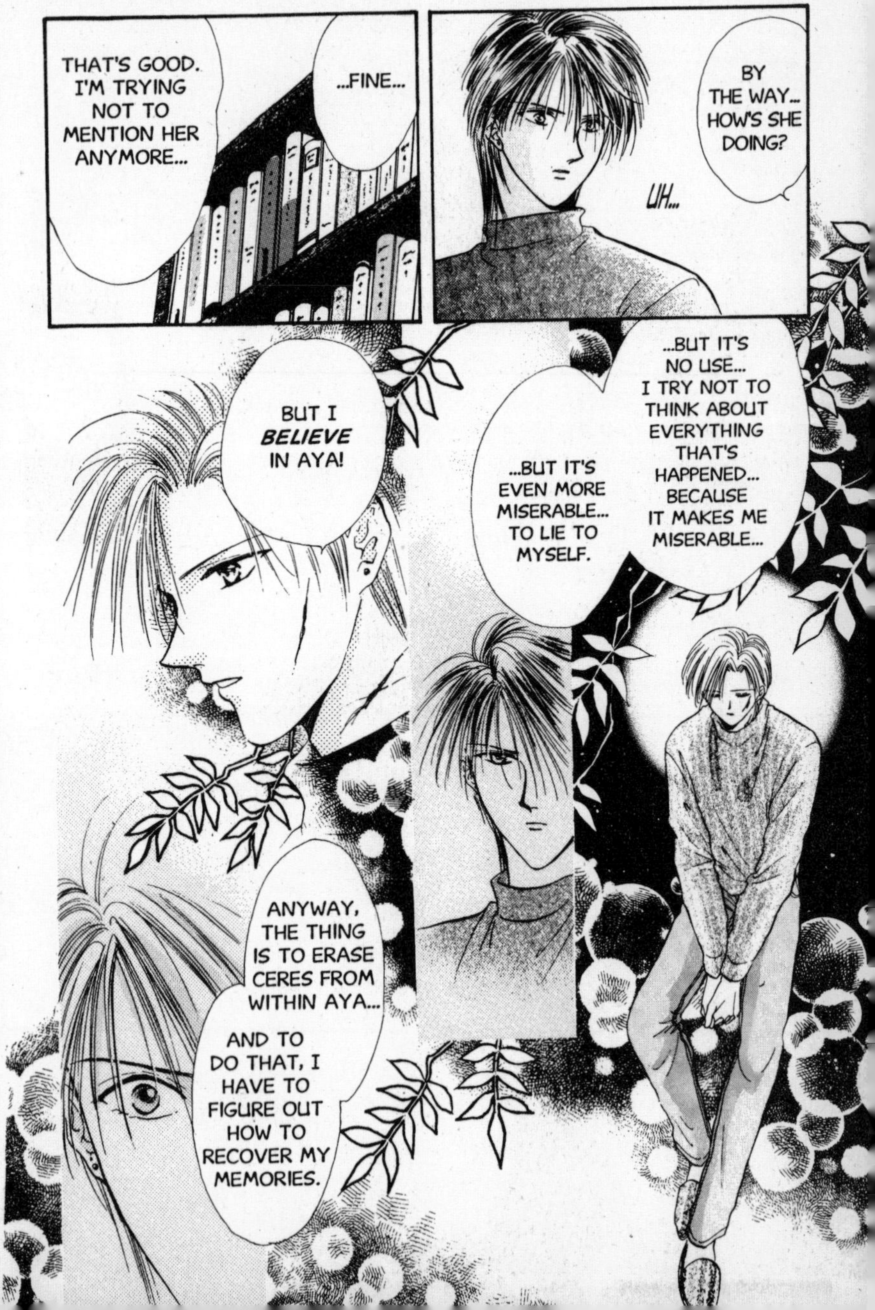
BY THE WAY... HOW'S SHE DOING?
UH...
...FINE...
THAT'S GOOD. I'M TRYING NOT TO MENTION HER ANYMORE...
...BUT IT'S NO USE... I TRY NOT TO THINK ABOUT EVERYTHING THAT'S HAPPENED... BECAUSE IT MAKES ME MISERABLE...
...BUT IT'S EVEN MORE MISERABLE... TO LIE TO MYSELF.
BUT I *BELIEVE* IN AYA!
ANYWAY, THE THING IS TO ERASE CERES FROM WITHIN AYA...
AND TO DO THAT, I HAVE TO FIGURE OUT HOW TO RECOVER MY MEMORIES.

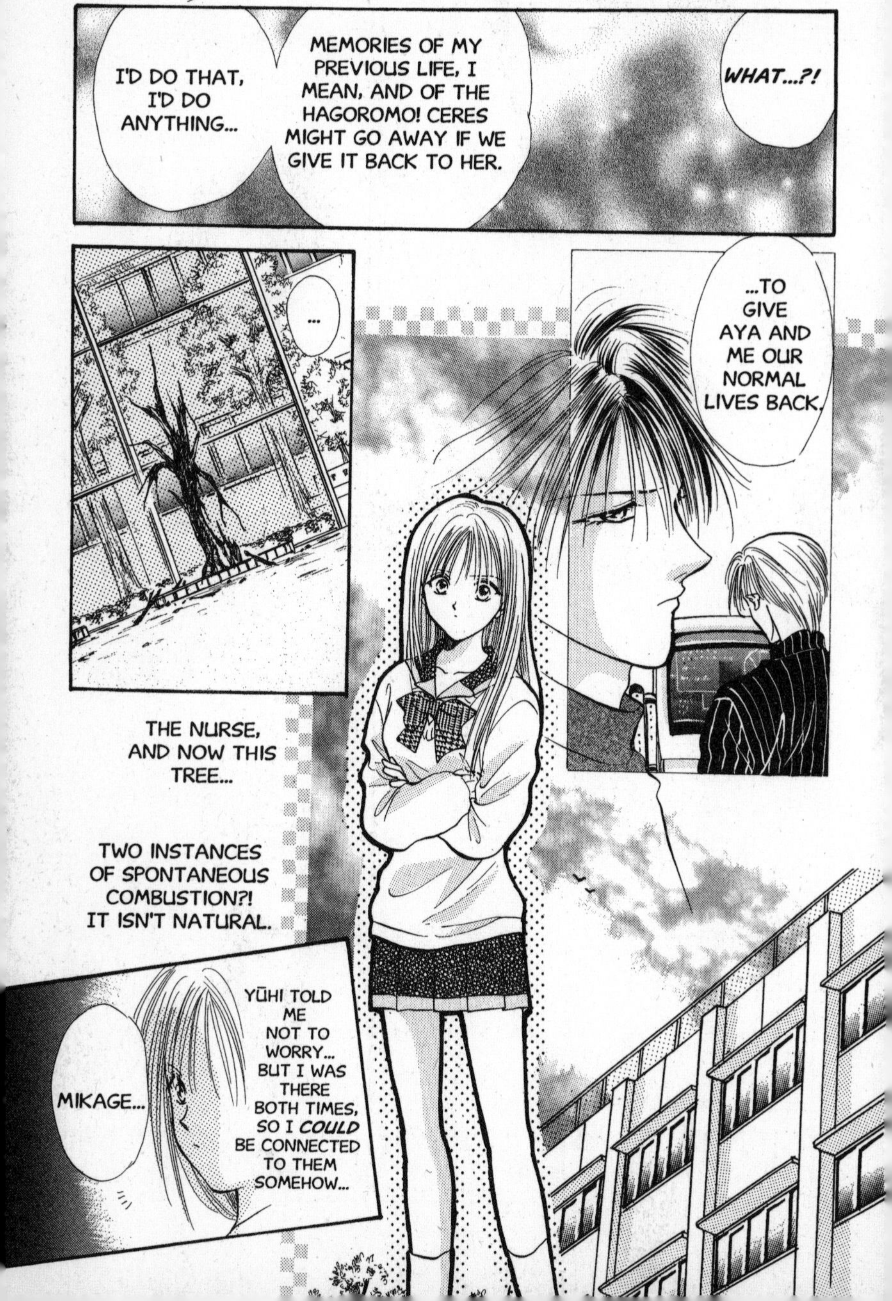
WHAT...?!
MEMORIES OF MY PREVIOUS LIFE, I MEAN, AND OF THE HAGOROMO! CERES MIGHT GO AWAY IF WE GIVE IT BACK TO HER.
I'D DO THAT, I'D DO ANYTHING...
...TO GIVE AYA AND ME OUR NORMAL LIVES BACK.
...
THE NURSE, AND NOW THIS TREE...
TWO INSTANCES OF SPONTANEOUS COMBUSTION?! IT ISN'T NATURAL.
YŪHI TOLD ME NOT TO WORRY... BUT I WAS THERE BOTH TIMES, SO I *COULD* BE CONNECTED TO THEM SOMEHOW...
MIKAGE...

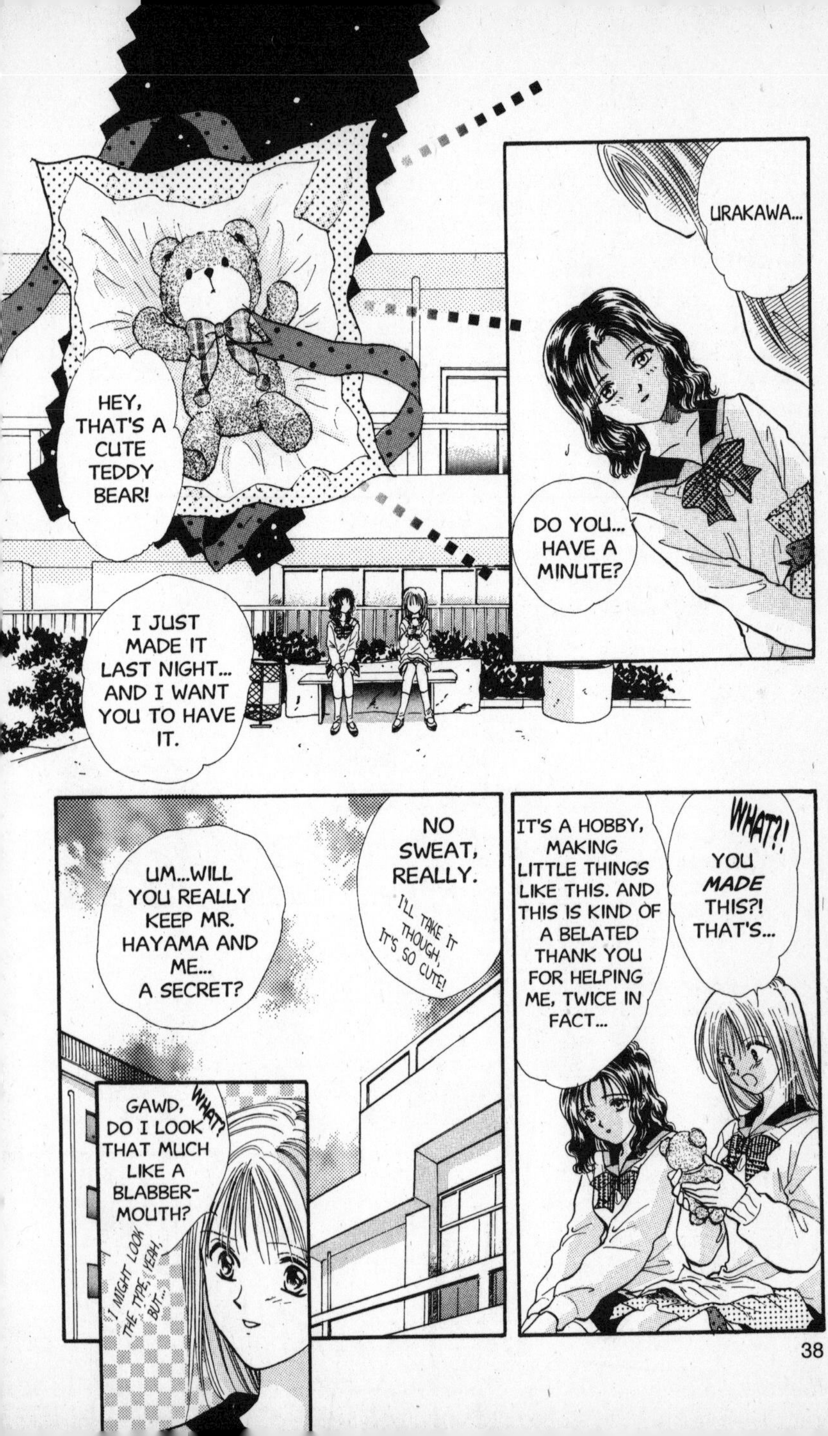
URAKAWA...
DO YOU... HAVE A MINUTE?
HEY, THAT'S A CUTE TEDDY BEAR!
I JUST MADE IT LAST NIGHT... AND I WANT YOU TO HAVE IT.
WHAT?!
YOU *MADE* THIS?! THAT'S...
IT'S A HOBBY, MAKING LITTLE THINGS LIKE THIS. AND THIS IS KIND OF A BELATED THANK YOU FOR HELPING ME, TWICE IN FACT...
NO SWEAT, REALLY.
I'LL TAKE IT THOUGH, IT'S SO CUTE!
UM...WILL YOU REALLY KEEP MR. HAYAMA AND ME... A SECRET?
WHAT?
GAWD, DO I LOOK THAT MUCH LIKE A BLABBER-MOUTH?
I MIGHT LOOK THE TYPE, YEAH, BUT...

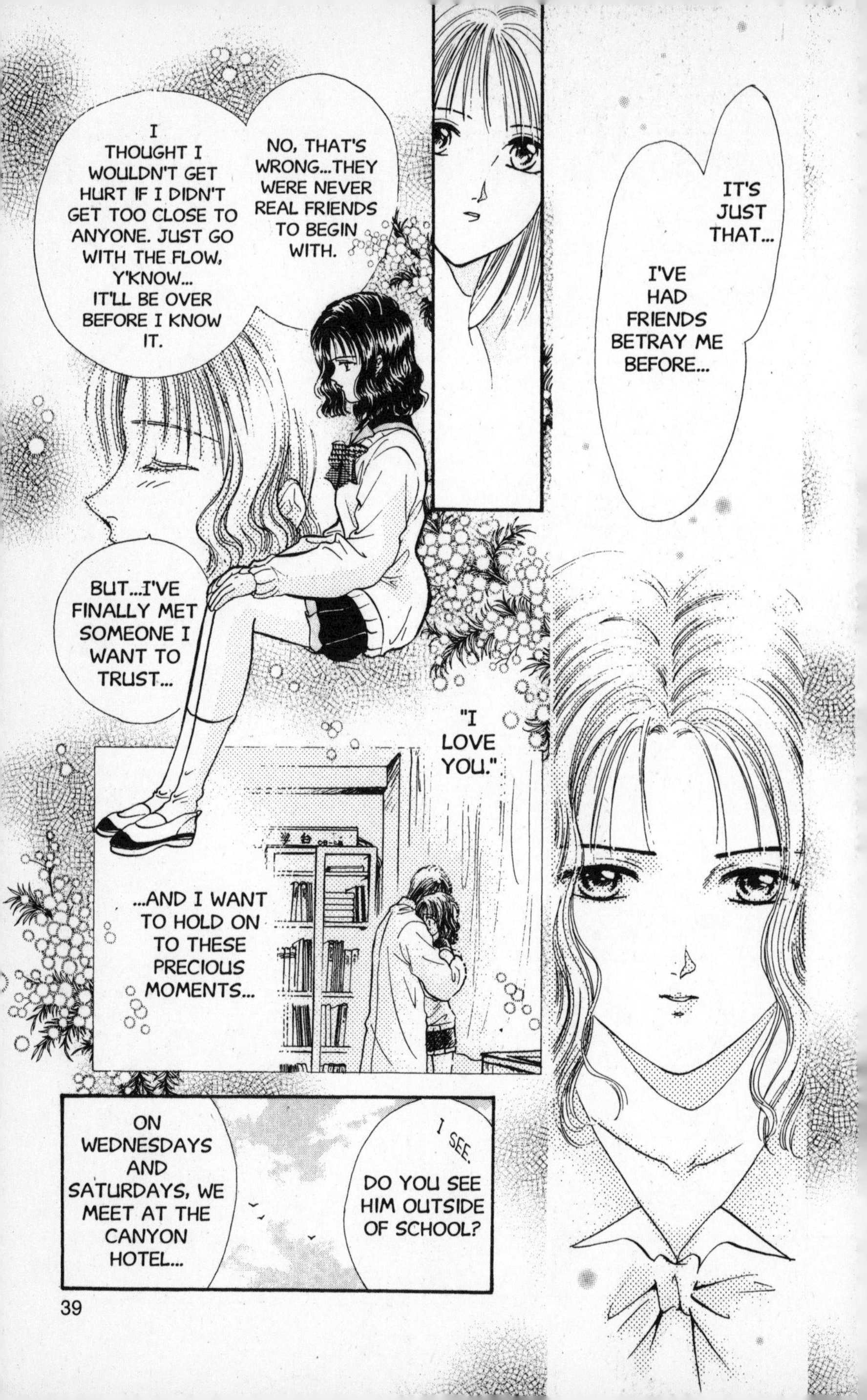
IT'S JUST THAT...
I'VE HAD FRIENDS BETRAY ME BEFORE...
NO, THAT'S WRONG...THEY WERE NEVER REAL FRIENDS TO BEGIN WITH.
I THOUGHT I WOULDN'T GET HURT IF I DIDN'T GET TOO CLOSE TO ANYONE. JUST GO WITH THE FLOW, Y'KNOW... IT'LL BE OVER BEFORE I KNOW IT.
BUT...I'VE FINALLY MET SOMEONE I WANT TO TRUST...
"I LOVE YOU."
...AND I WANT TO HOLD ON TO THESE PRECIOUS MOMENTS...
I SEE.
DO YOU SEE HIM OUTSIDE OF SCHOOL?
ON WEDNESDAYS AND SATURDAYS, WE MEET AT THE CANYON HOTEL...

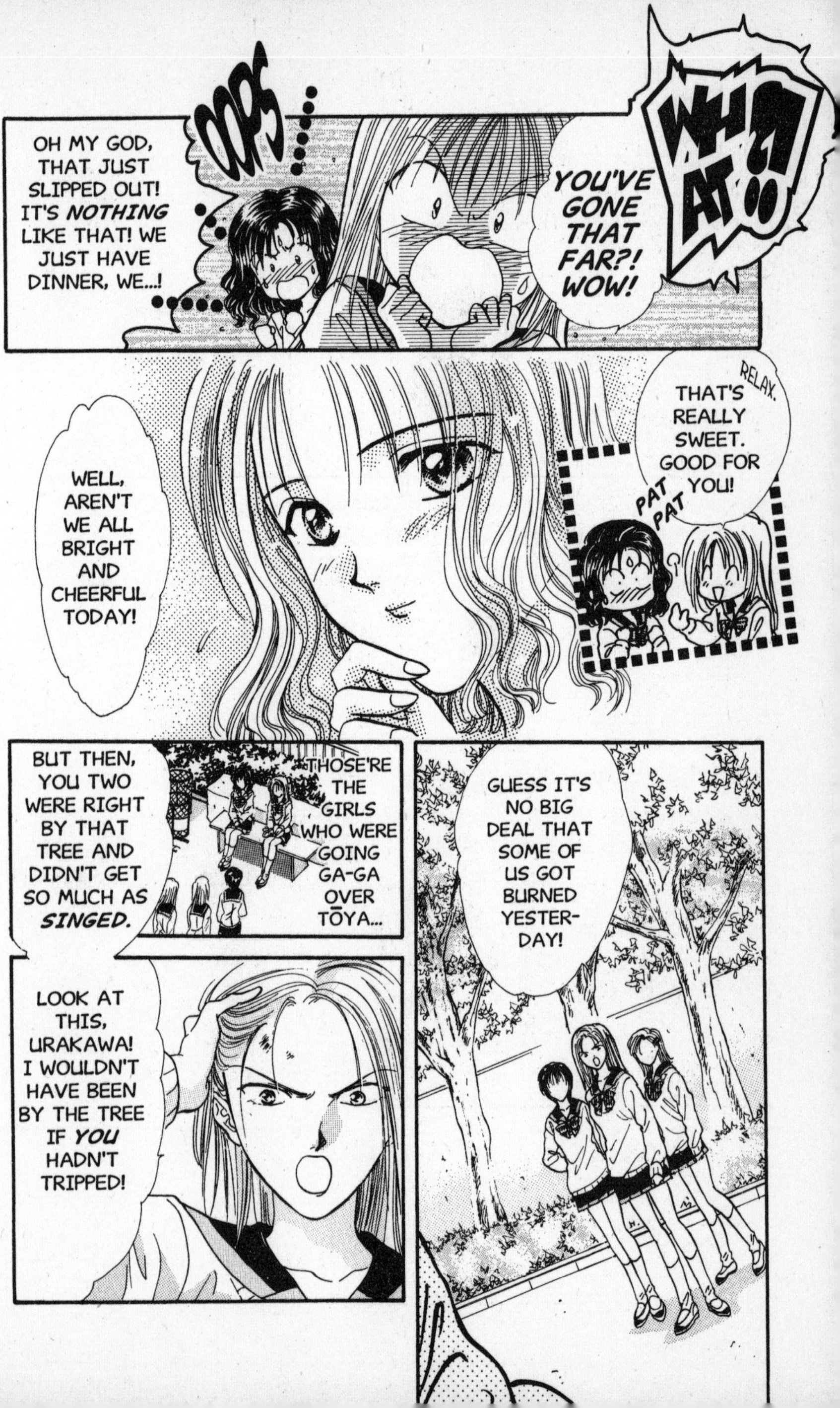
WHAT?!!
YOU'VE GONE THAT FAR?! WOW!
OOPS...
OH MY GOD, THAT JUST SLIPPED OUT! IT'S *NOTHING* LIKE THAT! WE JUST HAVE DINNER, WE...!
RELAX.
THAT'S REALLY SWEET. GOOD FOR YOU!
PAT PAT
WELL, AREN'T WE ALL BRIGHT AND CHEERFUL TODAY!
GUESS IT'S NO BIG DEAL THAT SOME OF US GOT BURNED YESTER-DAY!
THOSE'RE THE GIRLS WHO WERE GOING GA-GA OVER TŌYA...
BUT THEN, YOU TWO WERE RIGHT BY THAT TREE AND DIDN'T GET SO MUCH AS *SINGED.*
LOOK AT THIS, URAKAWA! I WOULDN'T HAVE BEEN BY THE TREE IF *YOU* HADN'T TRIPPED!

♦ SUZUMI ♦

I just had dinner! Phew. Now I can write with more coherence. But I'm still sleepy ♪ Oh, the first volume of the OAV for **FY part 2** is now on sale! (as of June '97) Please take a look at it! ♫ Vol.2 won't be out for a while, though... I really like the new opening and ending theme songs. ♡ So check out the CDs too! Come to think of it, they gave out CD singles as a free gift for readers in the April issue of Animedia. And speaking of CD singles, I participated (half hesitatingly) in the recording on the bonus CD that comes with buying all 3 volumes of the first OAV series. I always act for fun with my assistants, but I fell apart when I actually got up to the mic! I was so nervous. If someone was doing it for me, and I was demonstrating, "This is how you do it," I could've been more relaxed. Darnit.

Actually... on another note, I think in China, there's a pop group called "Ceres: Chinese Sugar Girls" (I think? Maybe I'm wrong.). There are 5 girls, and the group's name is Ceres! What a coincidence -I had to laugh. I've heard of them before, but they just recently came out with a photo book. I wonder how they decided on the name "Ceres"? Actually, Toyota had a car called "Ceres" too. I wonder if they were named for the same reasons.

Oh, about the question "Why does the tennyo from a Japanese legend have an English name?" I mean, she's from heaven. She's not Japanese. ...It sounds pretty too.

So what if it's English?

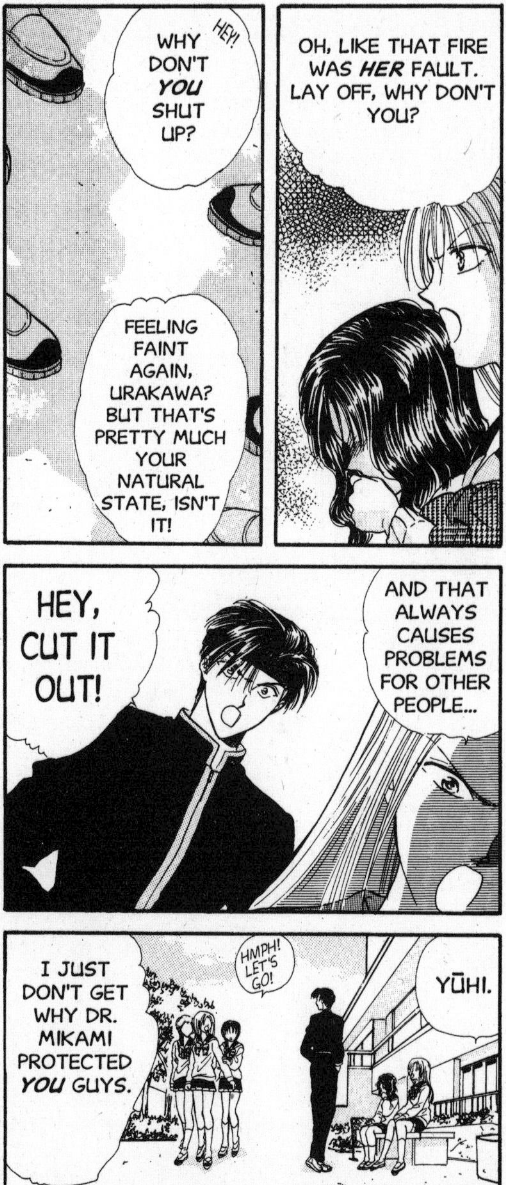
OH, LIKE THAT FIRE WAS HER FAULT. LAY OFF, WHY DON'T YOU?
HEY!
WHY DON'T YOU SHUT UP?
FEELING FAINT AGAIN, URAKAWA? BUT THAT'S PRETTY MUCH YOUR NATURAL STATE, ISN'T IT!
AND THAT ALWAYS CAUSES PROBLEMS FOR OTHER PEOPLE...
HEY, CUT IT OUT!
YŪHI.
HMPH! LET'S GO!
I JUST DON'T GET WHY DR. MIKAMI PROTECTED YOU GUYS.

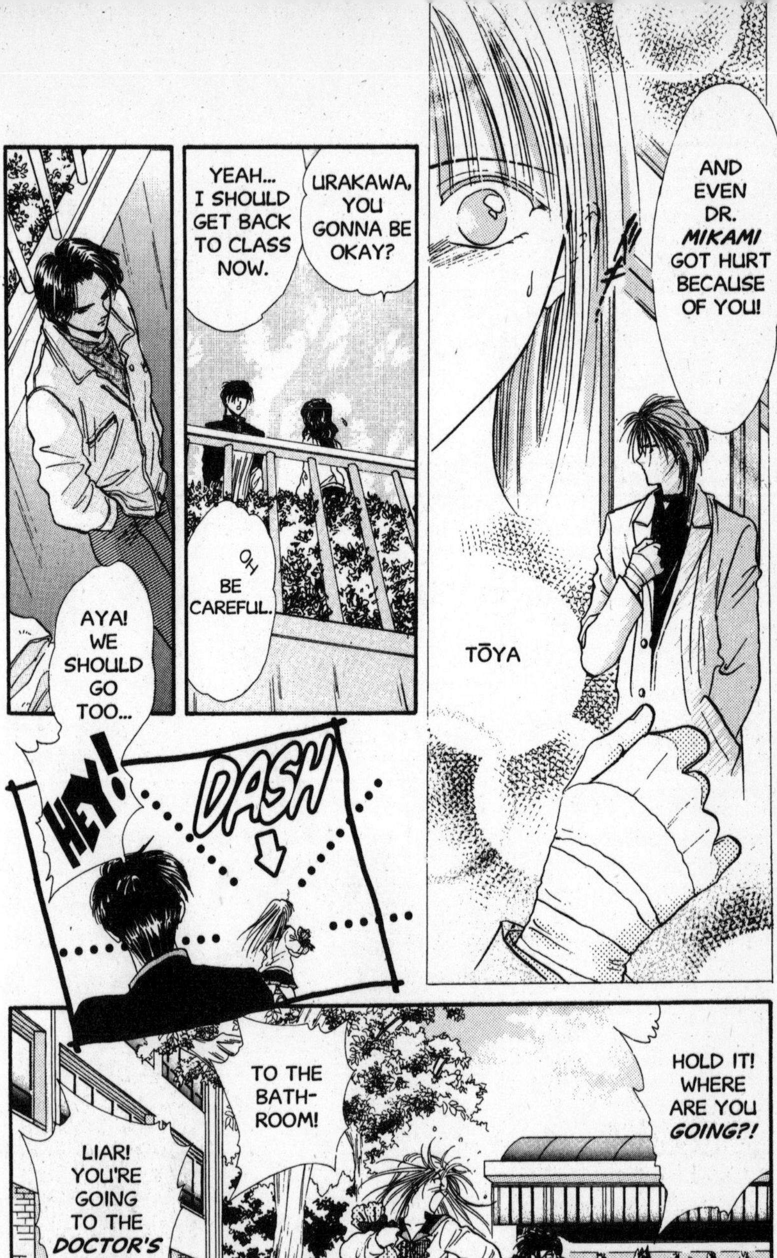
AND EVEN DR. *MIKAMI* GOT HURT BECAUSE OF YOU!
TŌYA
URAKAWA, YOU GONNA BE OKAY?
YEAH... I SHOULD GET BACK TO CLASS NOW.
OH
BE CAREFUL.
AYA! WE SHOULD GO TOO...
HEY!
DASH
HOLD IT! WHERE ARE YOU *GOING?!*
TO THE BATH-ROOM!
LIAR! YOU'RE GOING TO THE *DOCTOR'S* OFFICE!

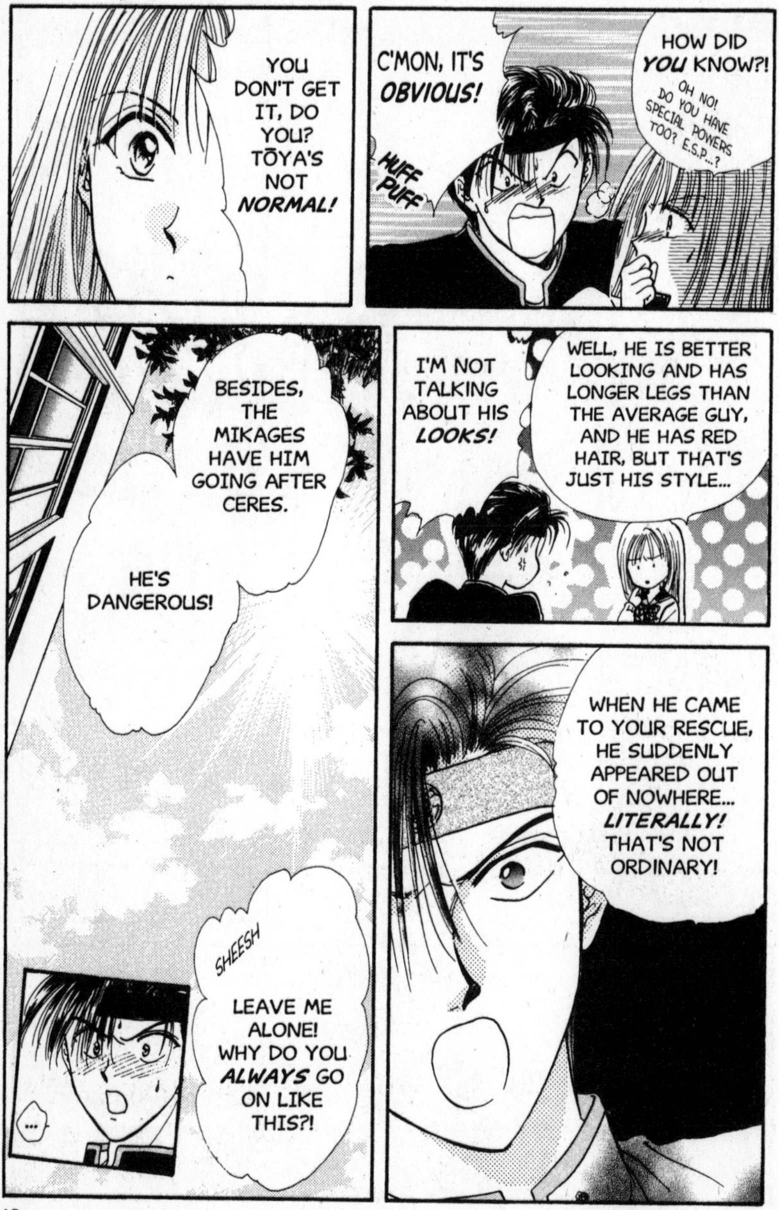
HOW DID *YOU* KNOW?!
OH NO! DO YOU HAVE SPECIAL POWERS TOO? E.S.P...?
C'MON, IT'S *OBVIOUS!*
HUFF PUFF
YOU DON'T GET IT, DO YOU? TŌYA'S NOT *NORMAL!*
WELL, HE IS BETTER LOOKING AND HAS LONGER LEGS THAN THE AVERAGE GUY, AND HE HAS RED HAIR, BUT THAT'S JUST HIS STYLE...
I'M NOT TALKING ABOUT HIS *LOOKS!*
WHEN HE CAME TO YOUR RESCUE, HE SUDDENLY APPEARED OUT OF NOWHERE... *LITERALLY!* THAT'S NOT ORDINARY!
BESIDES, THE MIKAGES HAVE HIM GOING AFTER CERES.
HE'S DANGEROUS!
SHEESH
LEAVE ME ALONE! WHY DO YOU *ALWAYS* GO ON LIKE THIS?!
...

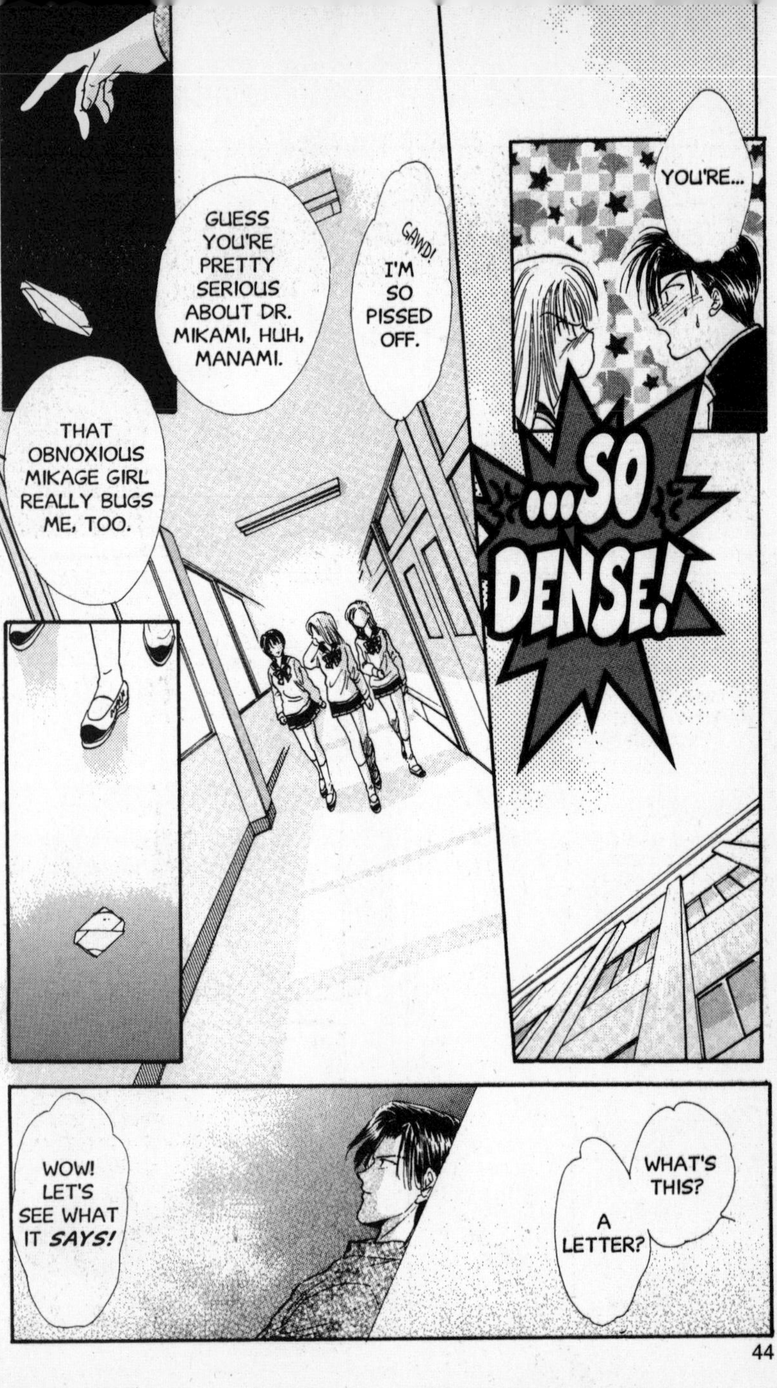
YOU'RE...
...SO DENSE!
GAWD!
I'M SO PISSED OFF.
GUESS YOU'RE PRETTY SERIOUS ABOUT DR. MIKAMI, HUH, MANAMI.
THAT OBNOXIOUS MIKAGE GIRL REALLY BUGS ME, TOO.
WHAT'S THIS?
A LETTER?
WOW! LET'S SEE WHAT IT *SAYS!*

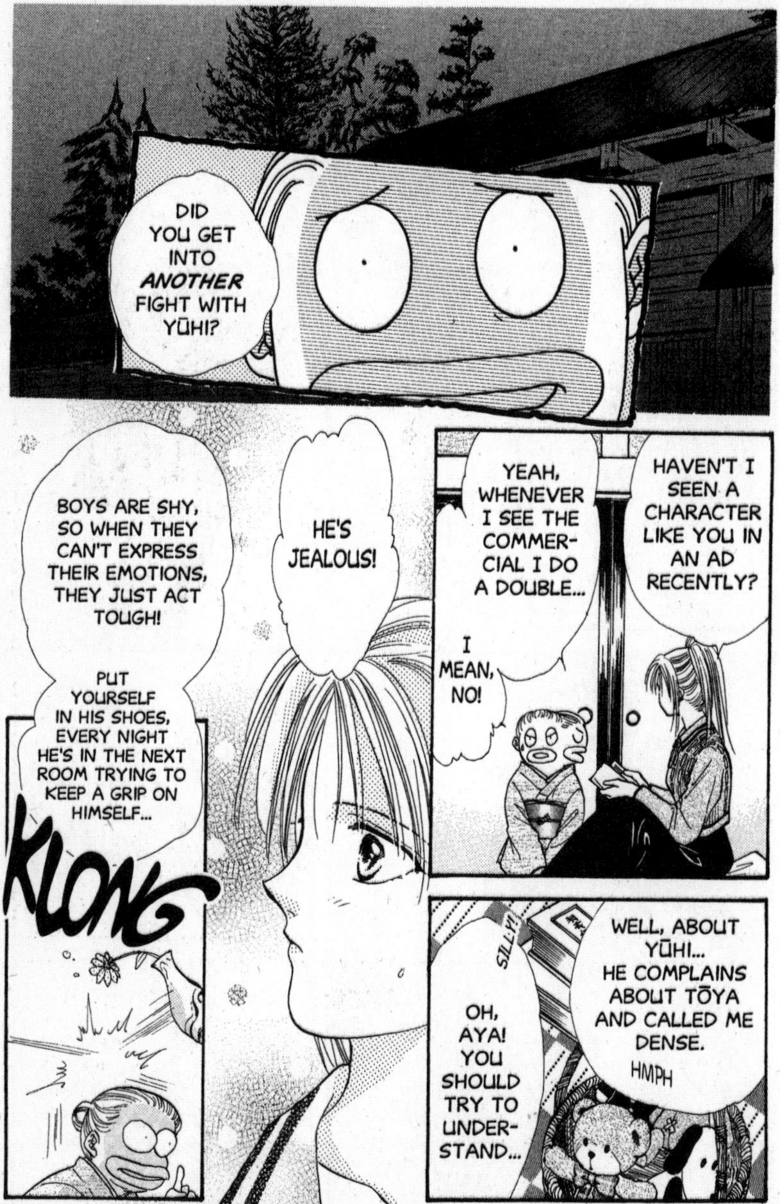
DID YOU GET INTO ANOTHER FIGHT WITH YŪHI?
HAVEN'T I SEEN A CHARACTER LIKE YOU IN AN AD RECENTLY?
YEAH, WHENEVER I SEE THE COMMERCIAL I DO A DOUBLE...
I MEAN, NO!
WELL, ABOUT YŪHI... HE COMPLAINS ABOUT TŌYA AND CALLED ME DENSE.
HMPH
SILLY!
OH, AYA! YOU SHOULD TRY TO UNDERSTAND...
HE'S JEALOUS!
BOYS ARE SHY, SO WHEN THEY CAN'T EXPRESS THEIR EMOTIONS, THEY JUST ACT TOUGH!
PUT YOURSELF IN HIS SHOES, EVERY NIGHT HE'S IN THE NEXT ROOM TRYING TO KEEP A GRIP ON HIMSELF...
KLONG

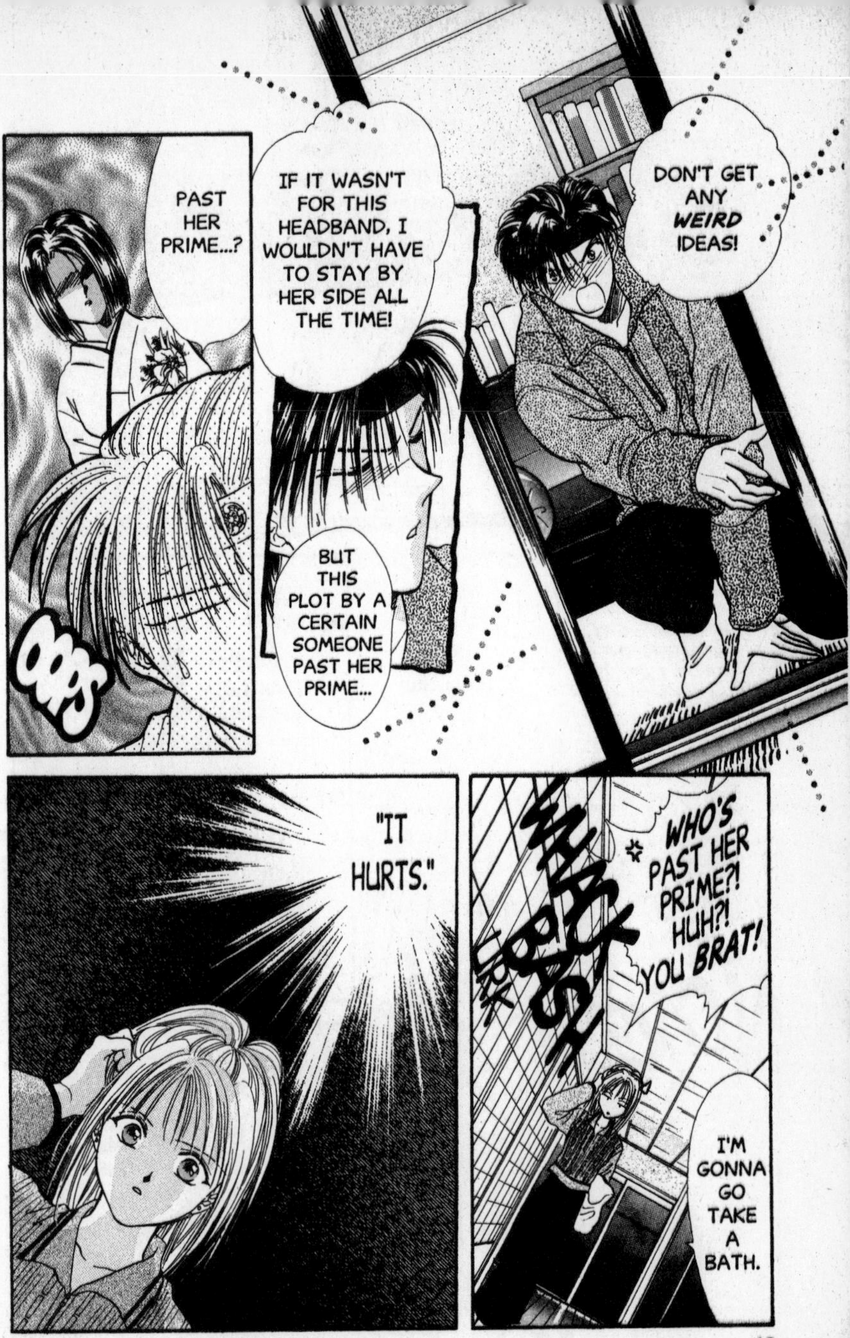
DON'T GET ANY *WEIRD* IDEAS!
IF IT WASN'T FOR THIS HEADBAND, I WOULDN'T HAVE TO STAY BY HER SIDE ALL THE TIME!
BUT THIS PLOT BY A CERTAIN SOMEONE PAST HER PRIME...
PAST HER PRIME...?
OOPS
WHO'S PAST HER PRIME?! HUH?! YOU *BRAT!*
WHACK
BASH
URK
I'M GONNA GO TAKE A BATH.
"IT HURTS."

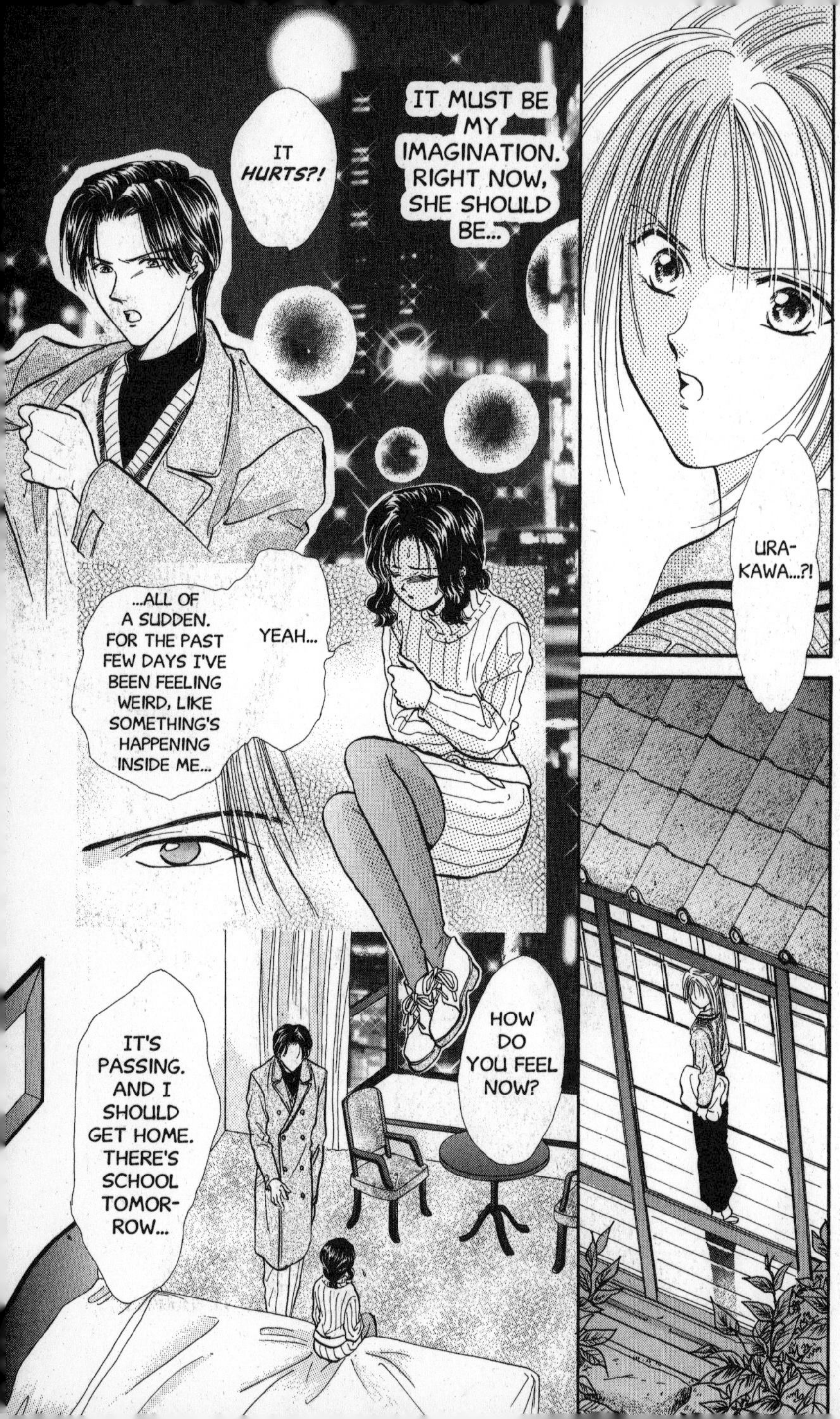
URA-KAWA...?!
IT MUST BE MY IMAGINATION. RIGHT NOW, SHE SHOULD BE...
IT HURTS?!
YEAH...
...ALL OF A SUDDEN. FOR THE PAST FEW DAYS I'VE BEEN FEELING WEIRD, LIKE SOMETHING'S HAPPENING INSIDE ME...
HOW DO YOU FEEL NOW?
IT'S PASSING. AND I SHOULD GET HOME. THERE'S SCHOOL TOMOR-ROW...

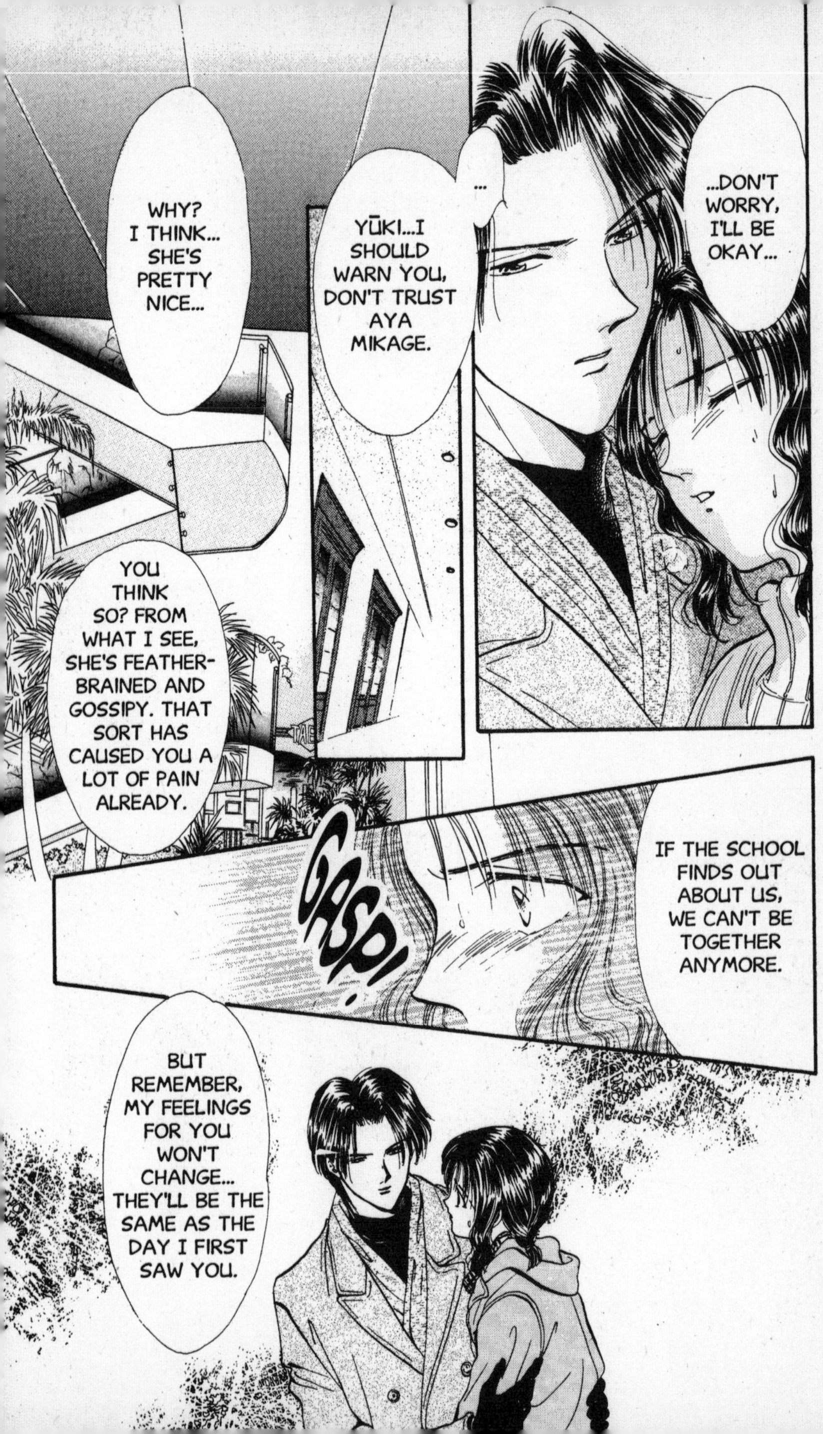
...DON'T WORRY, I'LL BE OKAY...
...
YŪKI...I SHOULD WARN YOU, DON'T TRUST AYA MIKAGE.
WHY? I THINK... SHE'S PRETTY NICE...
YOU THINK SO? FROM WHAT I SEE, SHE'S FEATHER-BRAINED AND GOSSIPY. THAT SORT HAS CAUSED YOU A LOT OF PAIN ALREADY.
IF THE SCHOOL FINDS OUT ABOUT US, WE CAN'T BE TOGETHER ANYMORE.
GASP!
BUT REMEMBER, MY FEELINGS FOR YOU WON'T CHANGE... THEY'LL BE THE SAME AS THE DAY I FIRST SAW YOU.

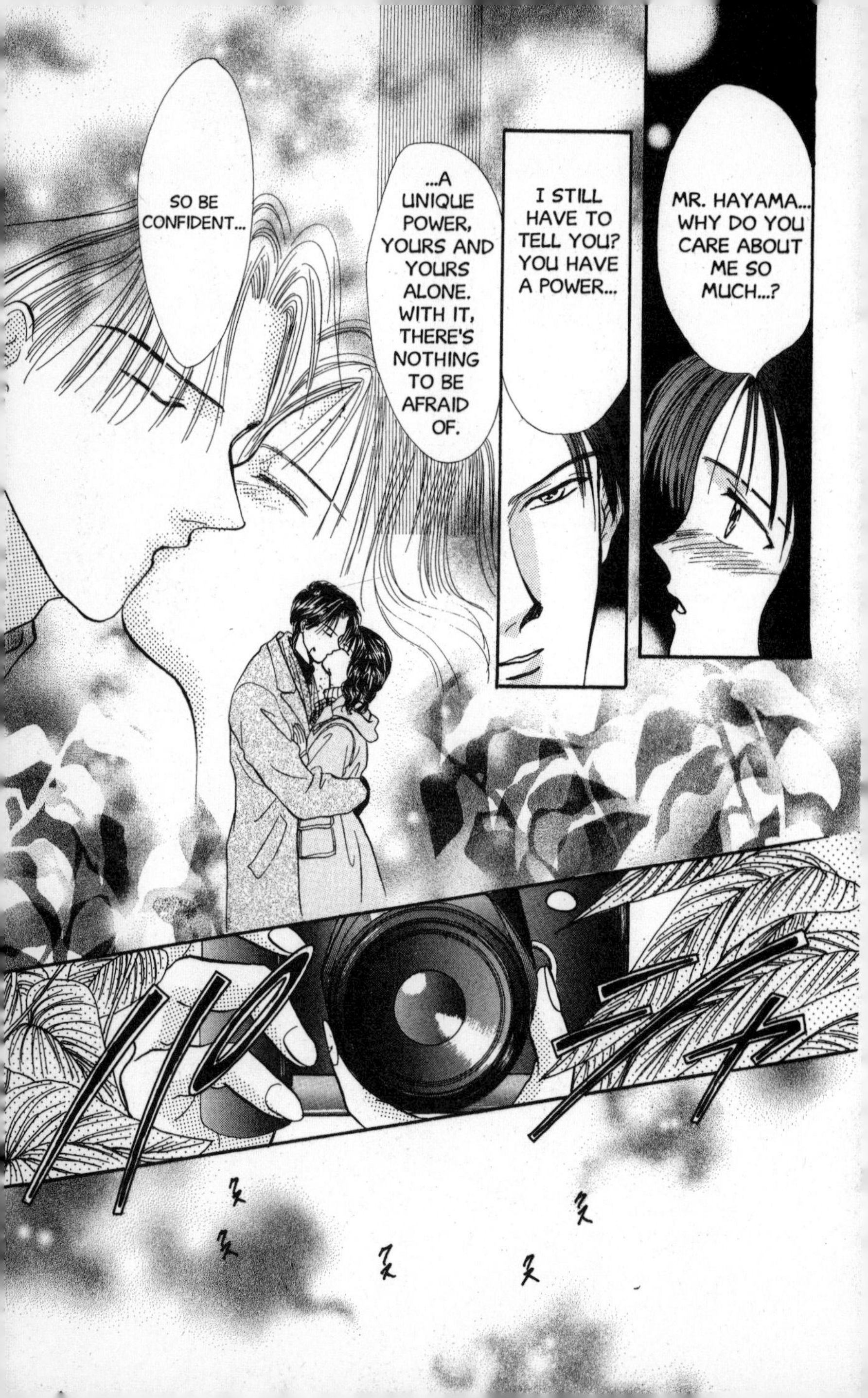
MR. HAYAMA... WHY DO YOU CARE ABOUT ME SO MUCH...?
I STILL HAVE TO TELL YOU? YOU HAVE A POWER...
...A UNIQUE POWER, YOURS AND YOURS ALONE. WITH IT, THERE'S NOTHING TO BE AFRAID OF.
SO BE CONFIDENT...

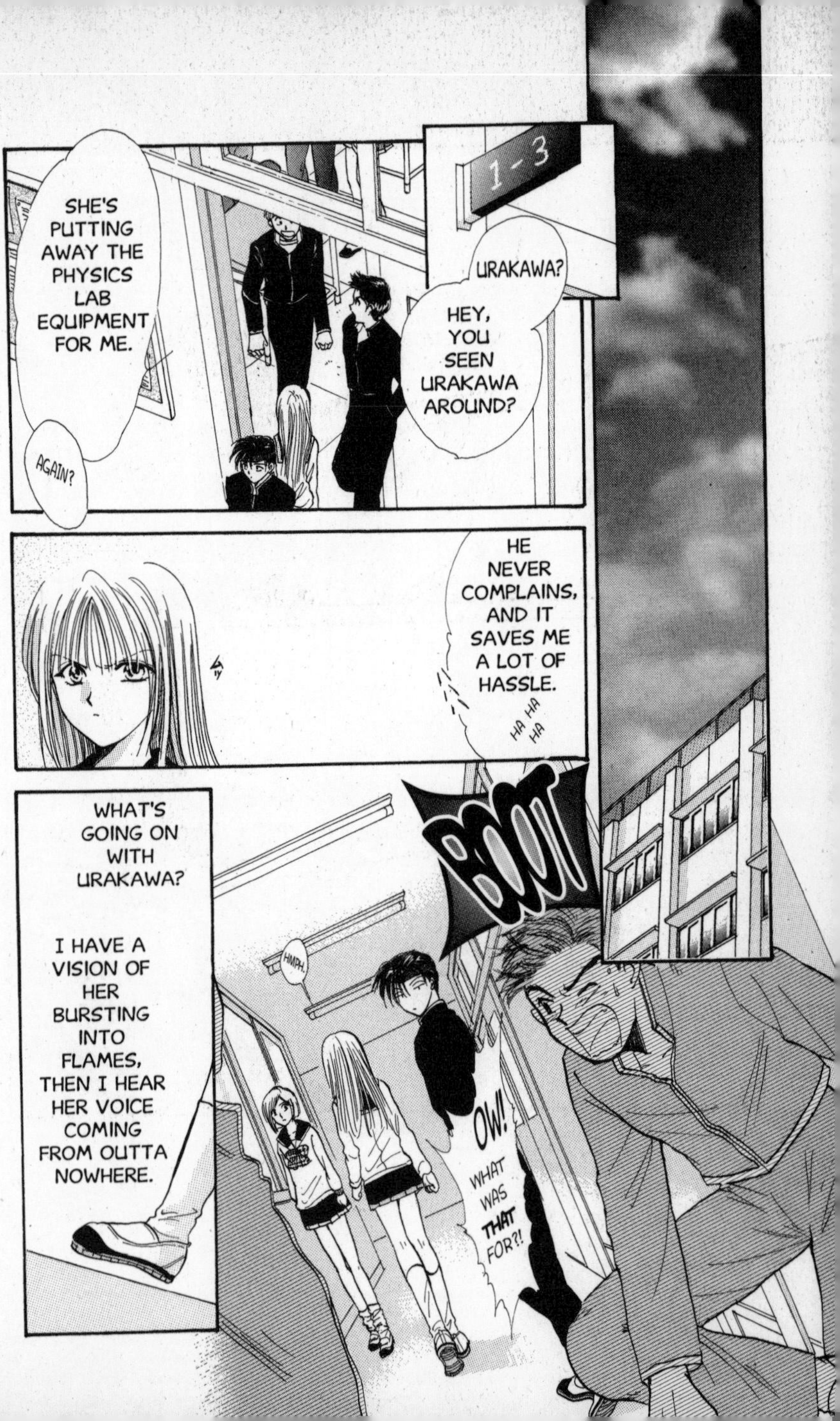
1-3
URAKAWA?
HEY, YOU SEEN URAKAWA AROUND?
SHE'S PUTTING AWAY THE PHYSICS LAB EQUIPMENT FOR ME.
AGAIN?
HE NEVER COMPLAINS, AND IT SAVES ME A LOT OF HASSLE.
HA HA HA
ムッ
BOOT
OW!
WHAT WAS THAT FOR?!
HMPH.
WHAT'S GOING ON WITH URAKAWA?
I HAVE A VISION OF HER BURSTING INTO FLAMES, THEN I HEAR HER VOICE COMING FROM OUTTA NOWHERE.

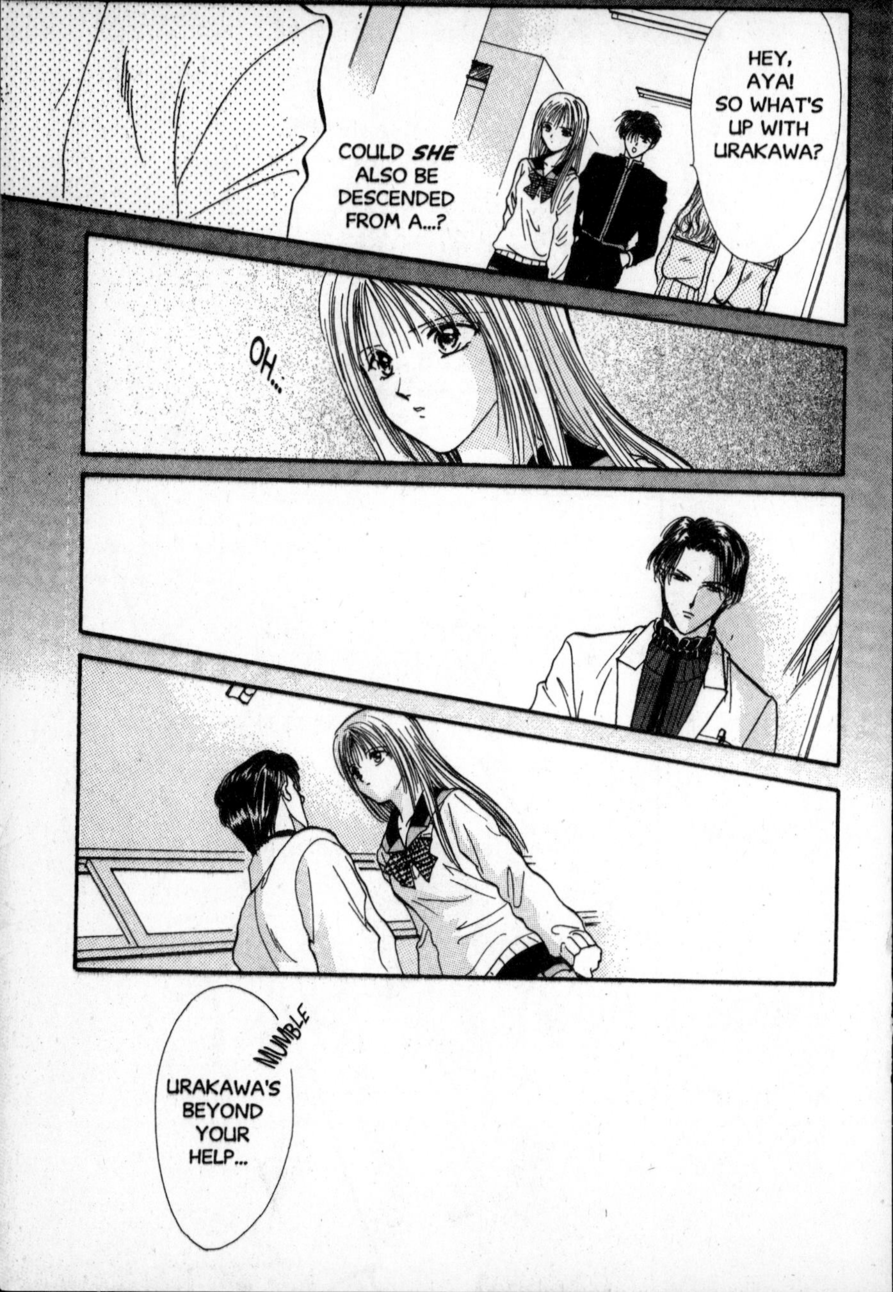
HEY, AYA! SO WHAT'S UP WITH URAKAWA?
COULD *SHE* ALSO BE DESCENDED FROM A...?
OH...
MUMBLE
URAKAWA'S BEYOND YOUR HELP...

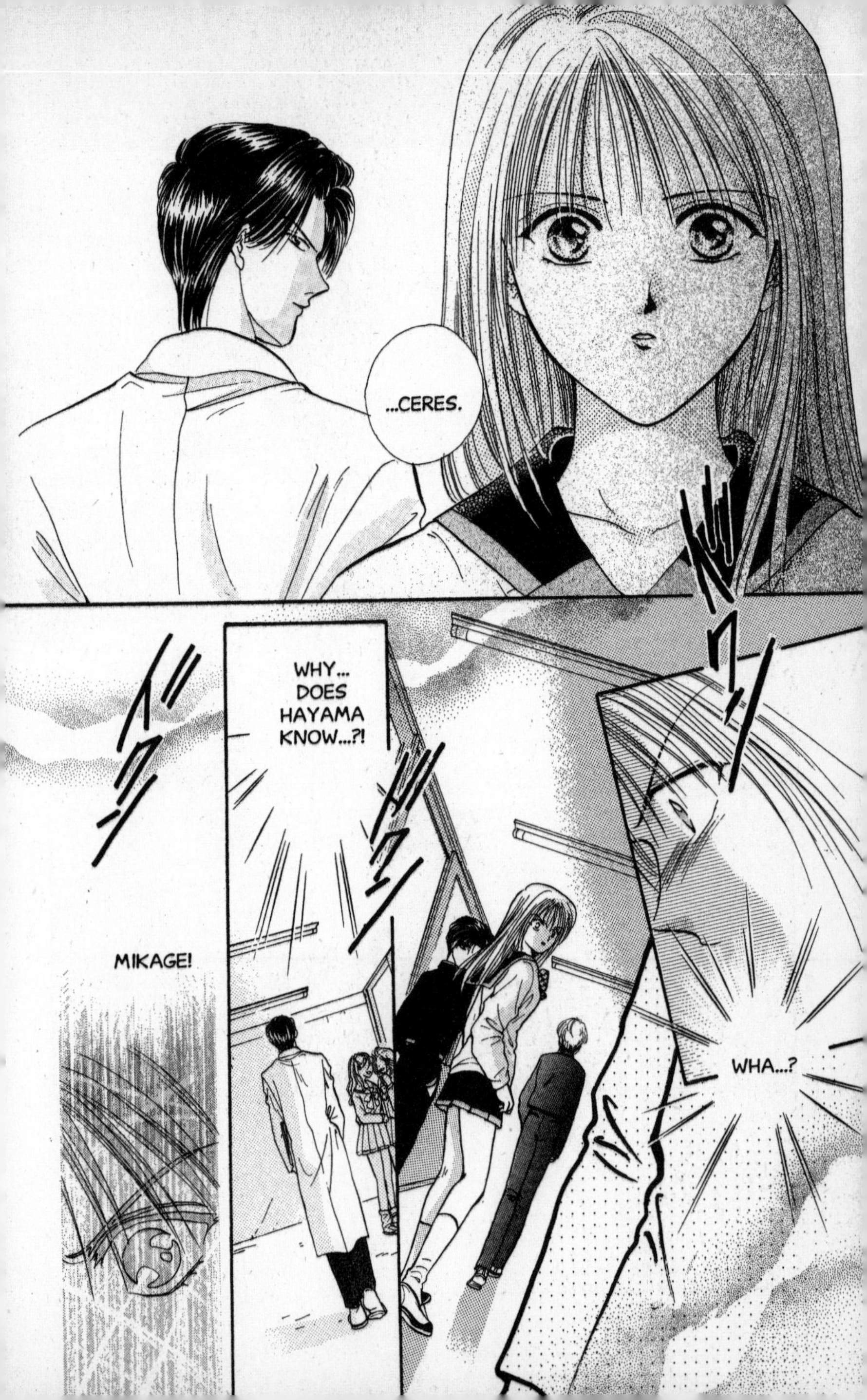
...CERES.
WHA...?
WHY... DOES HAYAMA KNOW...?!
MIKAGE!

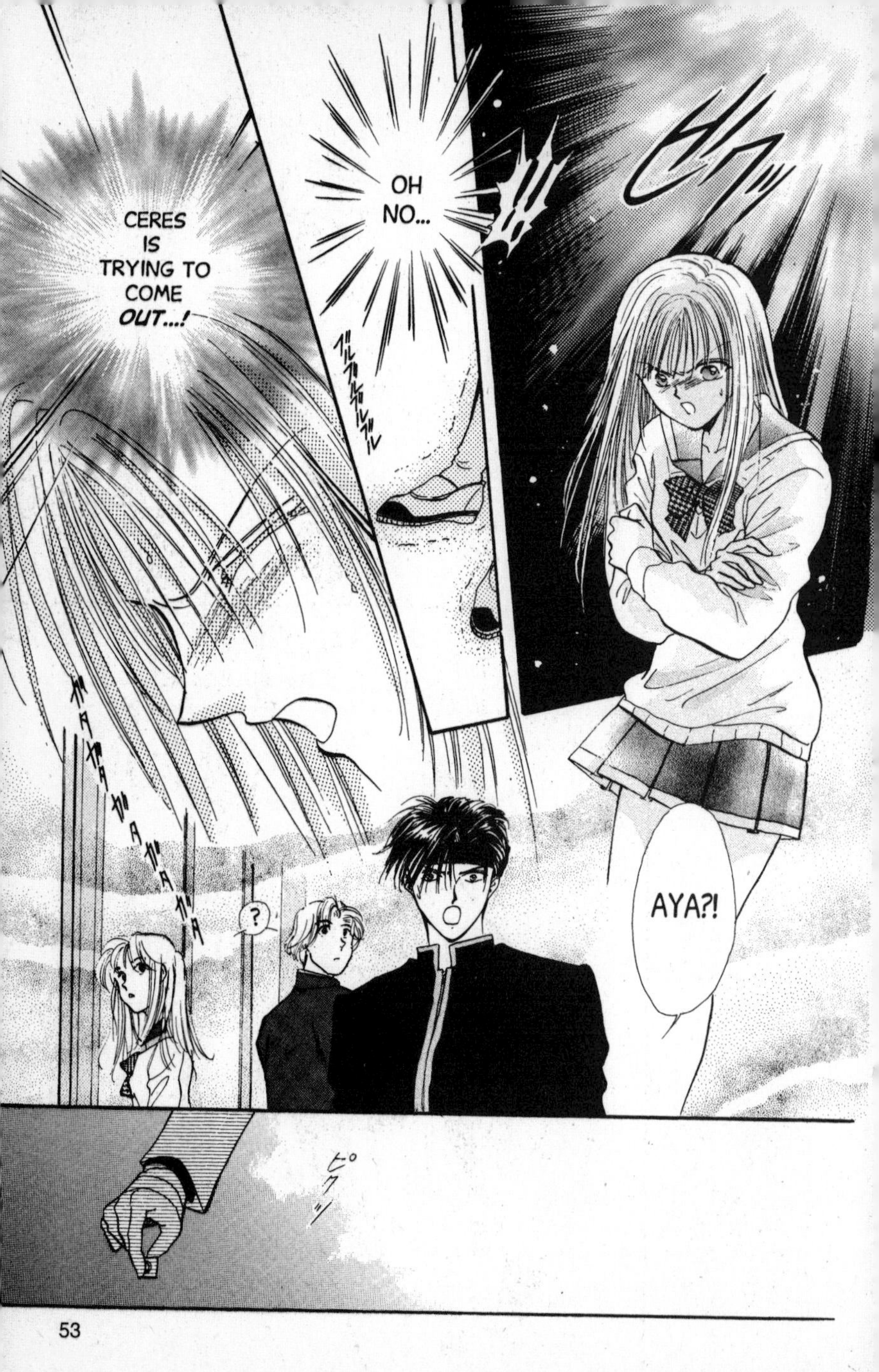
OH NO...
CERES IS TRYING TO COME *OUT*...!
AYA?!
?

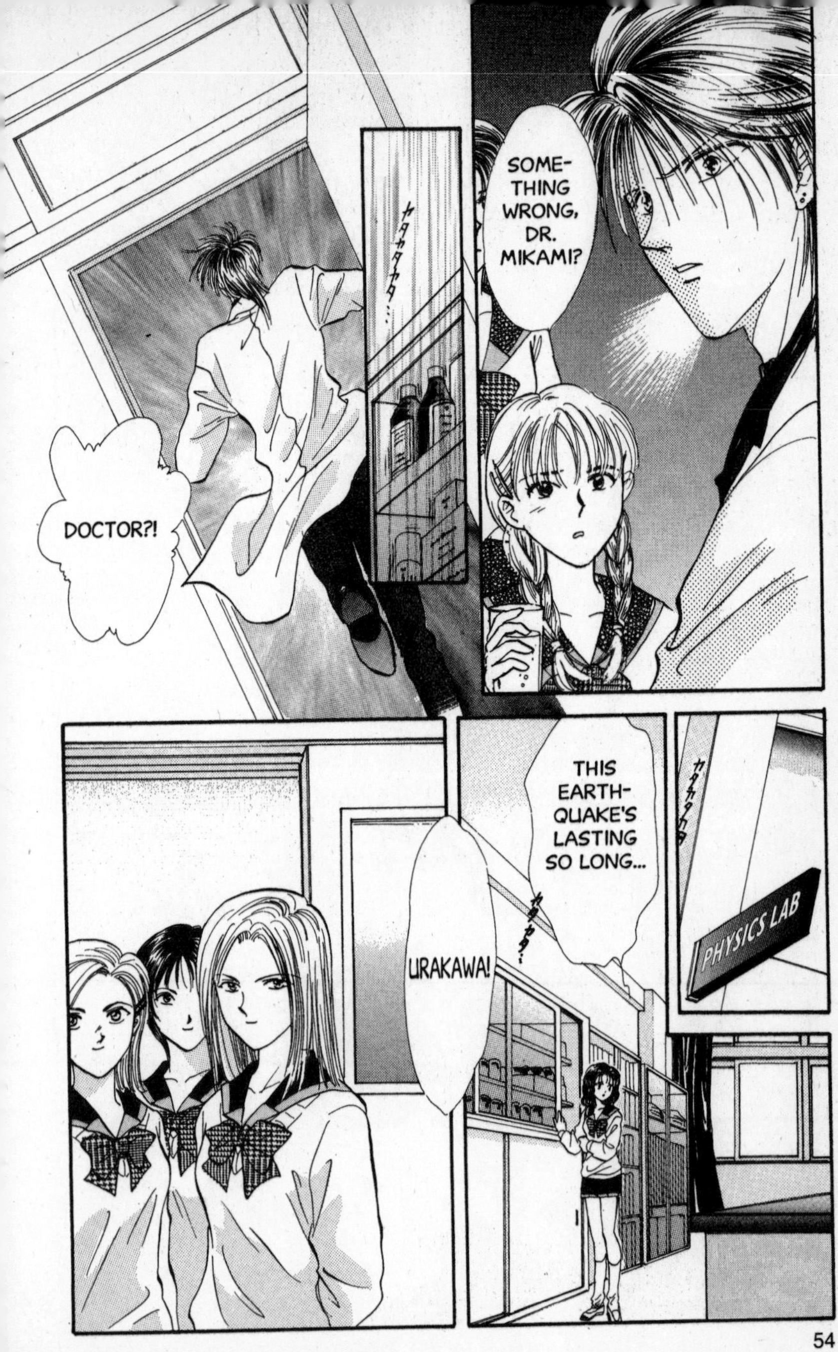
SOME-THING WRONG, DR. MIKAMI?
DOCTOR?!
PHYSICS LAB
THIS EARTH-QUAKE'S LASTING SO LONG...
URAKAWA!

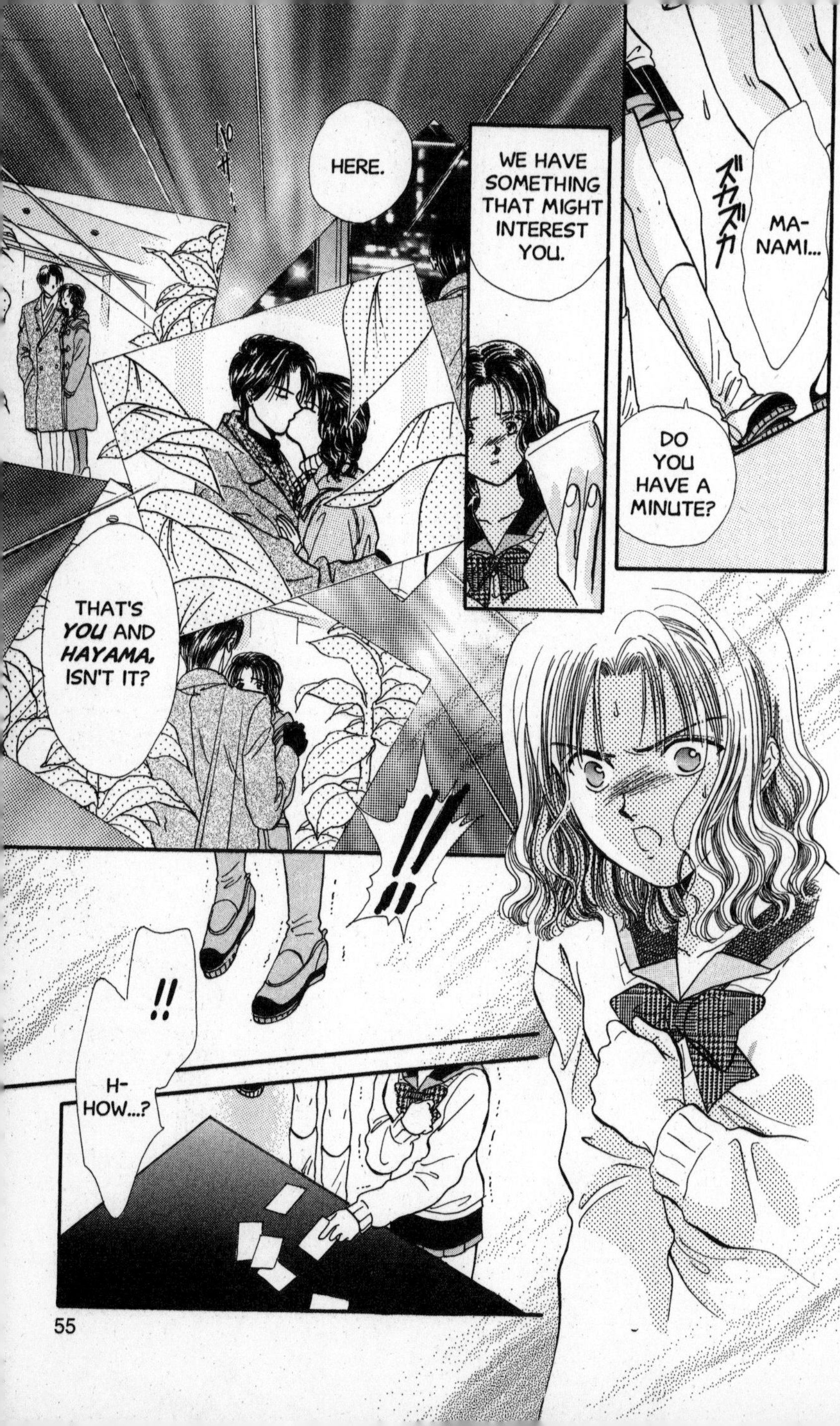

ズカズカ
MA-NAMI...
DO YOU HAVE A MINUTE?
WE HAVE SOMETHING THAT MIGHT INTEREST YOU.
HERE.
パサ…
THAT'S *YOU* AND *HAYAMA,* ISN'T IT?
!!
!!
H-HOW...?

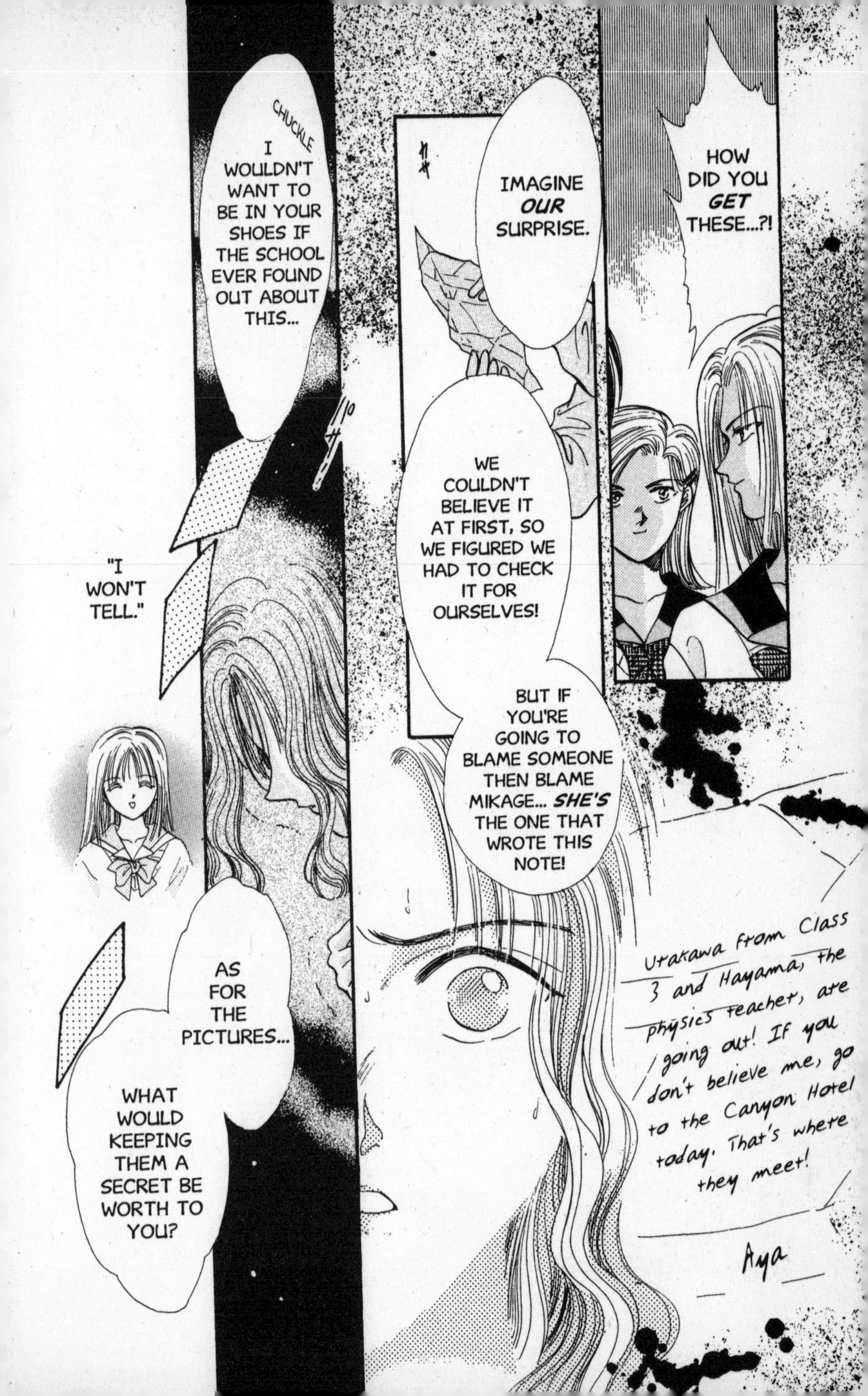
HOW DID YOU GET THESE...?!
IMAGINE OUR SURPRISE.
WE COULDN'T BELIEVE IT AT FIRST, SO WE FIGURED WE HAD TO CHECK IT FOR OURSELVES!
BUT IF YOU'RE GOING TO BLAME SOMEONE THEN BLAME MIKAGE... SHE'S THE ONE THAT WROTE THIS NOTE!
Utakawa from Class 3 and Hayama, the physics teacher, are going out! If you don't believe me, go to the Canyon Hotel today. That's where they meet!
Aya
CHUCKLE
I WOULDN'T WANT TO BE IN YOUR SHOES IF THE SCHOOL EVER FOUND OUT ABOUT THIS...
"I WON'T TELL."
AS FOR THE PICTURES...
WHAT WOULD KEEPING THEM A SECRET BE WORTH TO YOU?

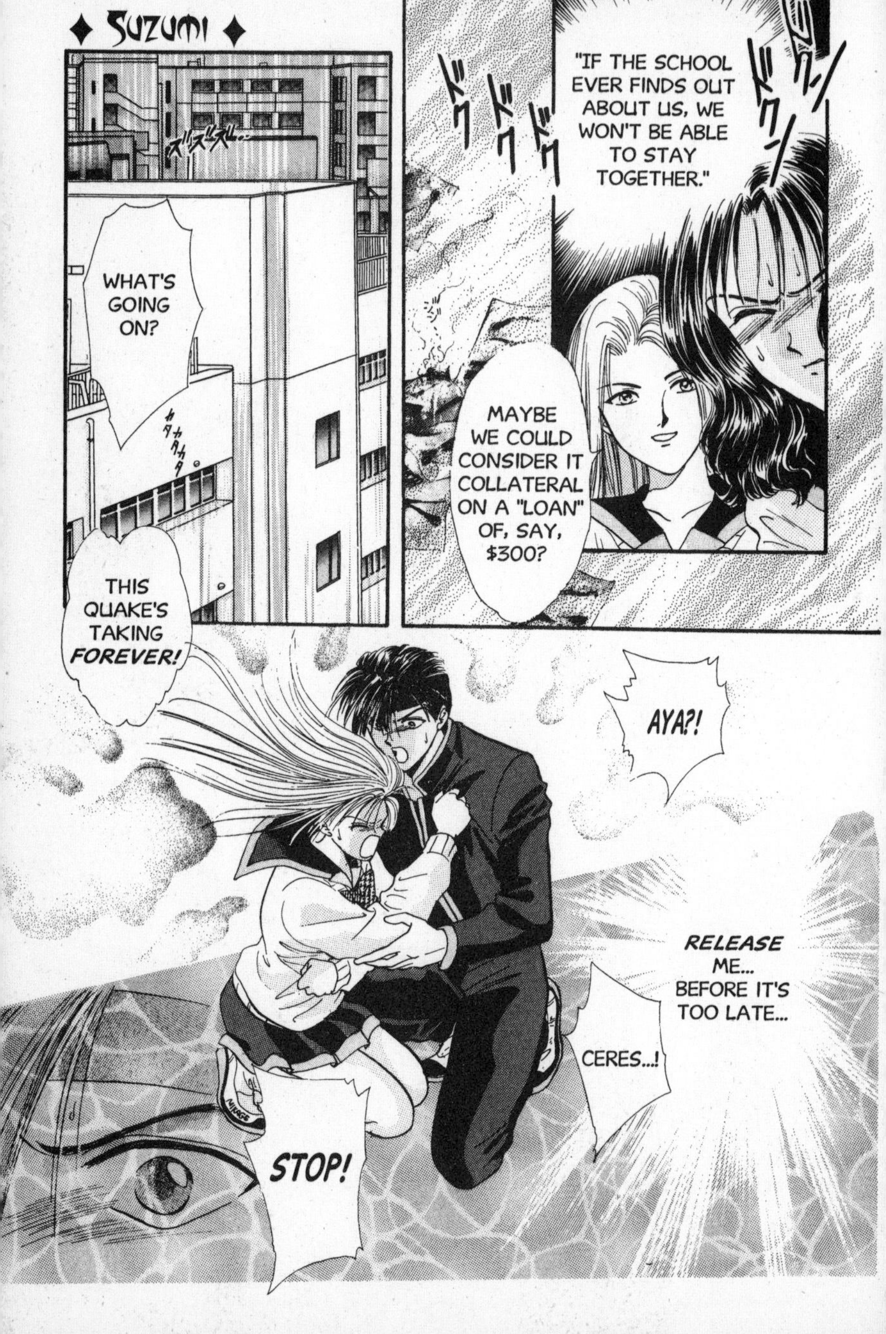
SUZUMI
"IF THE SCHOOL EVER FINDS OUT ABOUT US, WE WON'T BE ABLE TO STAY TOGETHER."
MAYBE WE COULD CONSIDER IT COLLATERAL ON A "LOAN" OF, SAY, $300?
WHAT'S GOING ON?
THIS QUAKE'S TAKING *FOREVER!*
AYA?!
RELEASE ME... BEFORE IT'S TOO LATE...
CERES...!
STOP!

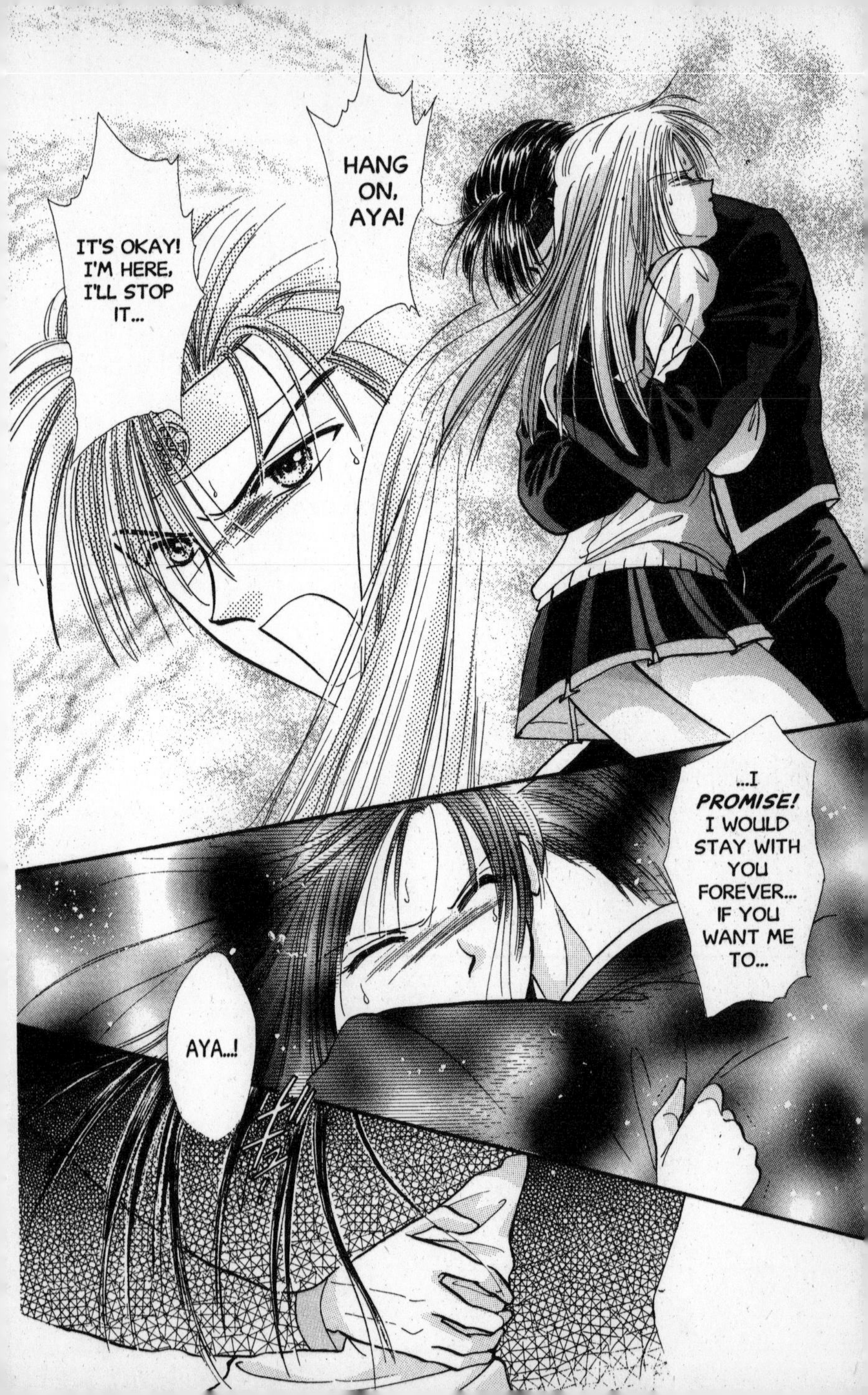
HANG ON, AYA!
IT'S OKAY! I'M HERE, I'LL STOP IT...
...I *PROMISE!* I WOULD STAY WITH YOU FOREVER... IF YOU WANT ME TO...
AYA..!

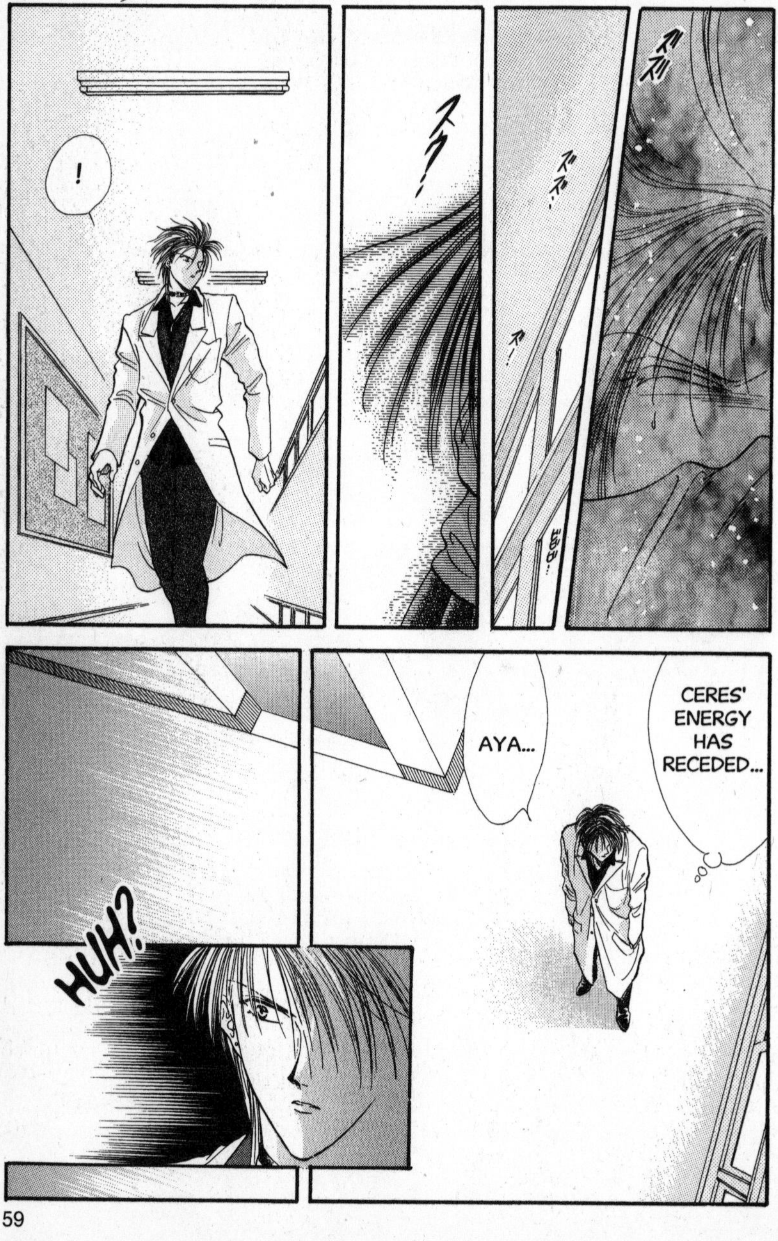
ズズ
ズズ…
ズ…
スク!!
!
CERES' ENERGY HAS RECEDED...
AYA...
HUH?

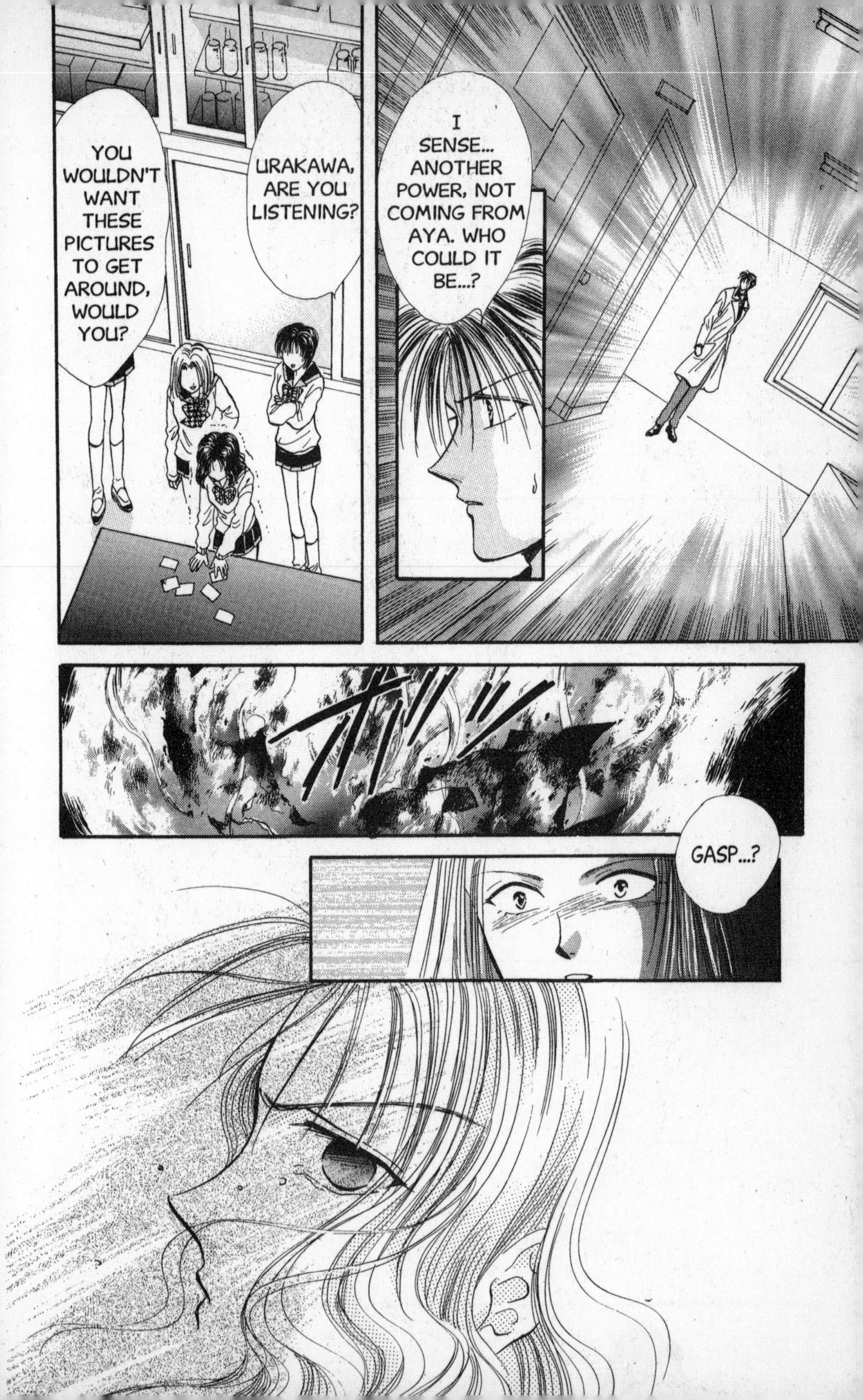
I SENSE... ANOTHER POWER, NOT COMING FROM AYA. WHO COULD IT BE...?
URAKAWA, ARE YOU LISTENING?
YOU WOULDN'T WANT THESE PICTURES TO GET AROUND, WOULD YOU?
GASP...?

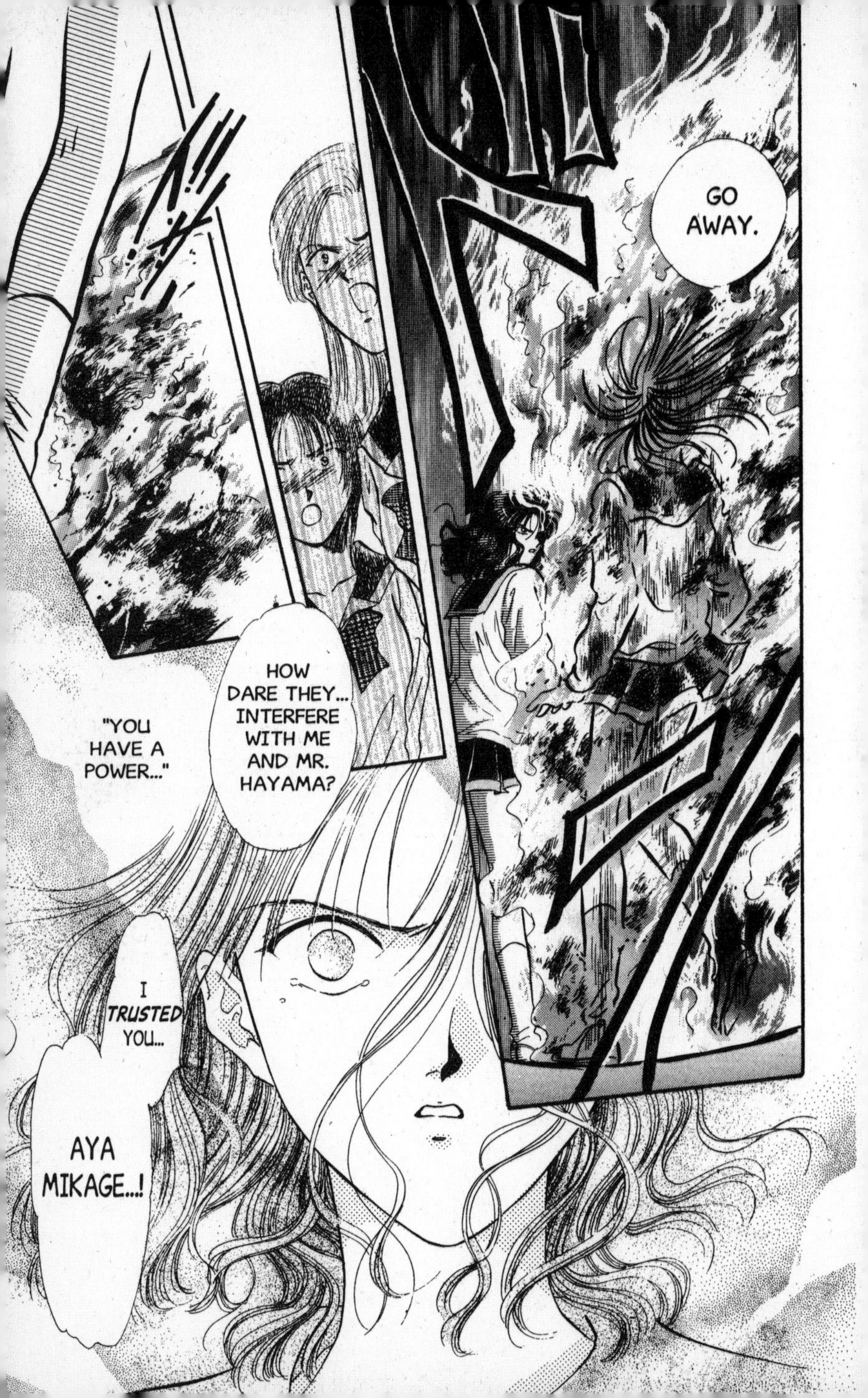
GO AWAY.
HOW DARE THEY... INTERFERE WITH ME AND MR. HAYAMA?
"YOU HAVE A POWER..."
I *TRUSTED* YOU...
AYA MIKAGE...!

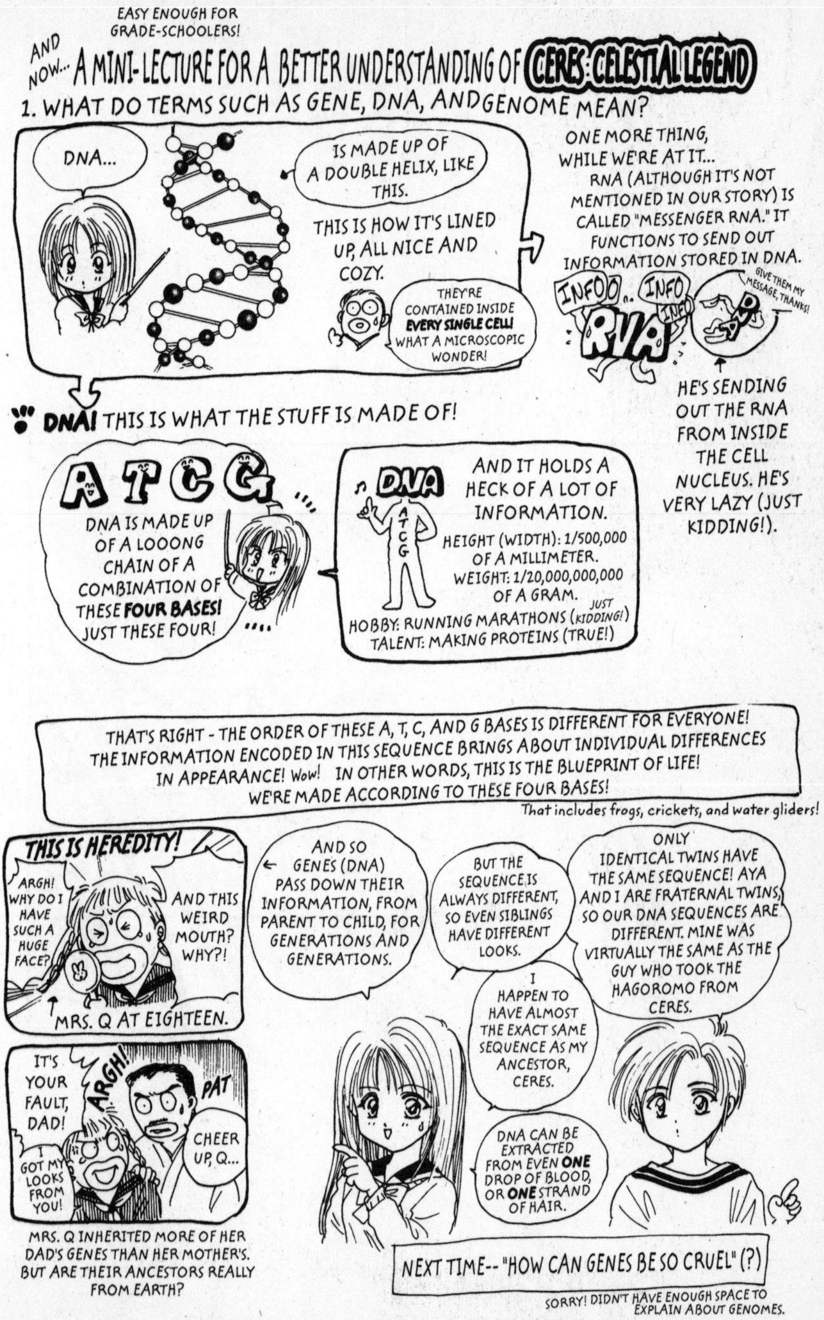

EASY ENOUGH FOR GRADE-SCHOOLERS!
AND NOW... A MINI-LECTURE FOR A BETTER UNDERSTANDING OF CERES: CELESTIAL LEGEND
1. WHAT DO TERMS SUCH AS GENE, DNA, ANDGENOME MEAN?
DNA...
IS MADE UP OF A DOUBLE HELIX, LIKE THIS.
THIS IS HOW IT'S LINED UP, ALL NICE AND COZY.
THEY'RE CONTAINED INSIDE EVERY SINGLE CELL! WHAT A MICROSCOPIC WONDER!
ONE MORE THING, WHILE WE'RE AT IT... RNA (ALTHOUGH IT'S NOT MENTIONED IN OUR STORY) IS CALLED "MESSENGER RNA." IT FUNCTIONS TO SEND OUT INFORMATION STORED IN DNA.
INFO
INFO
INFO
RNA
GIVE THEM MY MESSAGE, THANKS!
DNA
HE'S SENDING OUT THE RNA FROM INSIDE THE CELL NUCLEUS. HE'S VERY LAZY (JUST KIDDING!).
DNA! THIS IS WHAT THE STUFF IS MADE OF!
A T C G
DNA IS MADE UP OF A LOOONG CHAIN OF A COMBINATION OF THESE FOUR BASES! JUST THESE FOUR!
DNA
A T C G
AND IT HOLDS A HECK OF A LOT OF INFORMATION.
HEIGHT (WIDTH): 1/500,000 OF A MILLIMETER.
WEIGHT: 1/20,000,000,000 OF A GRAM.
HOBBY: RUNNING MARATHONS (JUST KIDDING!)
TALENT: MAKING PROTEINS (TRUE!)
THAT'S RIGHT - THE ORDER OF THESE A, T, C, AND G BASES IS DIFFERENT FOR EVERYONE! THE INFORMATION ENCODED IN THIS SEQUENCE BRINGS ABOUT INDIVIDUAL DIFFERENCES IN APPEARANCE! Wow! IN OTHER WORDS, THIS IS THE BLUEPRINT OF LIFE! WE'RE MADE ACCORDING TO THESE FOUR BASES!
That includes frogs, crickets, and water gliders!
THIS IS HEREDITY!
PAT
ARGH! WHY DO I HAVE SUCH A HUGE FACE?
AND THIS WEIRD MOUTH? WHY?!
MRS. Q AT EIGHTEEN.
IT'S YOUR FAULT, DAD!
ARGH!
PAT
I GOT MY LOOKS FROM YOU!
CHEER UP, Q...
MRS. Q INHERITED MORE OF HER DAD'S GENES THAN HER MOTHER'S. BUT ARE THEIR ANCESTORS REALLY FROM EARTH?
AND SO GENES (DNA) PASS DOWN THEIR INFORMATION, FROM PARENT TO CHILD, FOR GENERATIONS AND GENERATIONS.
BUT THE SEQUENCE IS ALWAYS DIFFERENT, SO EVEN SIBLINGS HAVE DIFFERENT LOOKS.
ONLY IDENTICAL TWINS HAVE THE SAME SEQUENCE! AYA AND I ARE FRATERNAL TWINS, SO OUR DNA SEQUENCES ARE DIFFERENT. MINE WAS VIRTUALLY THE SAME AS THE GUY WHO TOOK THE HAGOROMO FROM CERES.
I HAPPEN TO HAVE ALMOST THE EXACT SAME SEQUENCE AS MY ANCESTOR, CERES.
DNA CAN BE EXTRACTED FROM EVEN ONE DROP OF BLOOD, OR ONE STRAND OF HAIR.
NEXT TIME-- "HOW CAN GENES BE SO CRUEL" (?)
SORRY! DIDN'T HAVE ENOUGH SPACE TO EXPLAIN ABOUT GENOMES.

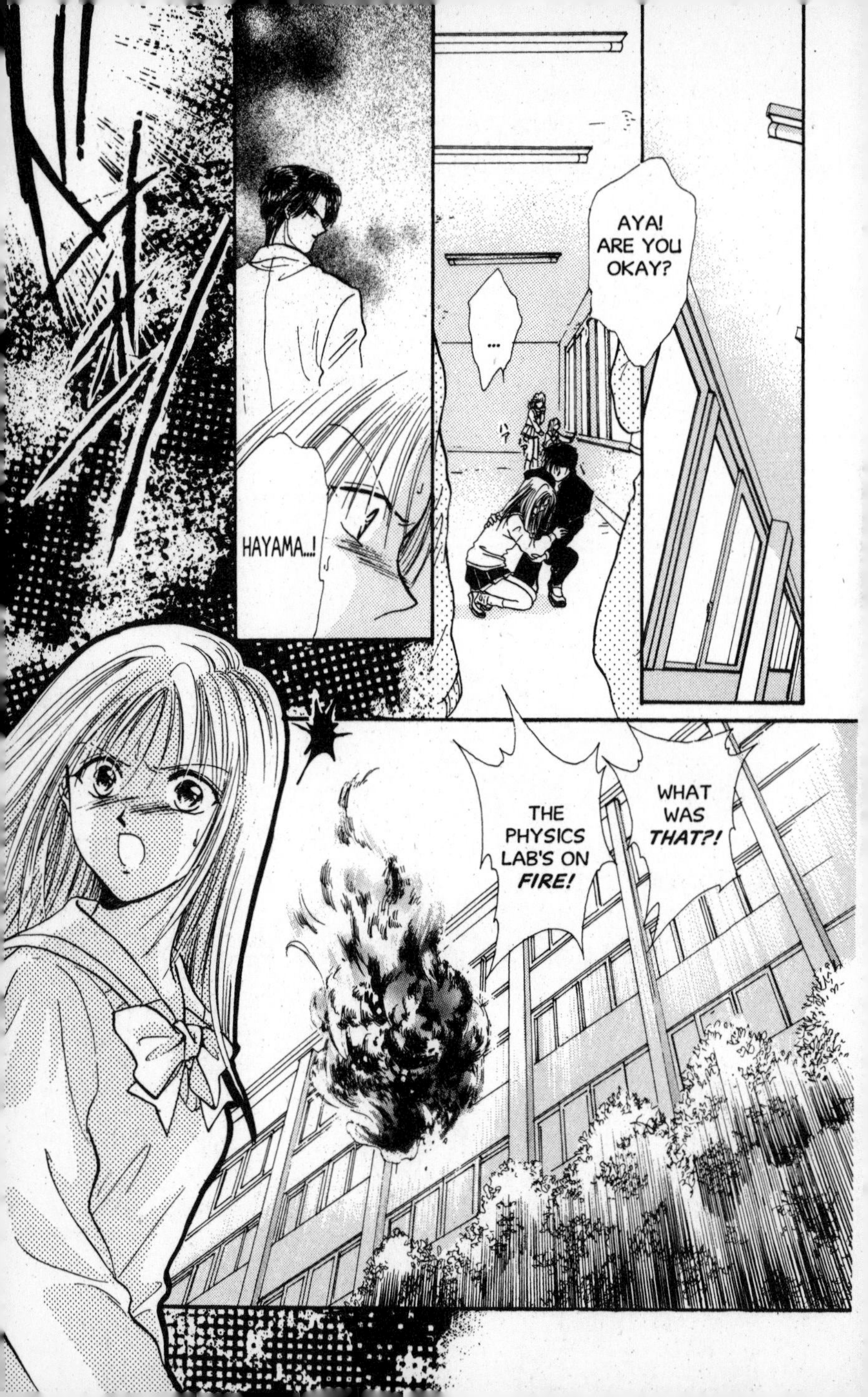
AYA! ARE YOU OKAY?
...
HAYAMA...!
WHAT WAS *THAT?!*
THE PHYSICS LAB'S ON *FIRE!*

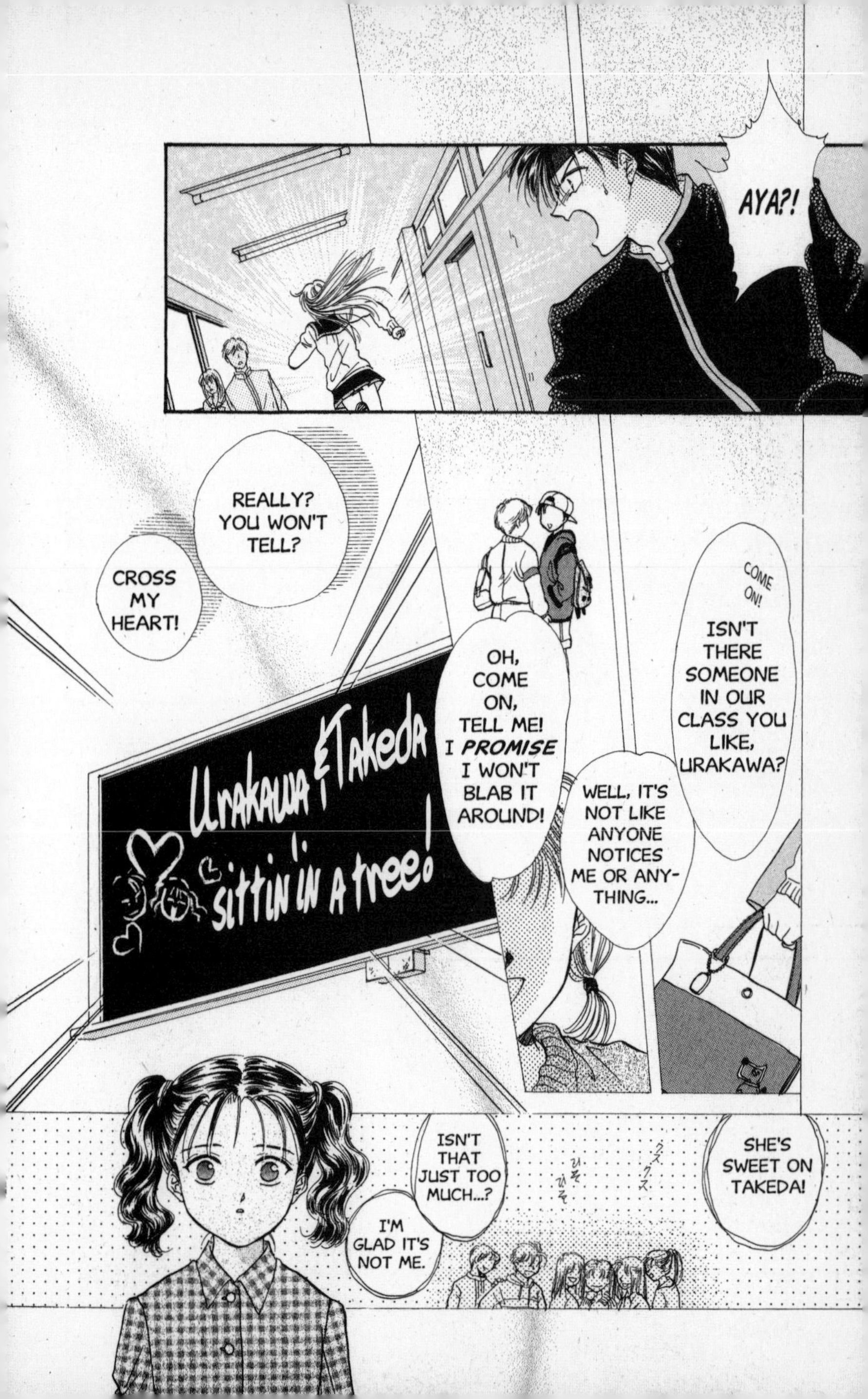
AYA?!
COME ON!
ISN'T THERE SOMEONE IN OUR CLASS YOU LIKE, URAKAWA?
WELL, IT'S NOT LIKE ANYONE NOTICES ME OR ANYTHING...
OH, COME ON, TELL ME! I *PROMISE* I WON'T BLAB IT AROUND!
REALLY? YOU WON'T TELL?
CROSS MY HEART!
Urakawa & Takeda
sittin' in a tree!
SHE'S SWEET ON TAKEDA!
クスクス
ひそひそ
ISN'T THAT JUST TOO MUCH...?
I'M GLAD IT'S NOT ME.

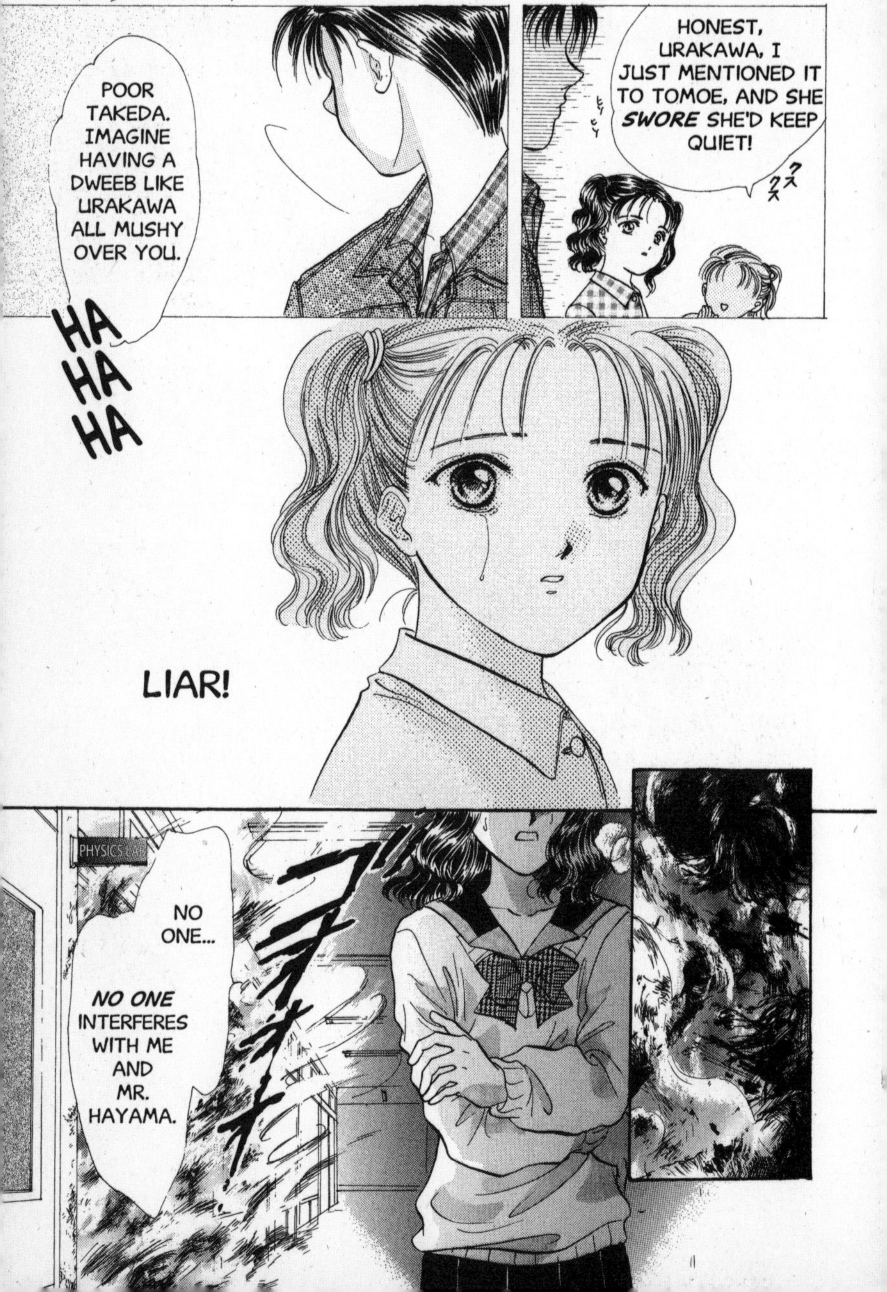
HONEST, URAKAWA, I JUST MENTIONED IT TO TOMOE, AND SHE *SWORE* SHE'D KEEP QUIET!
POOR TAKEDA. IMAGINE HAVING A DWEEB LIKE URAKAWA ALL MUSHY OVER YOU.
HA HA HA
LIAR!
PHYSICS LAB
NO ONE...
NO ONE INTERFERES WITH ME AND MR. HAYAMA.

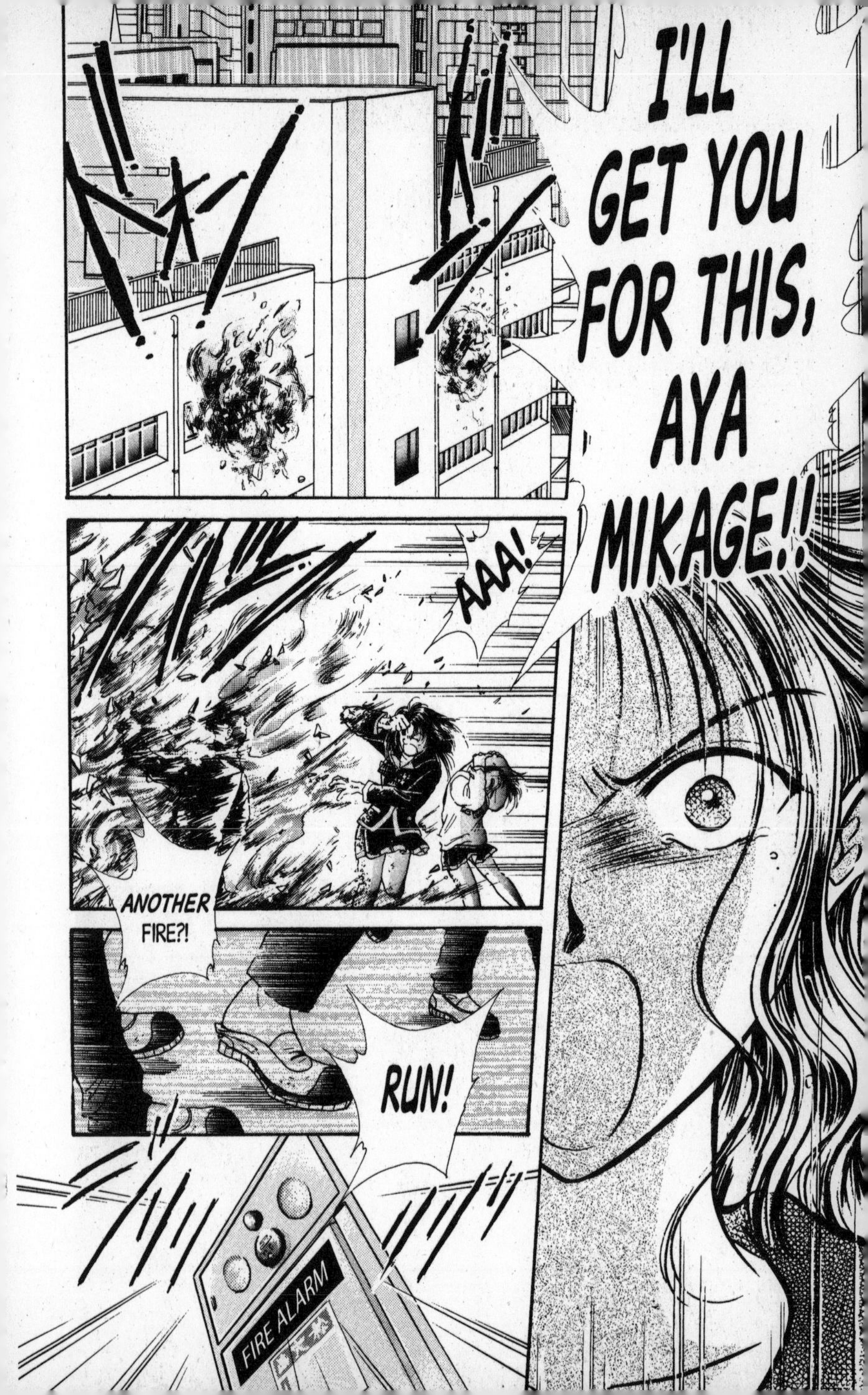
I'LL GET YOU FOR THIS, AYA MIKAGE!!
AAA!
ANOTHER FIRE?!
RUN!
FIRE ALARM

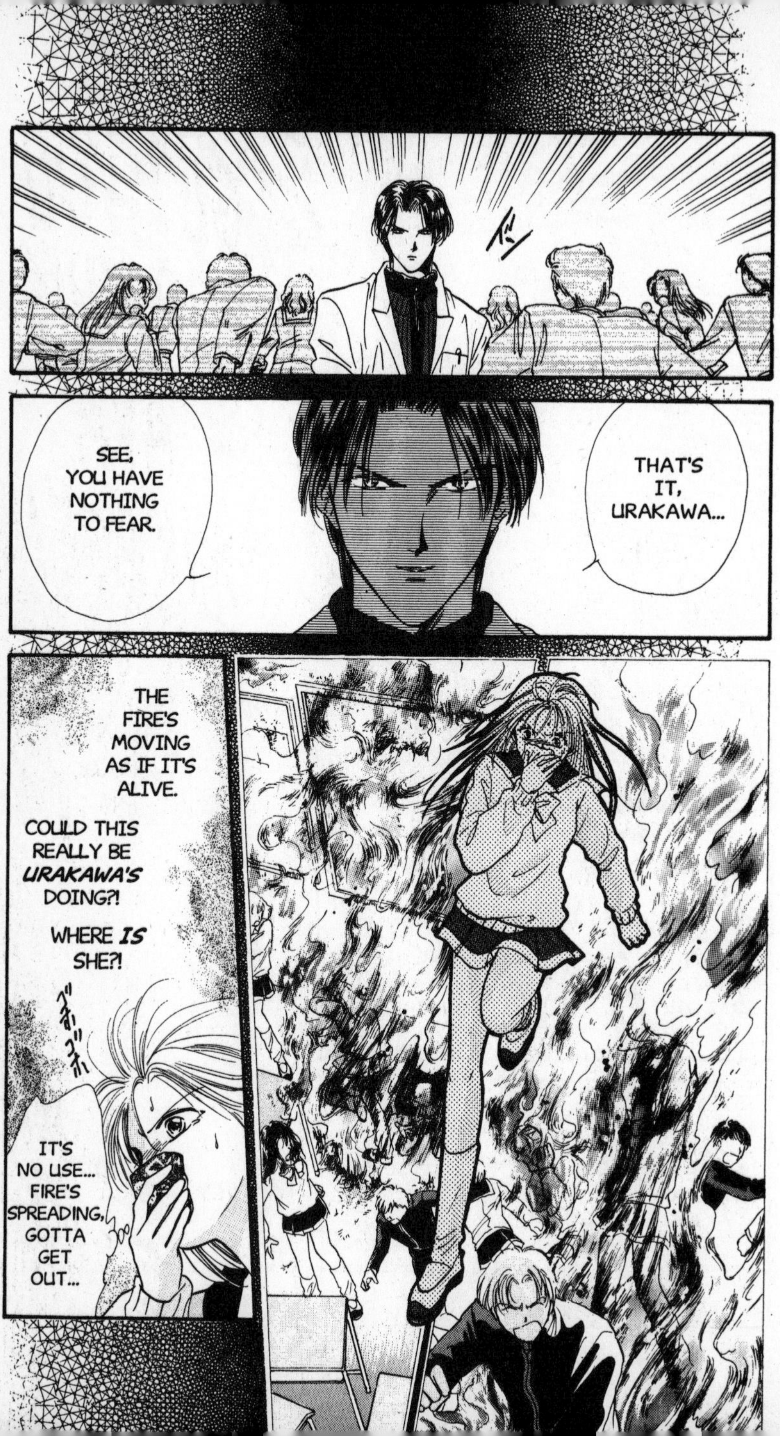
THAT'S IT, URAKAWA...
SEE, YOU HAVE NOTHING TO FEAR.
THE FIRE'S MOVING AS IF IT'S ALIVE.
COULD THIS REALLY BE *URAKAWA'S* DOING?!
WHERE *IS* SHE?!
IT'S NO USE... FIRE'S SPREADING, GOTTA GET OUT...

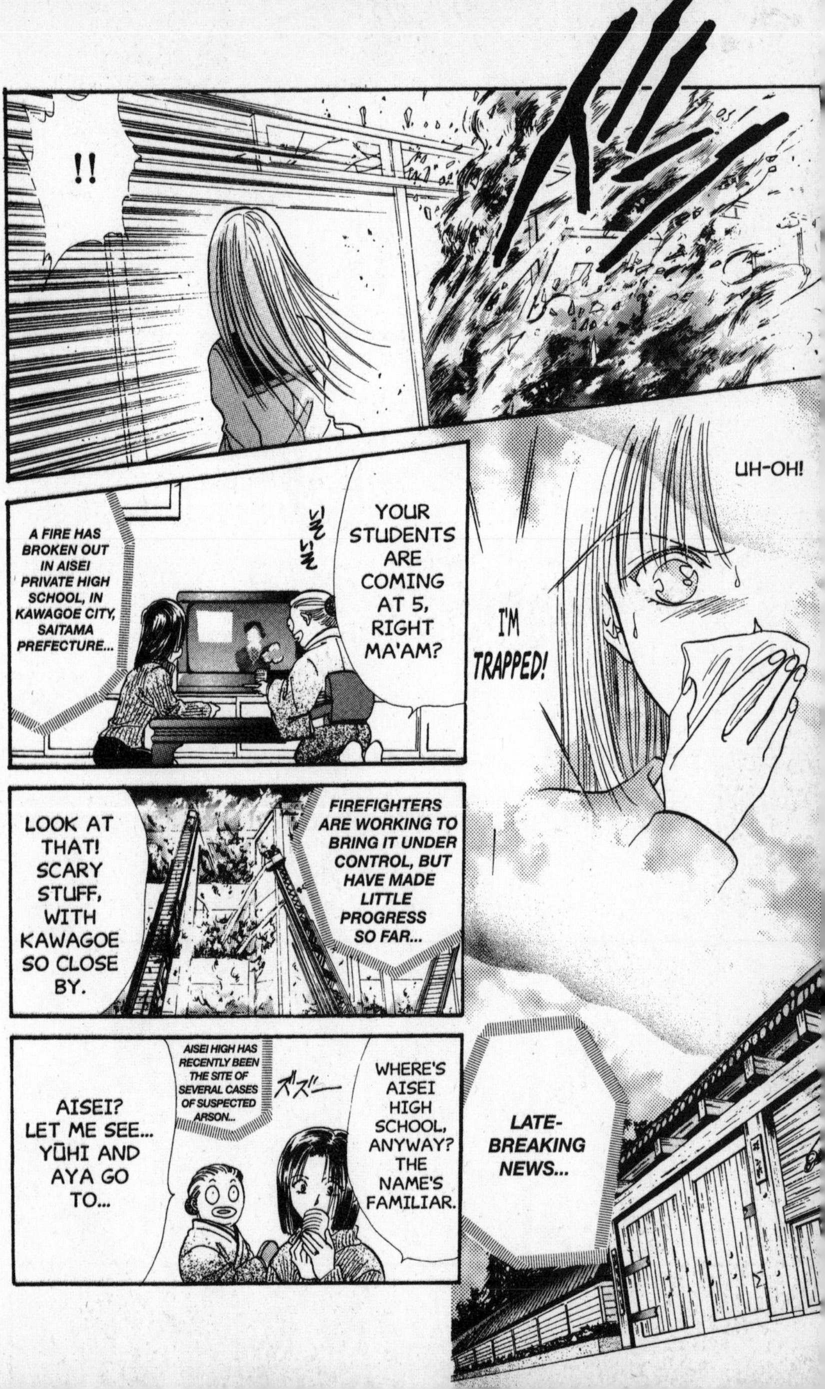
!!
UH-OH!
I'M TRAPPED!
LATE-BREAKING NEWS...
YOUR STUDENTS ARE COMING AT 5, RIGHT MA'AM?
A FIRE HAS BROKEN OUT IN AISEI PRIVATE HIGH SCHOOL, IN KAWAGOE CITY, SAITAMA PREFECTURE...
FIREFIGHTERS ARE WORKING TO BRING IT UNDER CONTROL, BUT HAVE MADE LITTLE PROGRESS SO FAR...
LOOK AT THAT! SCARY STUFF, WITH KAWAGOE SO CLOSE BY.
WHERE'S AISEI HIGH SCHOOL, ANYWAY? THE NAME'S FAMILIAR.
AISEI HIGH HAS RECENTLY BEEN THE SITE OF SEVERAL CASES OF SUSPECTED ARSON...
AISEI? LET ME SEE... YŪHI AND AYA GO TO...

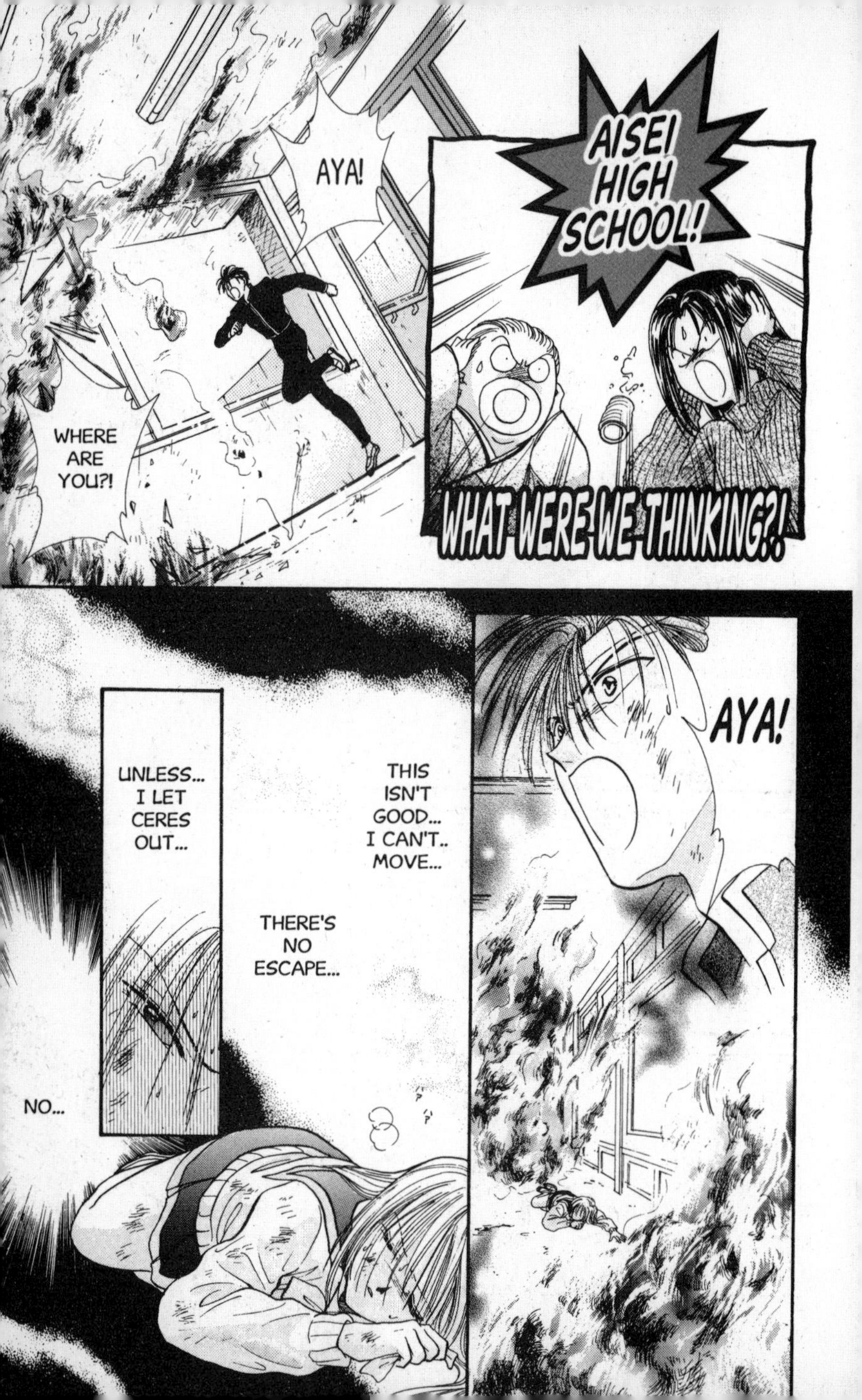
AISEI HIGH SCHOOL!
WHAT WERE WE THINKING?!
AYA!
WHERE ARE YOU?!
AYA!
THIS ISN'T GOOD... I CAN'T.. MOVE...
UNLESS... I LET CERES OUT...
THERE'S NO ESCAPE...
NO...

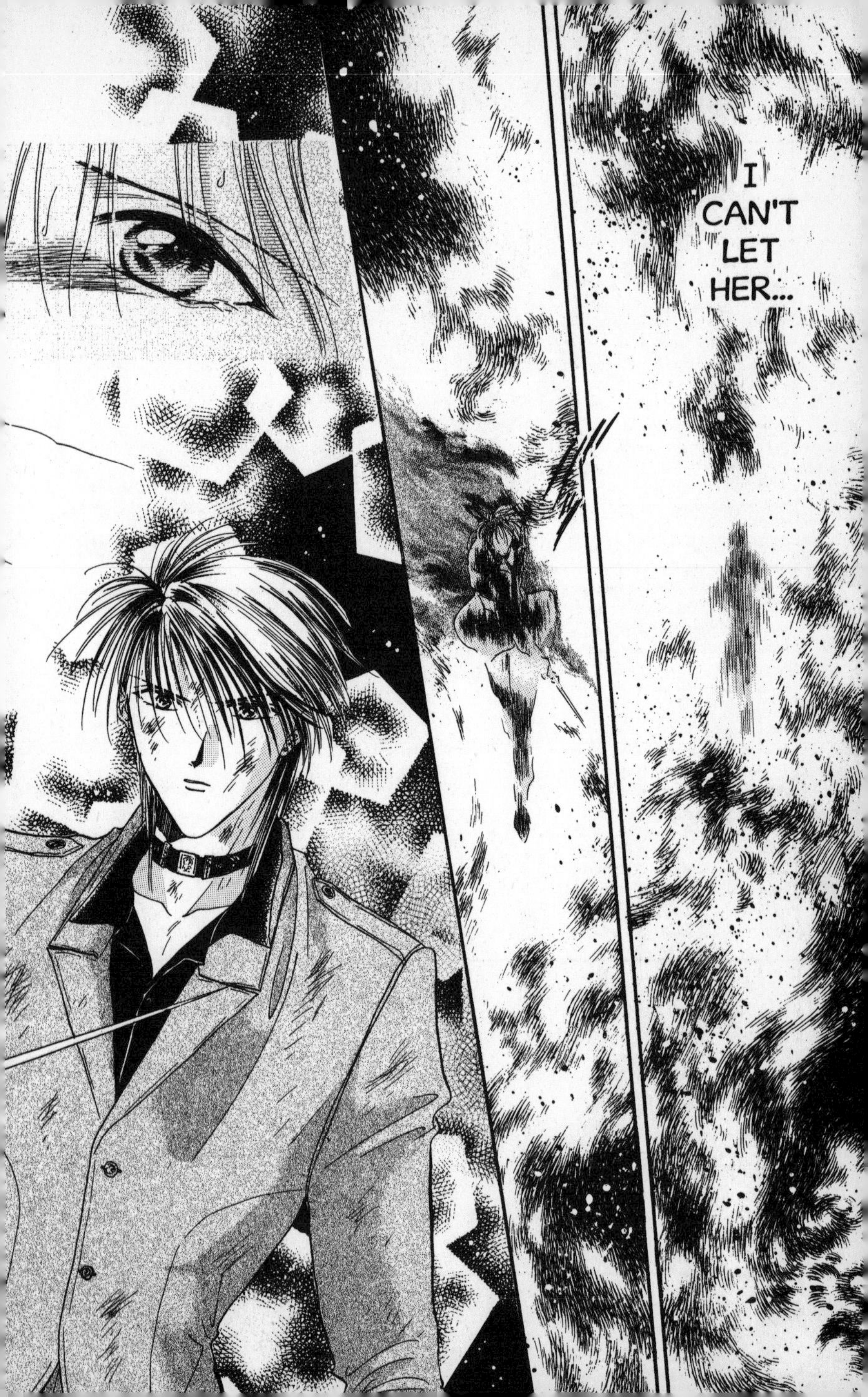
I CAN'T LET HER...

Ceres: 3

By the way... My assistant H, my editor, and I went on a field trip. Where? *Heh heh...* "The Mitsubishi Chemical Research Laboratory"! I gained a lot of knowledge there, and I was able to feel smart for a few days after the visit. ☺
It's (supposedly) one of the top five labs in the world. I was nervous at first, but they were all very nice there, and answered all my silly questions. It was a great educational experience. Thank you so much. One of the researchers explained celestial maiden genetics for me, and even drew some diagrams on the chalkboard. It was great! ☺
And so, I've clarified (I think) whether or not the logistics I created for the story make scientific sense. Now at least half of Ceres has the official stamp of approval from scientists! (oh, really?!) *well, let's just say it does.* The rest is fictional. ☺
People tend to think that genetics and biology use a lot of special terminology and that makes them hard to understand, but when you get to know even a little bit about the subjects, they're very interesting fields. I actually hated all the memorizing we had to do in high school science, but I liked biology and astronomy. The labs were a pain, but it was fun to get to use a microscope. At the Mitsubishi lab they let me use their microscope to take a peek at some mouse sperm. I also checked out mouse genes. I took pictures in a room that was minus 22°F. The whole time I was screaming about how cold it was...This is just a manga, but I should at least know about the fundamentals of science.
They also taught me about cloning, which was really interesting. There's been a lot of books out recently that look at men and women from a biological perspective. This is an age when society's eyes are turned towards the mysticism of life.

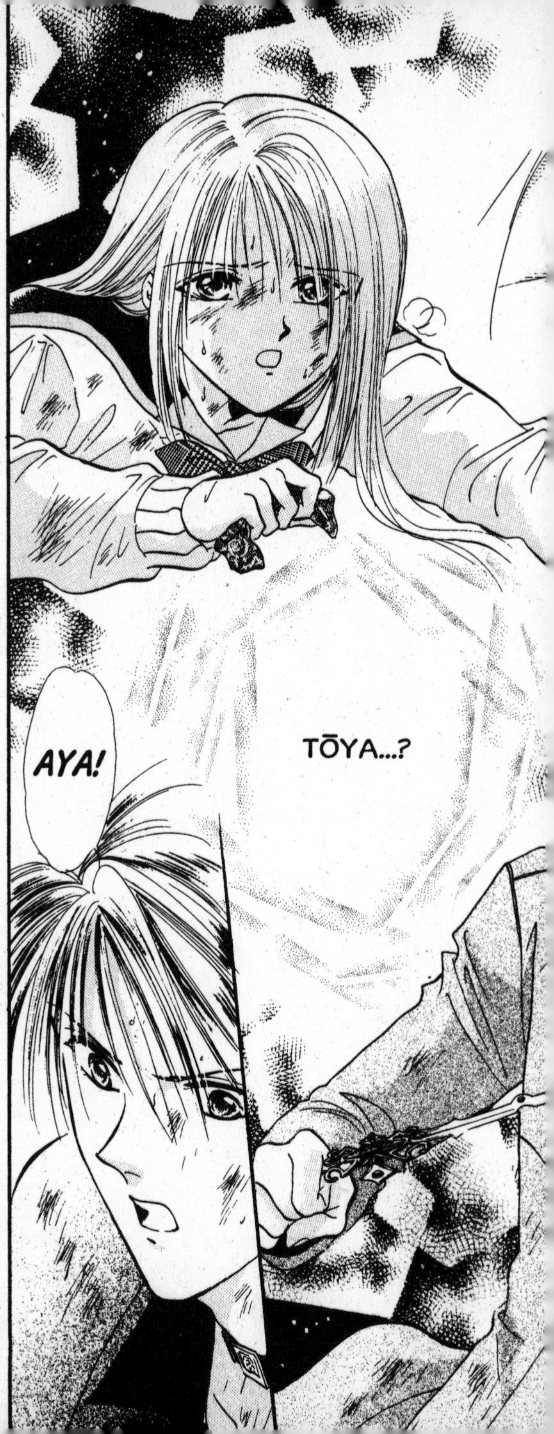
TŌYA...?
AYA!

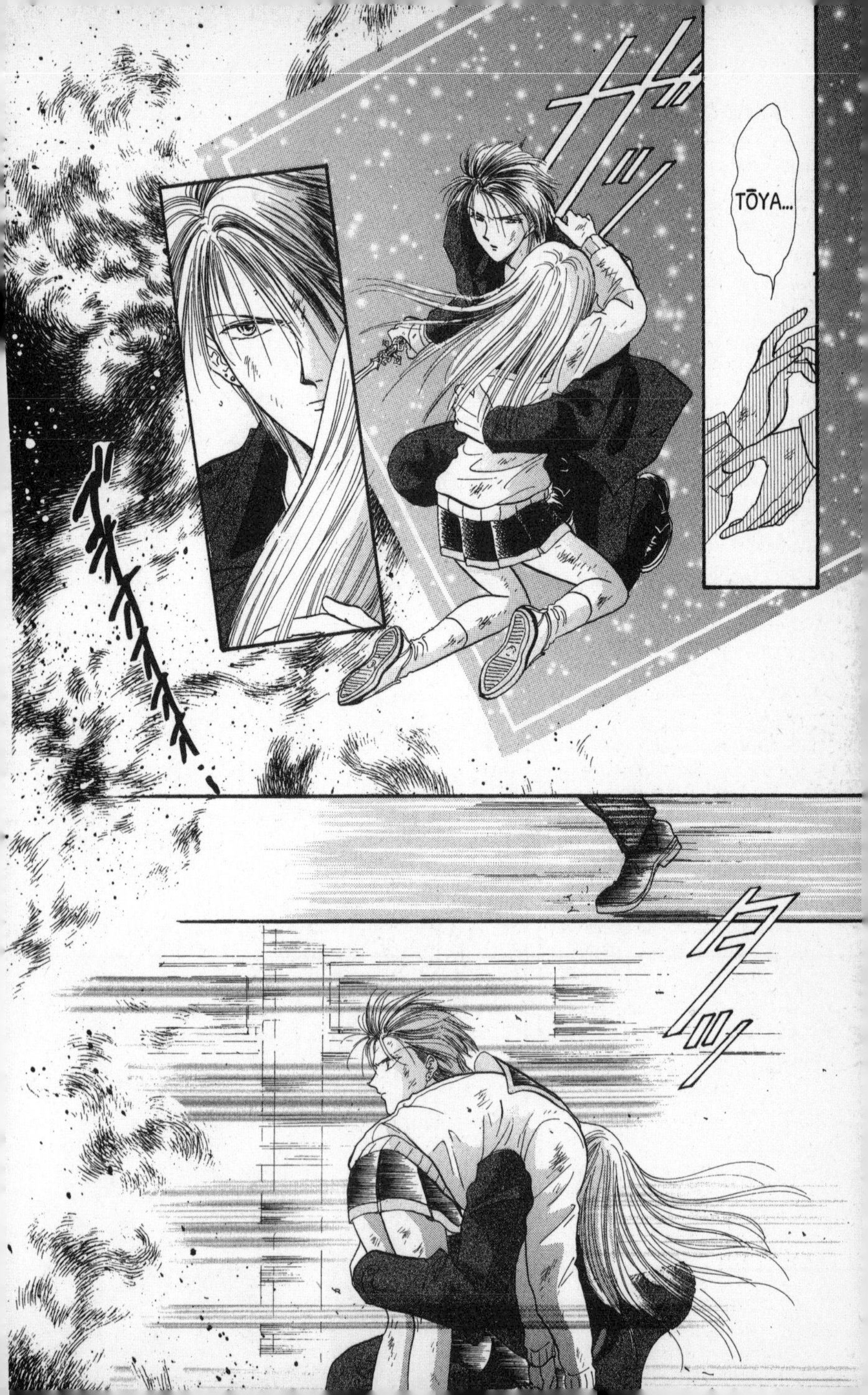
TŌYA...

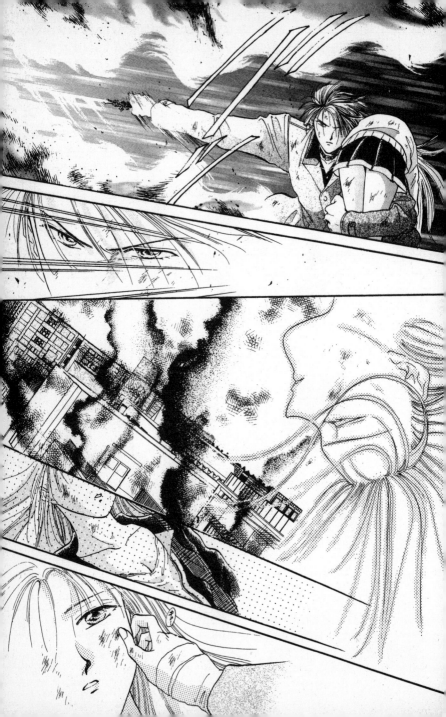

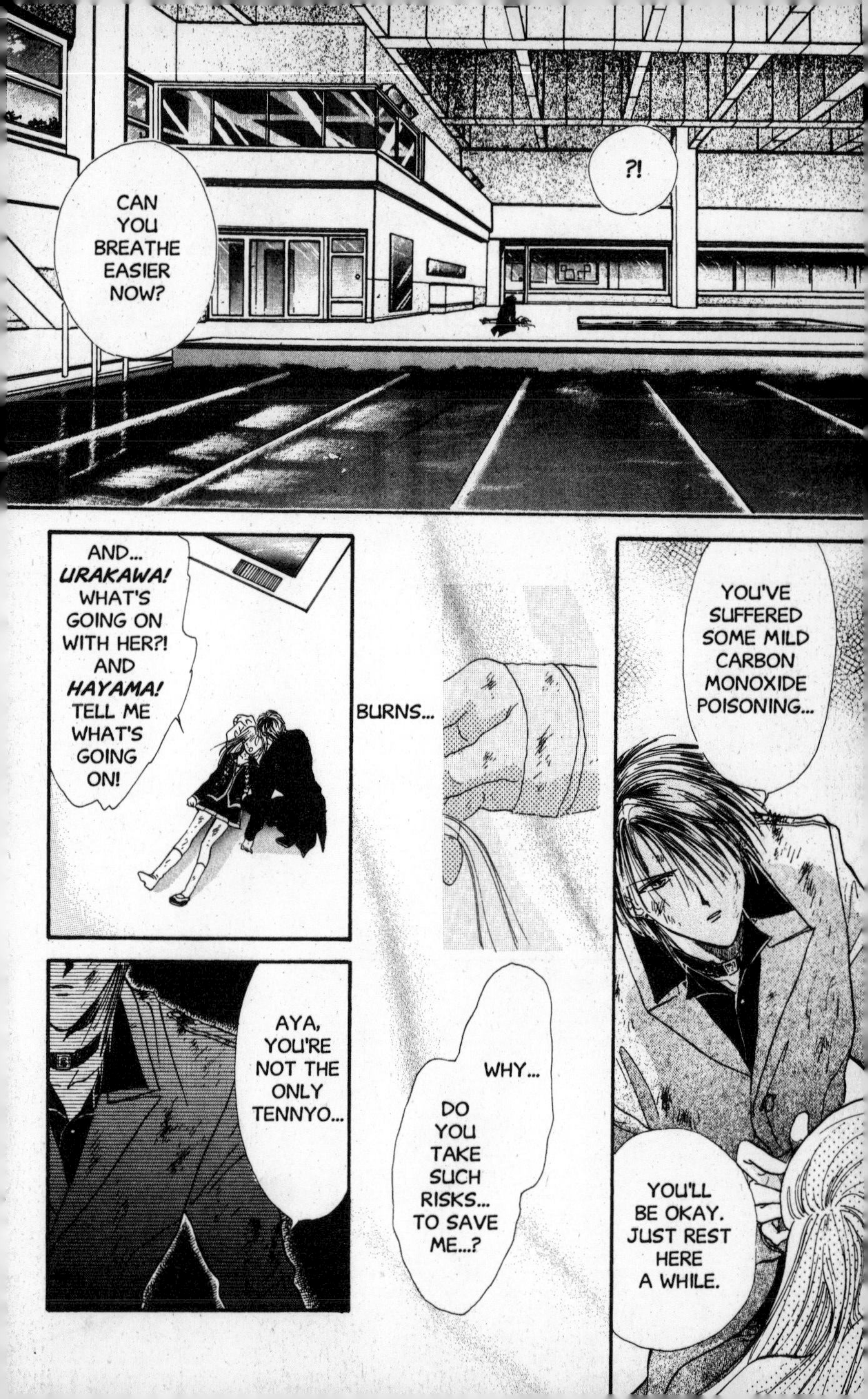
?!
CAN YOU BREATHE EASIER NOW?
YOU'VE SUFFERED SOME MILD CARBON MONOXIDE POISONING...
YOU'LL BE OKAY. JUST REST HERE A WHILE.
BURNS...
WHY...
DO YOU TAKE SUCH RISKS... TO SAVE ME...?
AND... *URAKAWA!* WHAT'S GOING ON WITH HER?! AND *HAYAMA!* TELL ME WHAT'S GOING ON!
AYA, YOU'RE NOT THE ONLY TENNYO...

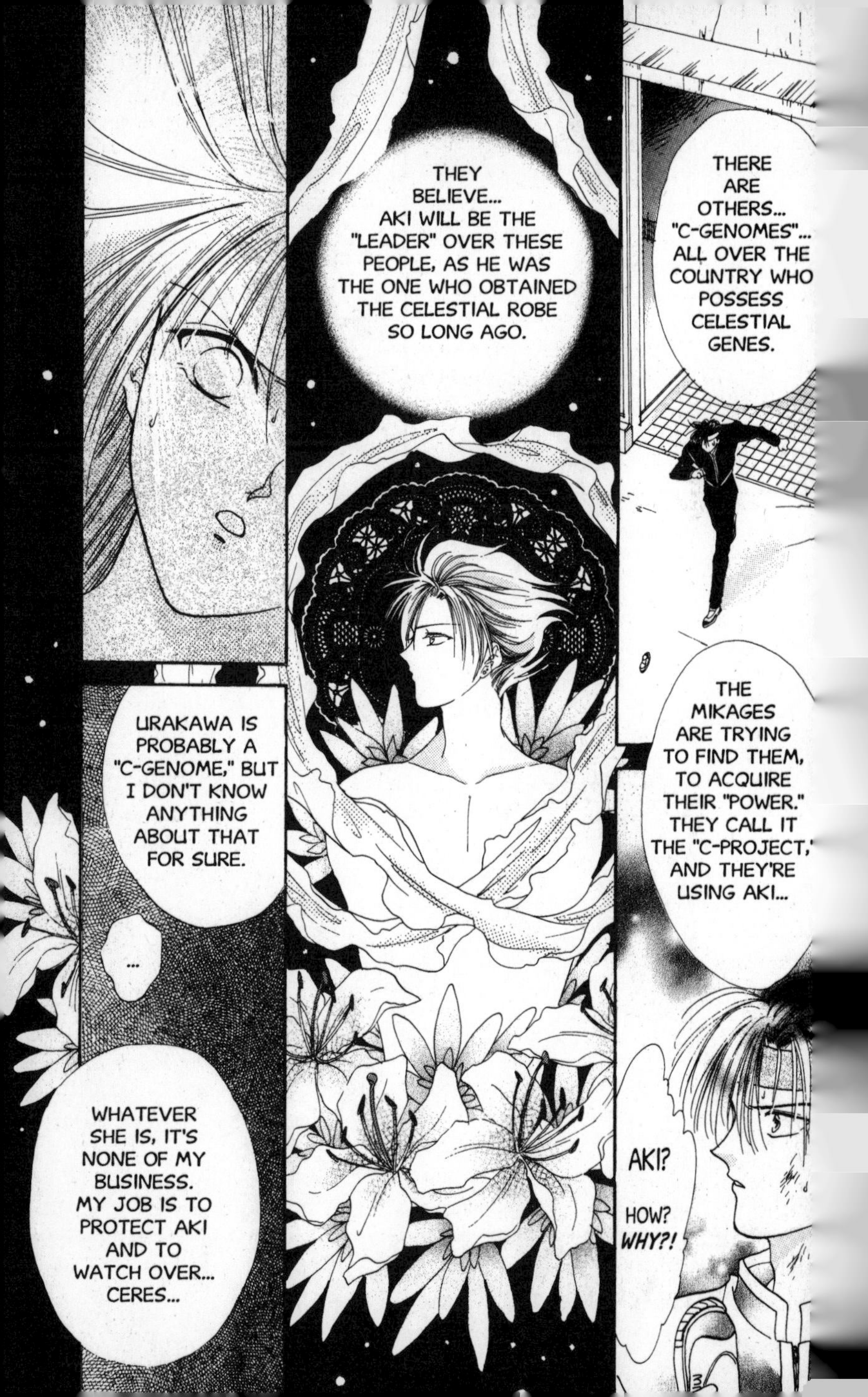
THERE ARE OTHERS... "C-GENOMES"... ALL OVER THE COUNTRY WHO POSSESS CELESTIAL GENES.
THE MIKAGES ARE TRYING TO FIND THEM, TO ACQUIRE THEIR "POWER." THEY CALL IT THE "C-PROJECT," AND THEY'RE USING AKI...
AKI?
HOW? *WHY?!*
THEY BELIEVE... AKI WILL BE THE "LEADER" OVER THESE PEOPLE, AS HE WAS THE ONE WHO OBTAINED THE CELESTIAL ROBE SO LONG AGO.
URAKAWA IS PROBABLY A "C-GENOME," BUT I DON'T KNOW ANYTHING ABOUT THAT FOR SURE.
...
WHATEVER SHE IS, IT'S NONE OF MY BUSINESS. MY JOB IS TO PROTECT AKI AND TO WATCH OVER... CERES...

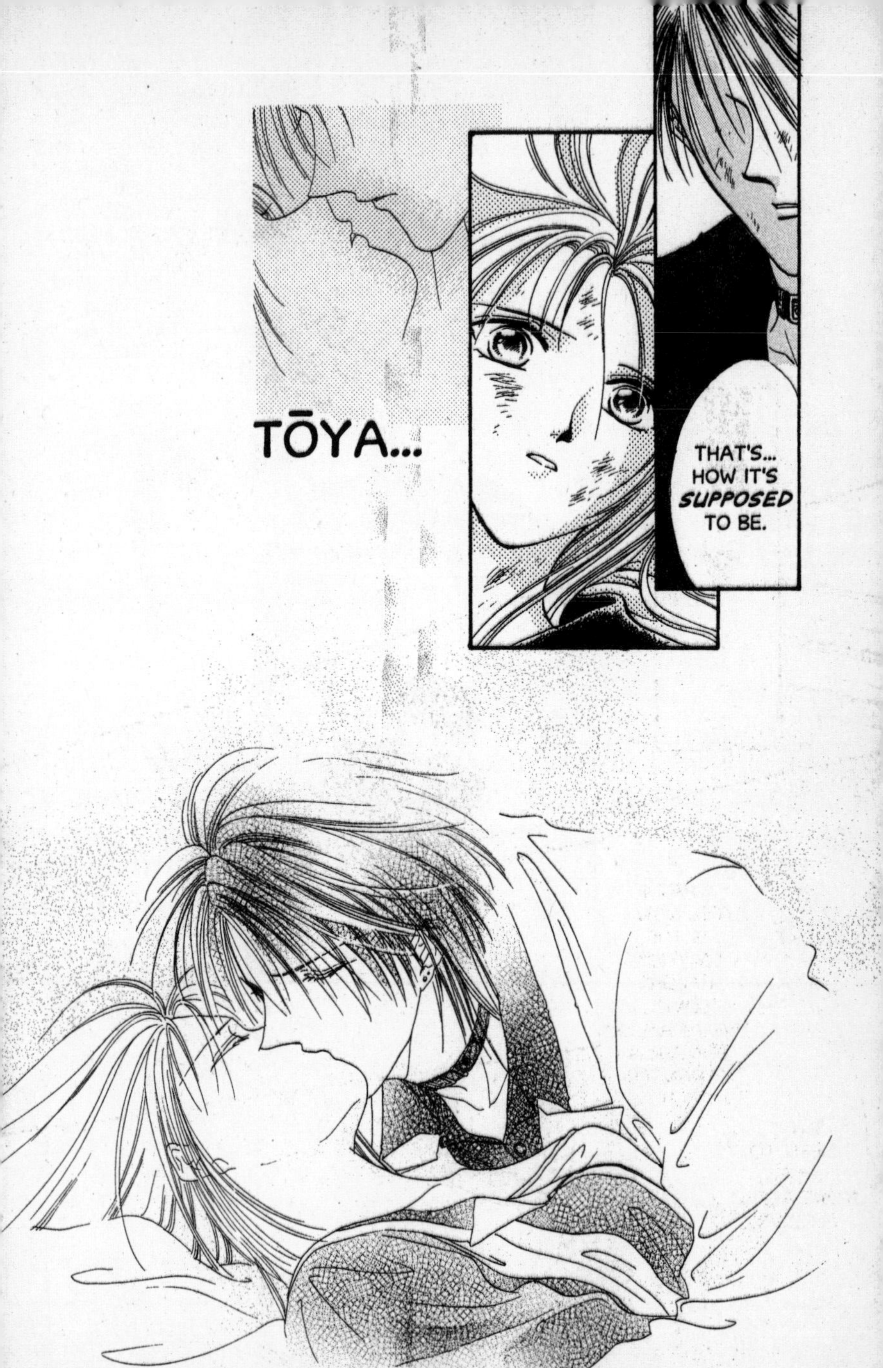
THAT'S... HOW IT'S *SUPPOSED* TO BE.
TŌYA...

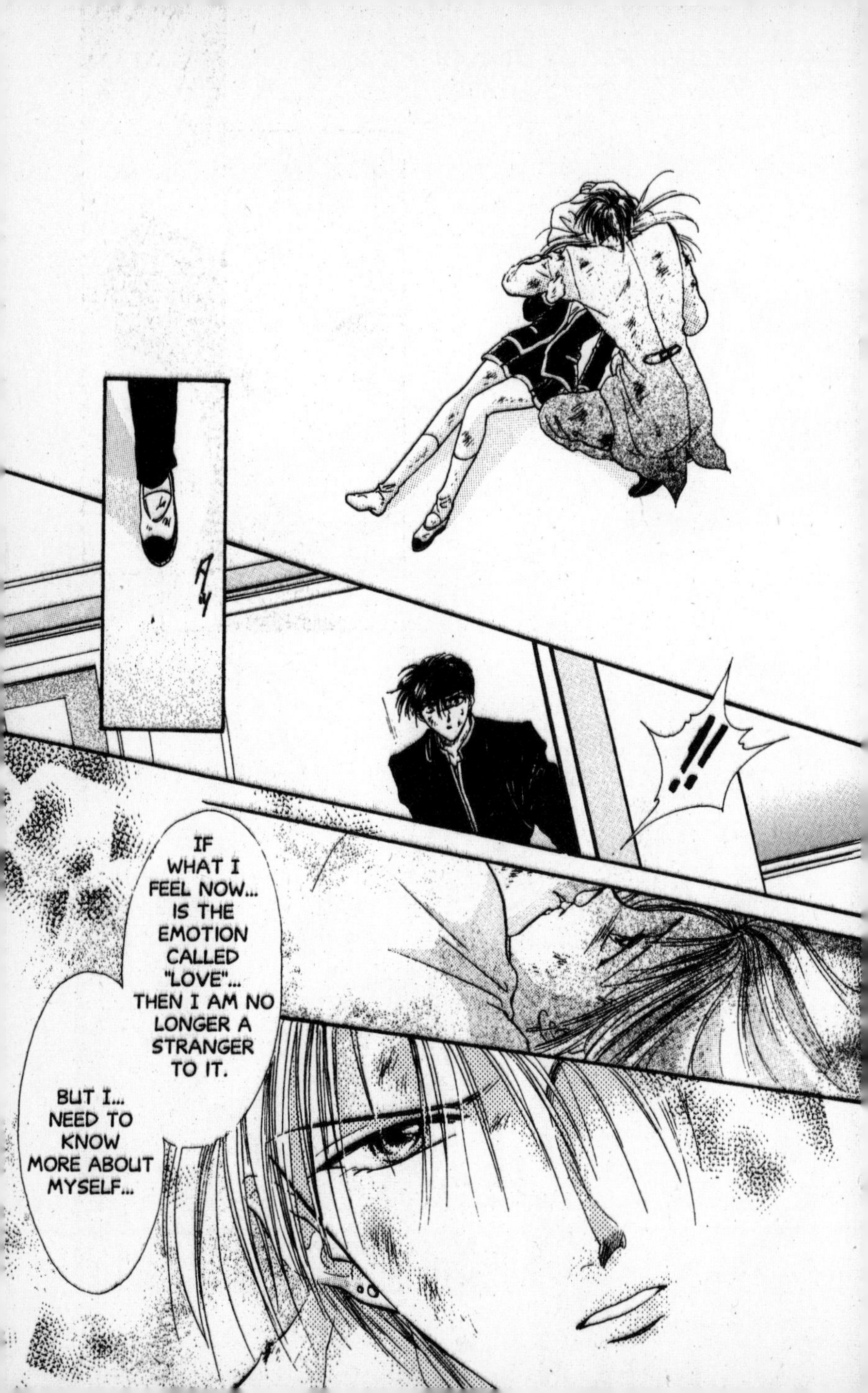
!!
IF WHAT I FEEL NOW... IS THE EMOTION CALLED "LOVE"... THEN I AM NO LONGER A STRANGER TO IT.
BUT I... NEED TO KNOW MORE ABOUT MYSELF...

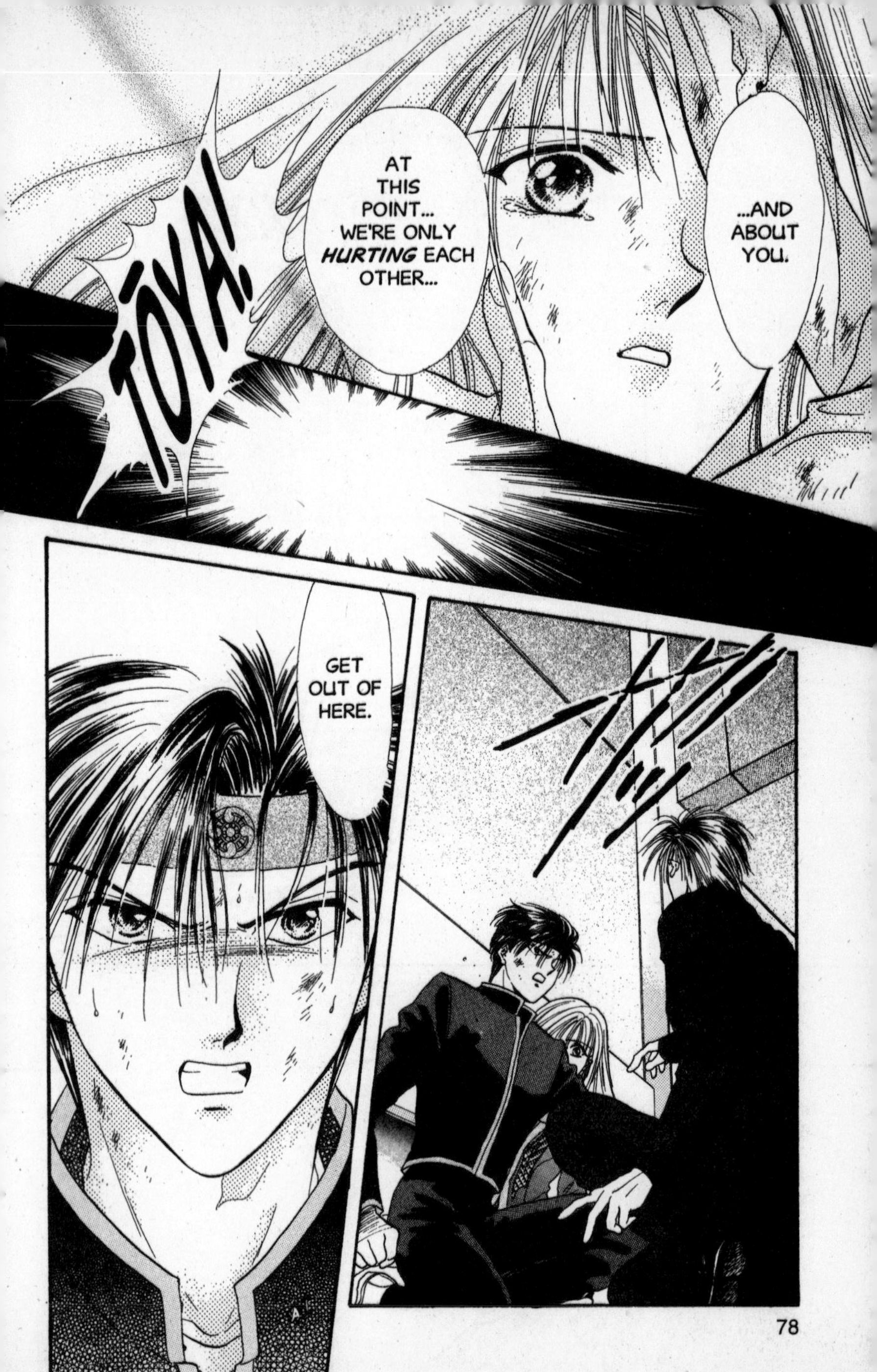
...AND ABOUT YOU.
AT THIS POINT... WE'RE ONLY *HURTING* EACH OTHER...
TŌYA!
GET OUT OF HERE.

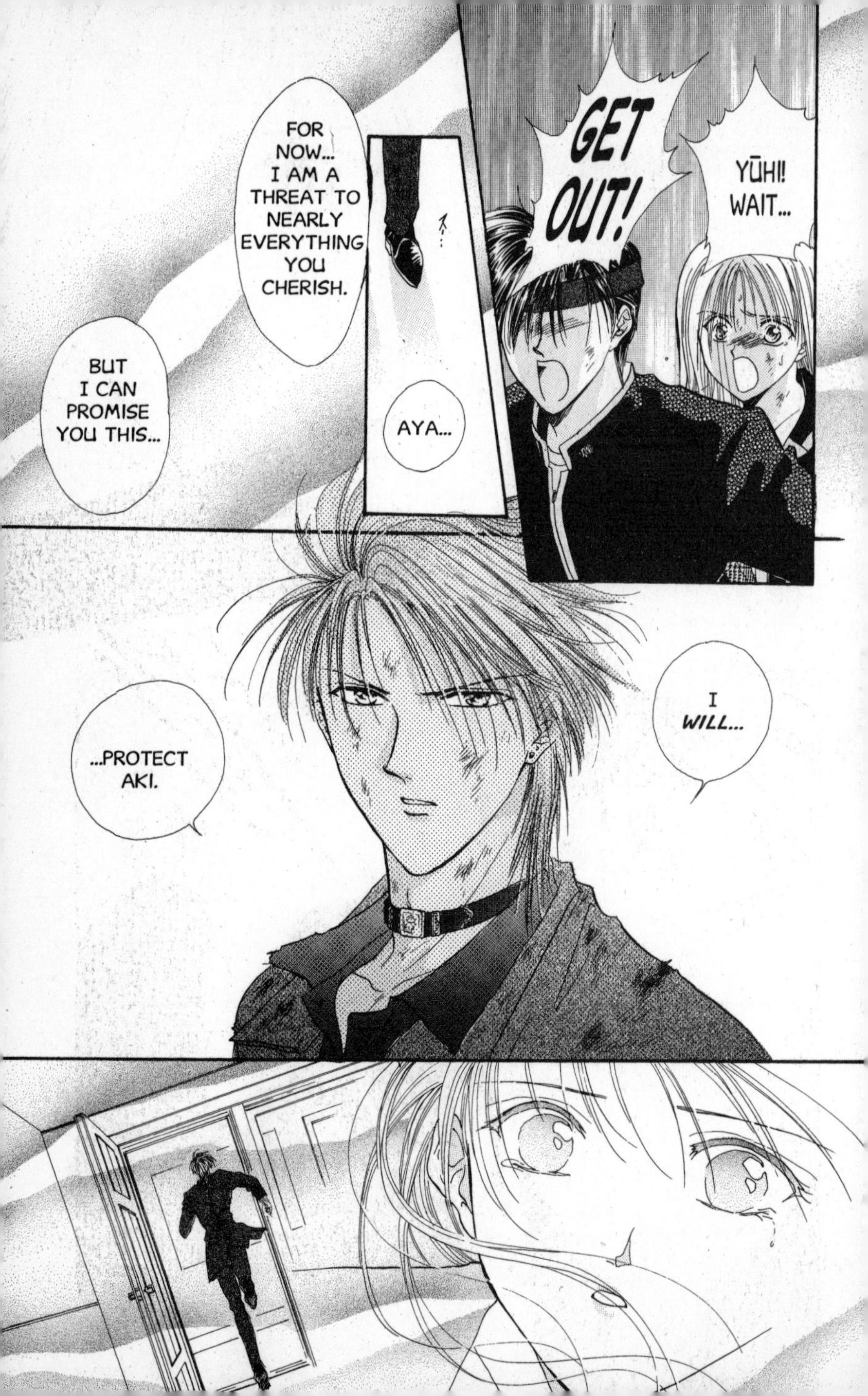
GET OUT!
YŪHI! WAIT...
AYA...
FOR NOW... I AM A THREAT TO NEARLY EVERYTHING YOU CHERISH.
BUT I CAN PROMISE YOU THIS...
I *WILL*...
...PROTECT AKI.

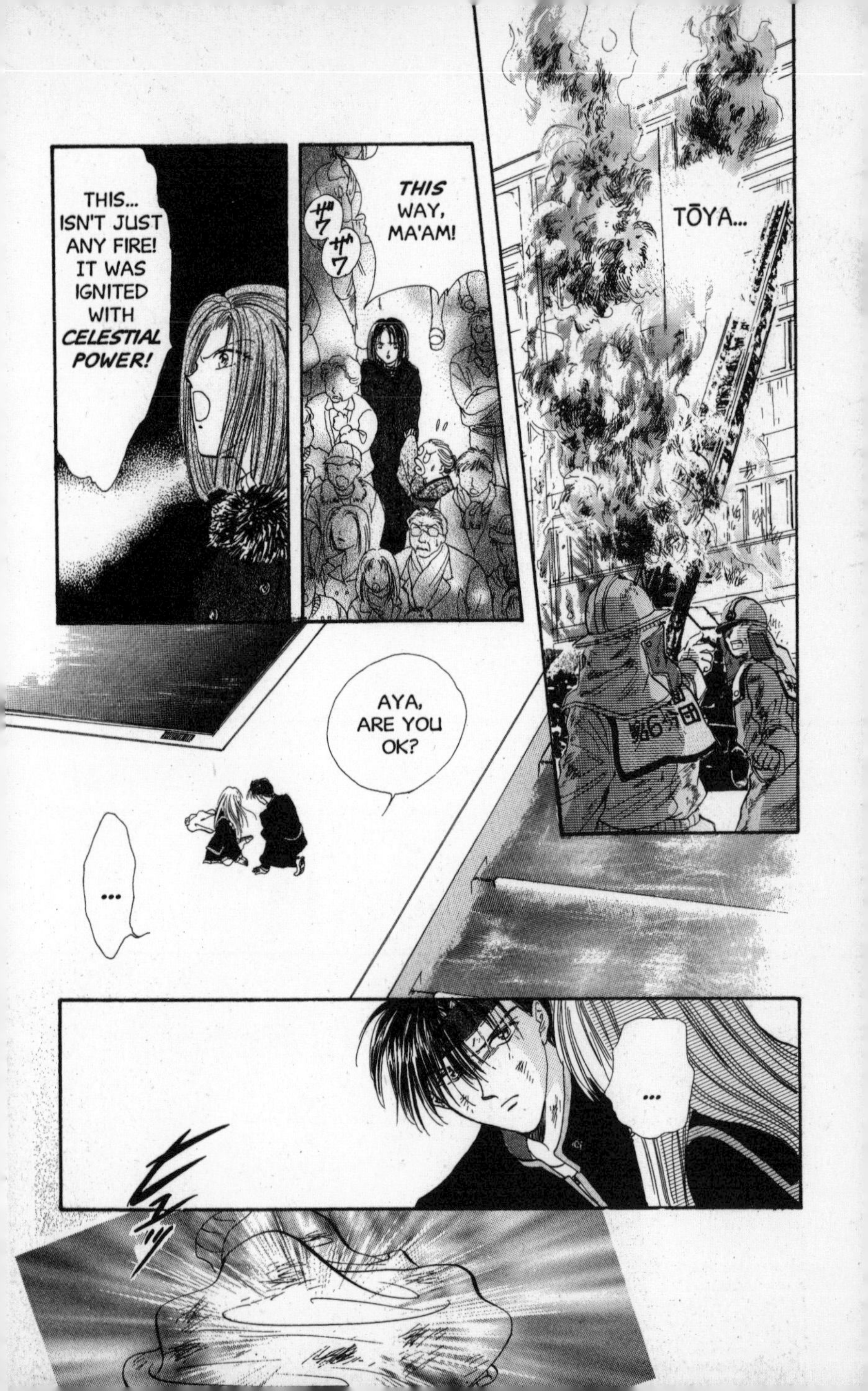
TŌYA...
THIS WAY, MA'AM!
ザワ ザワ
THIS... ISN'T JUST ANY FIRE! IT WAS IGNITED WITH CELESTIAL POWER!
AYA, ARE YOU OK?
...
...

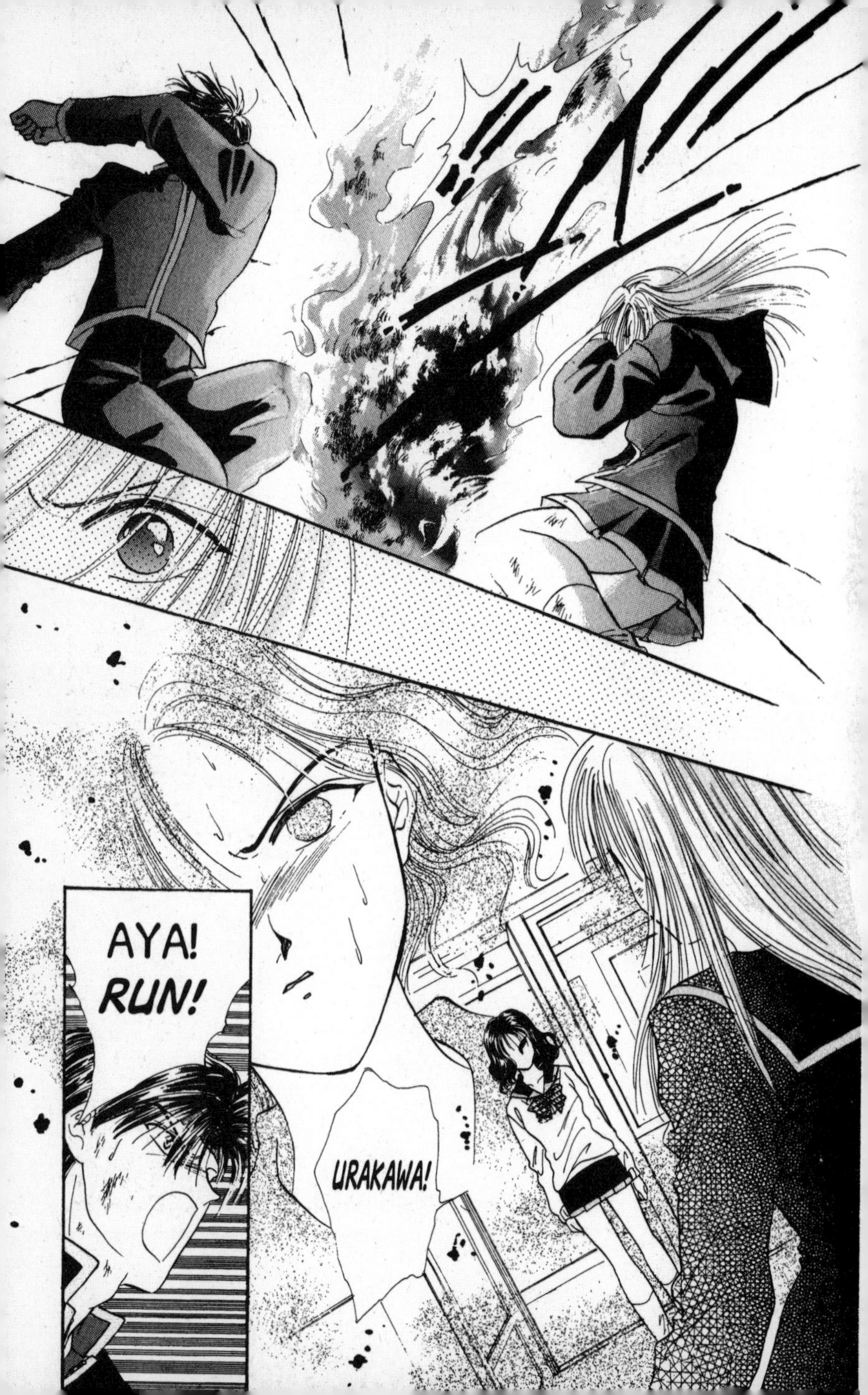
URAKAWA!
AYA! RUN!

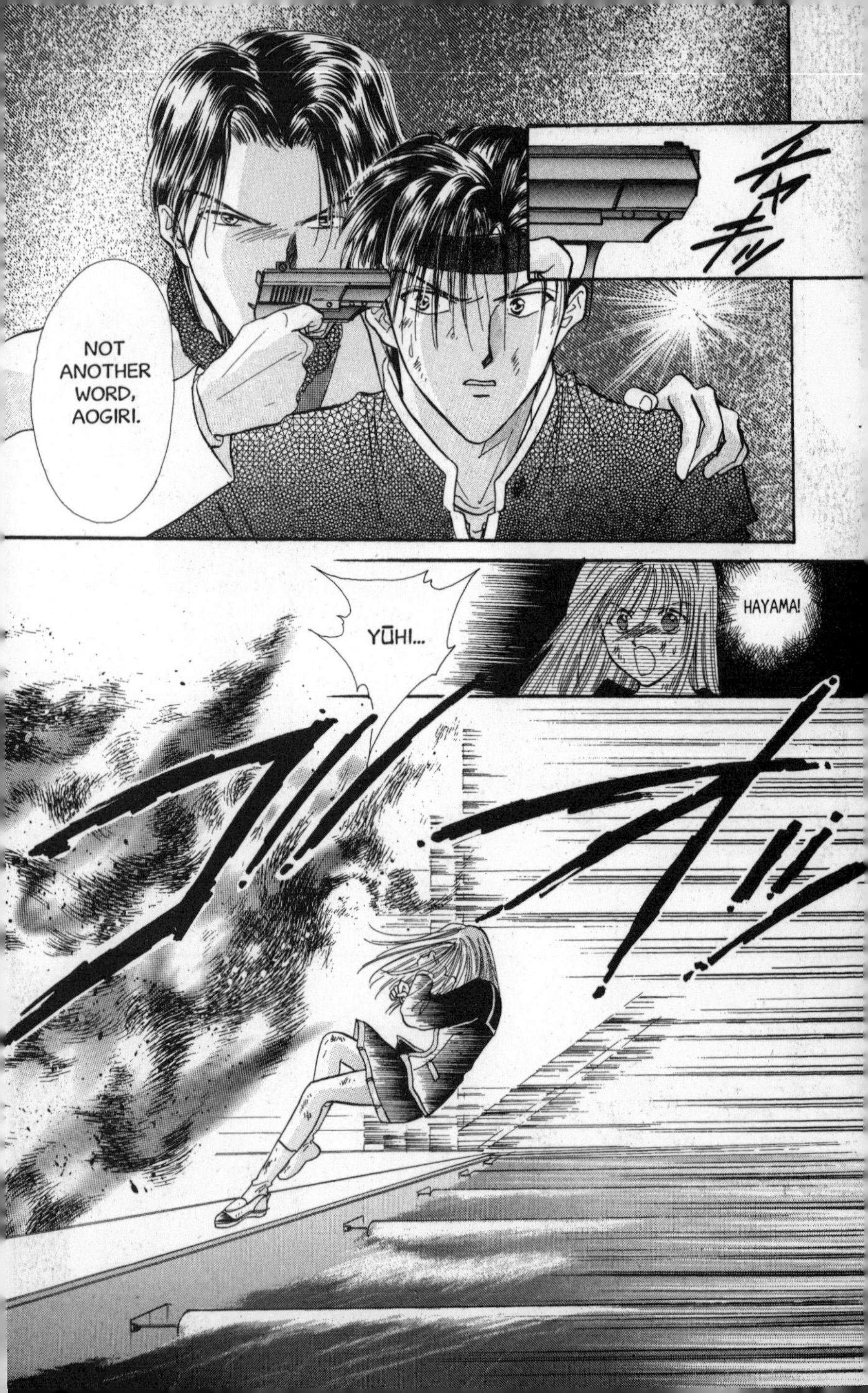
チャキッ
NOT ANOTHER WORD, AOGIRI.
HAYAMA!
YŪHI...

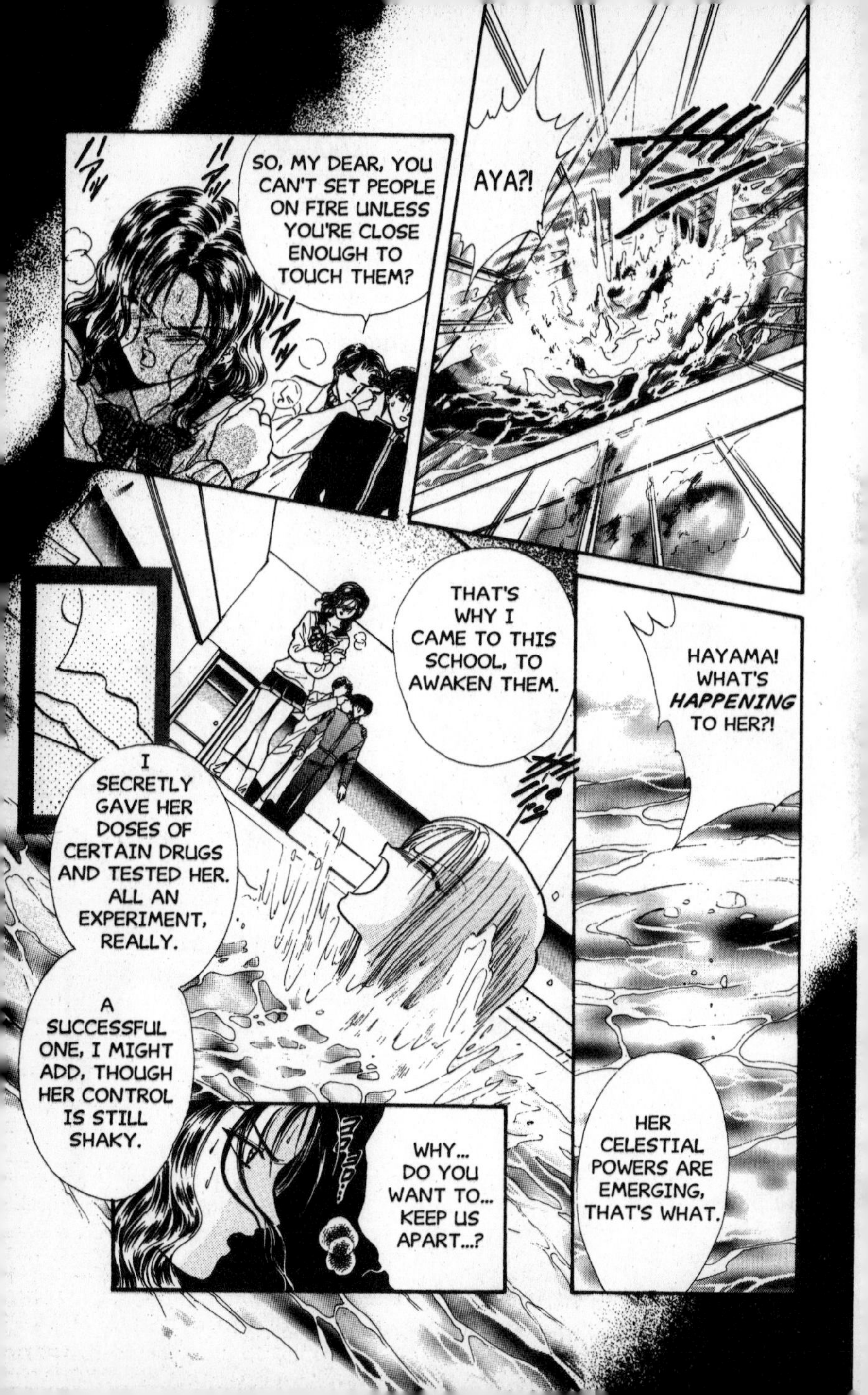
AYA?!
SO, MY DEAR, YOU CAN'T SET PEOPLE ON FIRE UNLESS YOU'RE CLOSE ENOUGH TO TOUCH THEM?
HAYAMA! WHAT'S *HAPPENING* TO HER?!
HER CELESTIAL POWERS ARE EMERGING, THAT'S WHAT.
THAT'S WHY I CAME TO THIS SCHOOL, TO AWAKEN THEM.
I SECRETLY GAVE HER DOSES OF CERTAIN DRUGS AND TESTED HER. ALL AN EXPERIMENT, REALLY.
A SUCCESSFUL ONE, I MIGHT ADD, THOUGH HER CONTROL IS STILL SHAKY.
WHY... DO YOU WANT TO... KEEP US APART...?

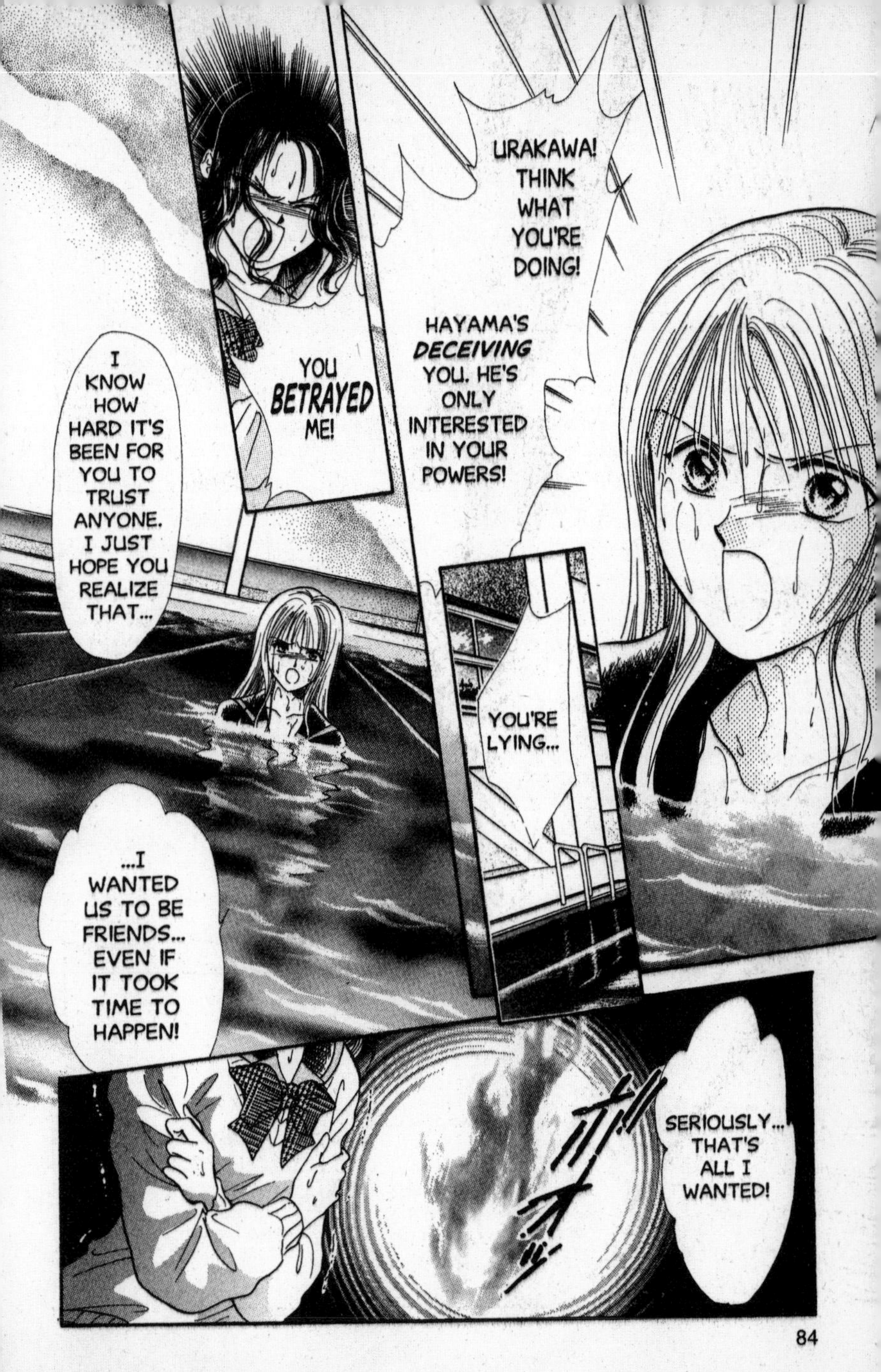
URAKAWA! THINK WHAT YOU'RE DOING!
HAYAMA'S *DECEIVING* YOU. HE'S ONLY INTERESTED IN YOUR POWERS!
YOU **BETRAYED** ME!
YOU'RE LYING...
I KNOW HOW HARD IT'S BEEN FOR YOU TO TRUST ANYONE. I JUST HOPE YOU REALIZE THAT...
...I WANTED US TO BE FRIENDS... EVEN IF IT TOOK TIME TO HAPPEN!
SERIOUSLY... THAT'S ALL I WANTED!

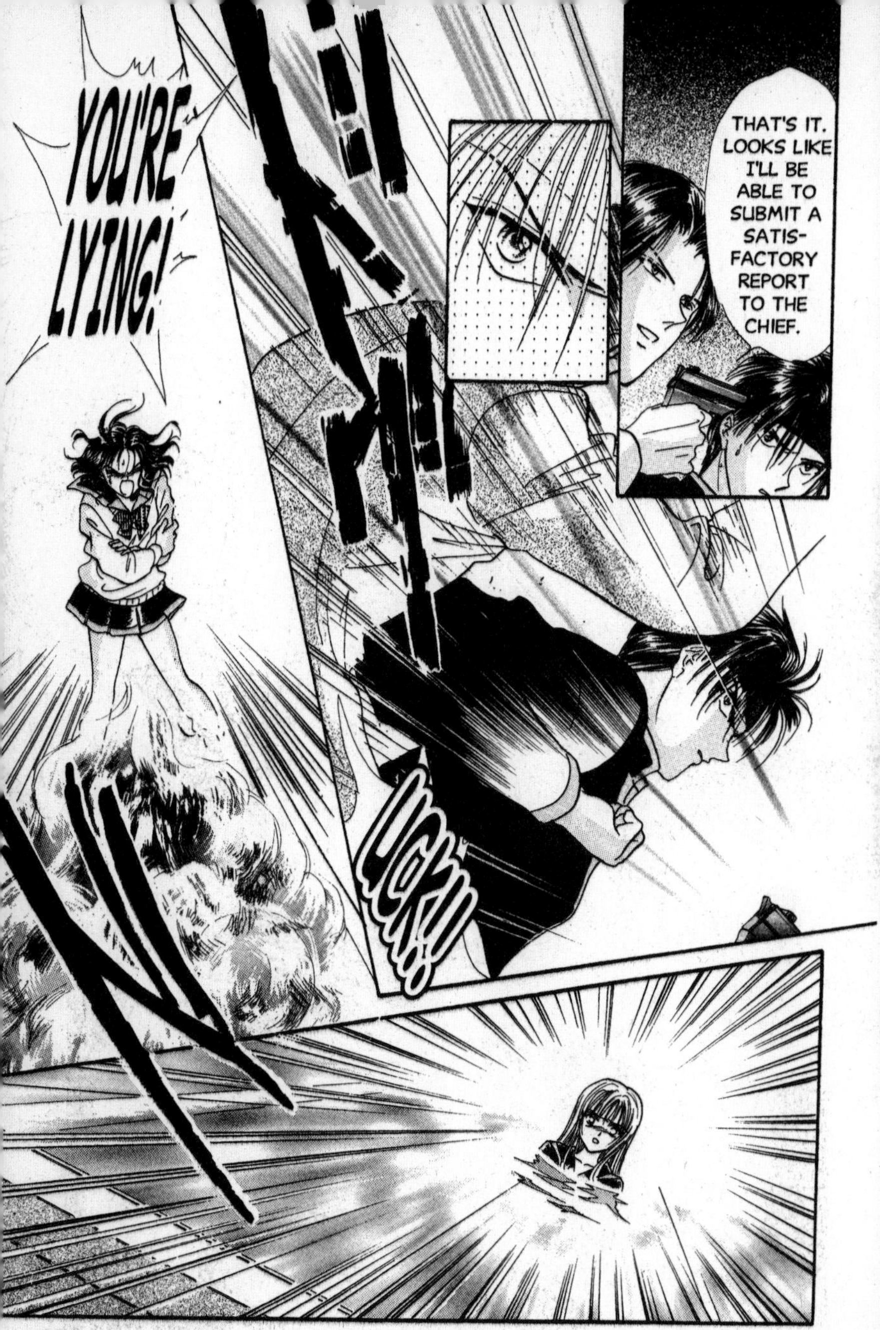
THAT'S IT. LOOKS LIKE I'LL BE ABLE TO SUBMIT A SATIS-FACTORY REPORT TO THE CHIEF.
UGH!!
YOU'RE LYING!

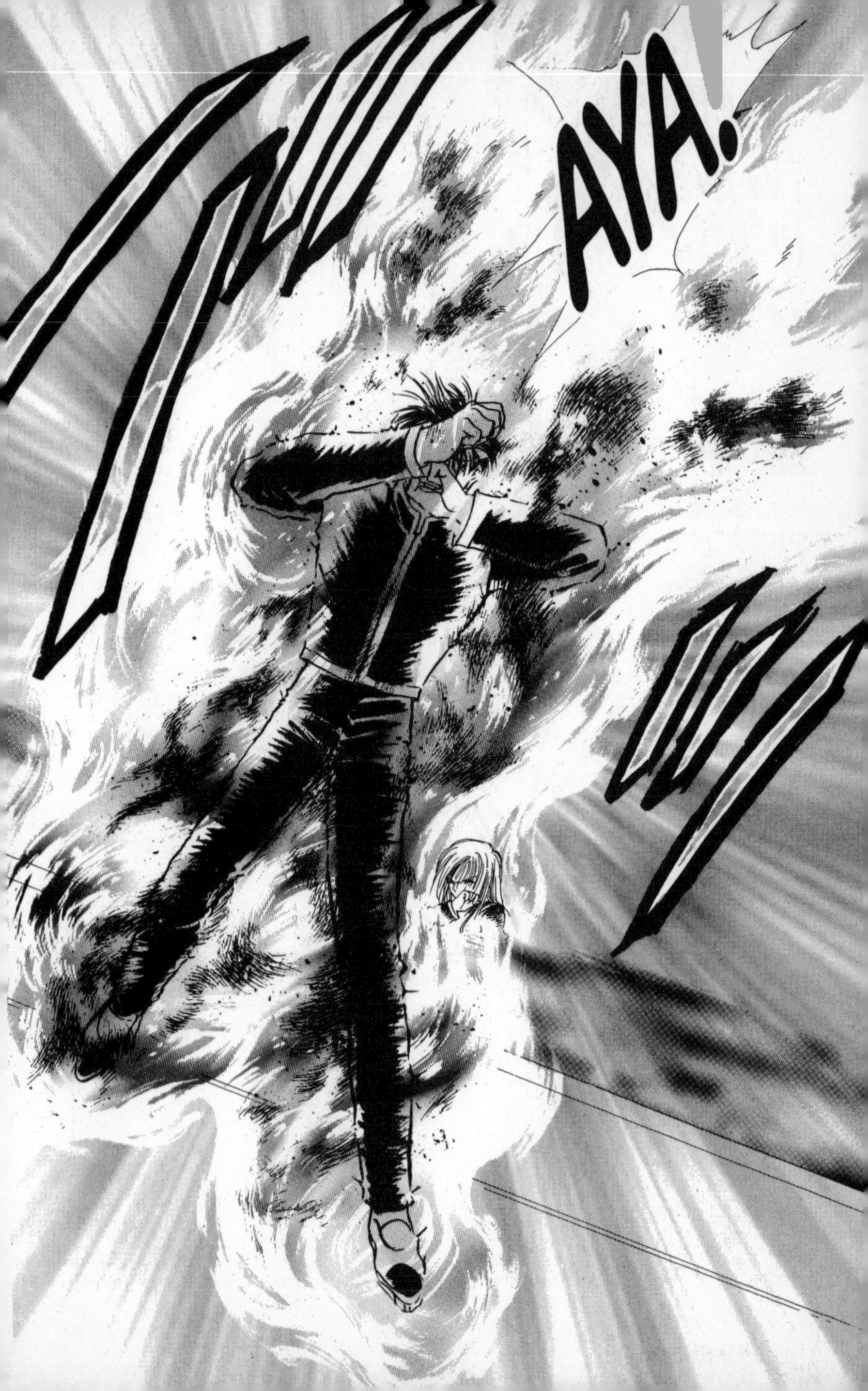
AYA!

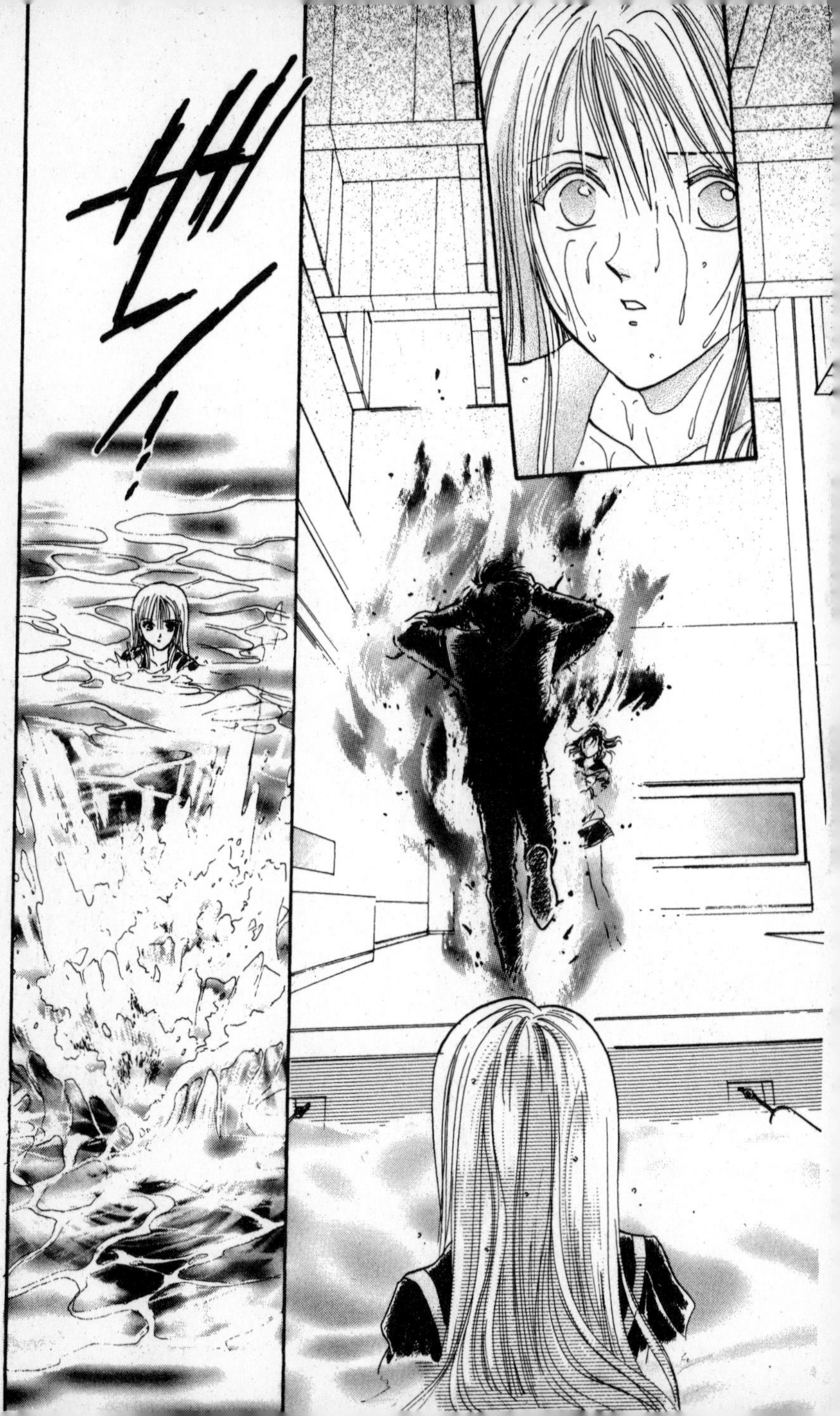

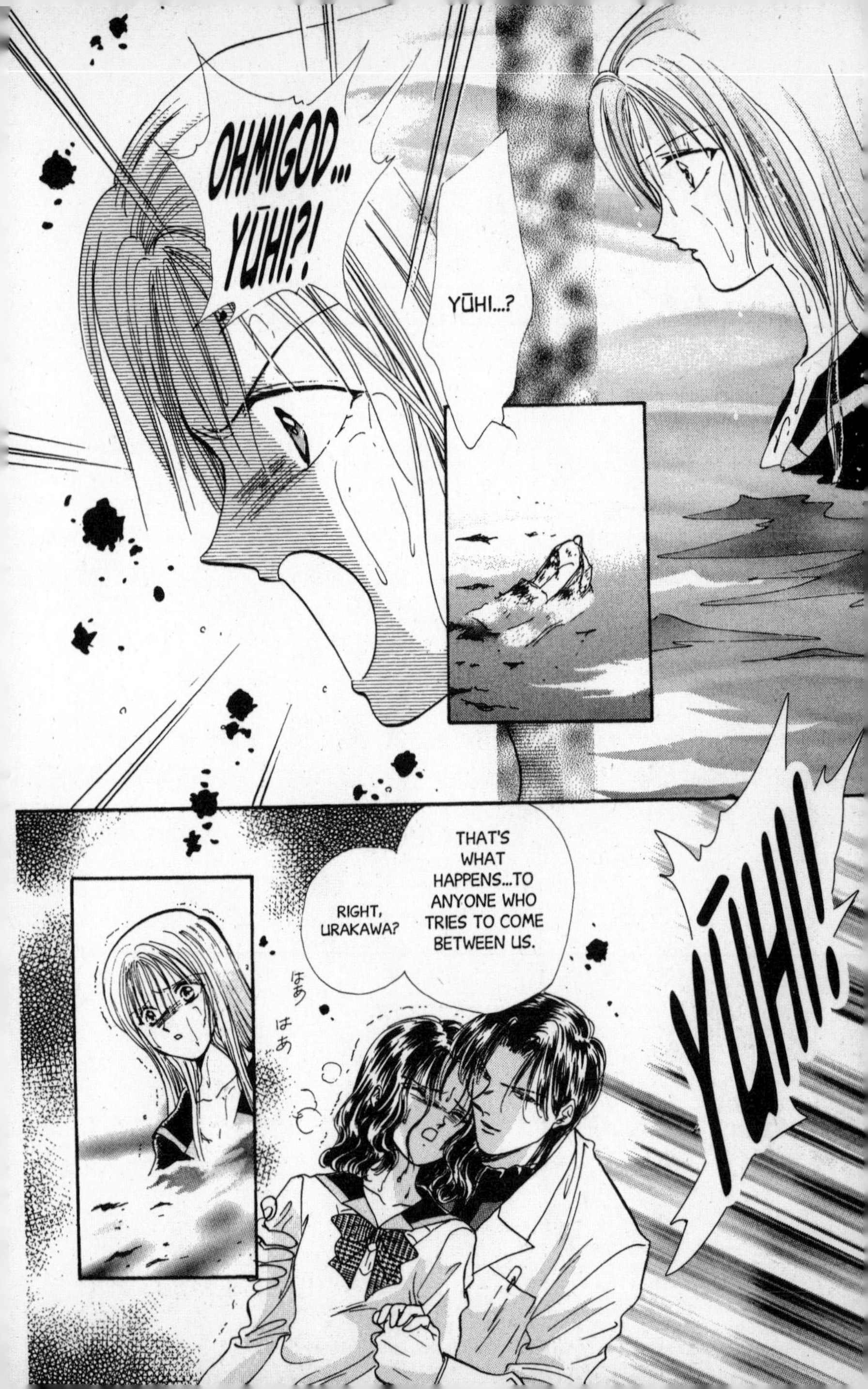
YŪHI...?
OHMIGOD... YŪHI?!
YŪHI!
THAT'S WHAT HAPPENS...TO ANYONE WHO TRIES TO COME BETWEEN US.
RIGHT, URAKAWA?
はあ はあ

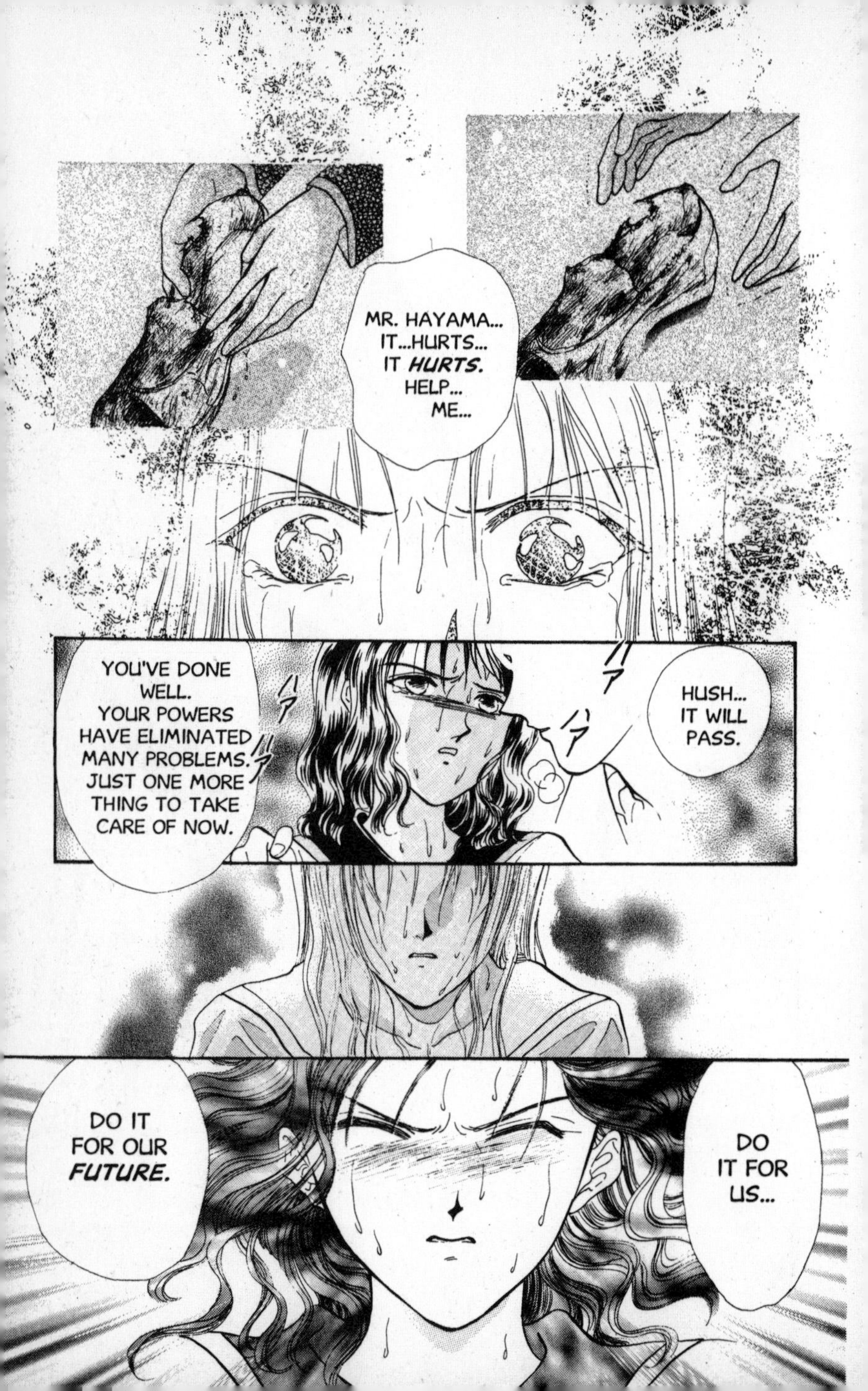
MR. HAYAMA... IT...HURTS... IT HURTS. HELP... ME...
HUSH... IT WILL PASS.
YOU'VE DONE WELL. YOUR POWERS HAVE ELIMINATED MANY PROBLEMS. JUST ONE MORE THING TO TAKE CARE OF NOW.
DO IT FOR US...
DO IT FOR OUR FUTURE.

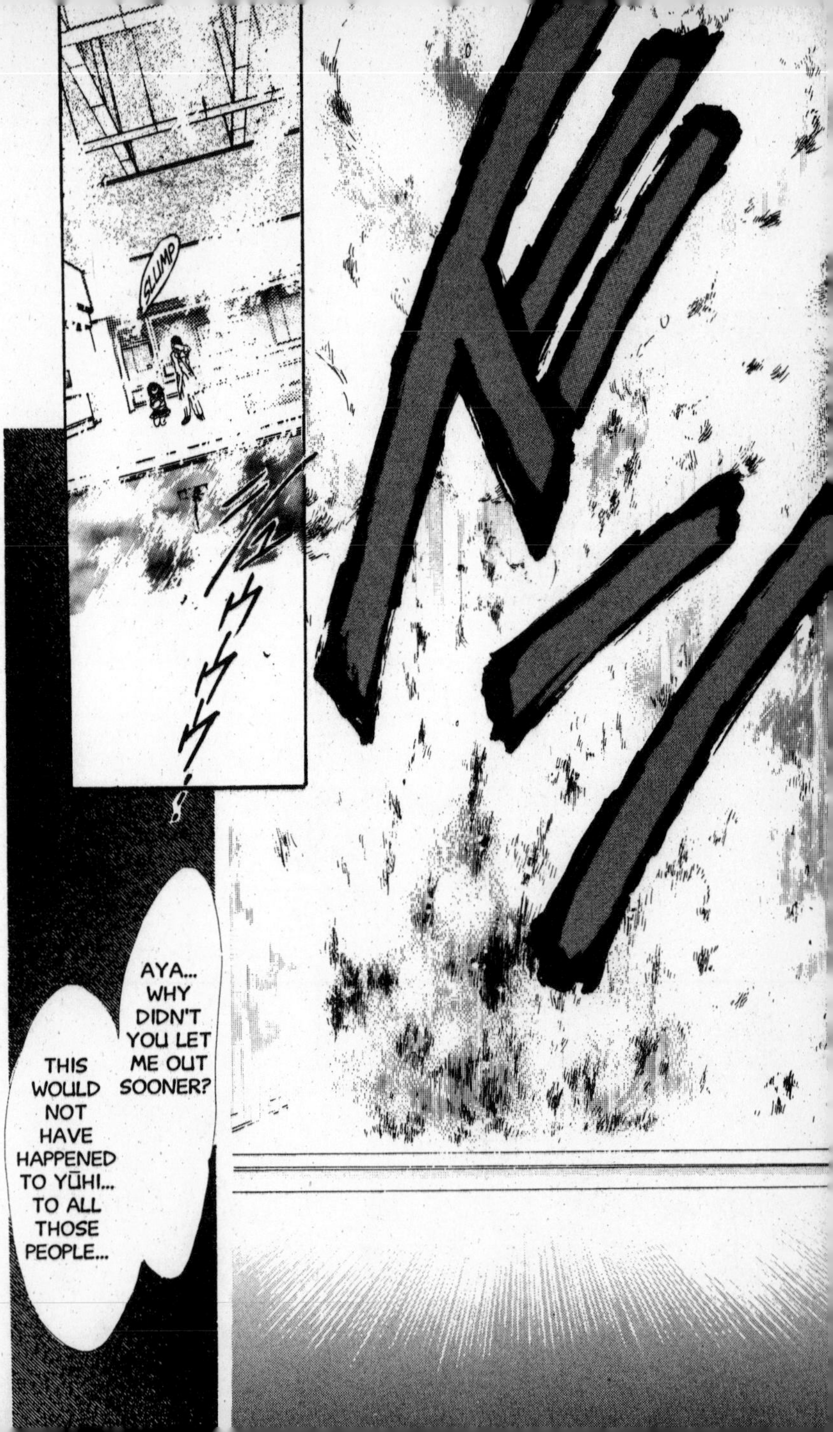
SLUMP
AYA... WHY DIDN'T YOU LET ME OUT SOONER?
THIS WOULD NOT HAVE HAPPENED TO YŪHI... TO ALL THOSE PEOPLE...

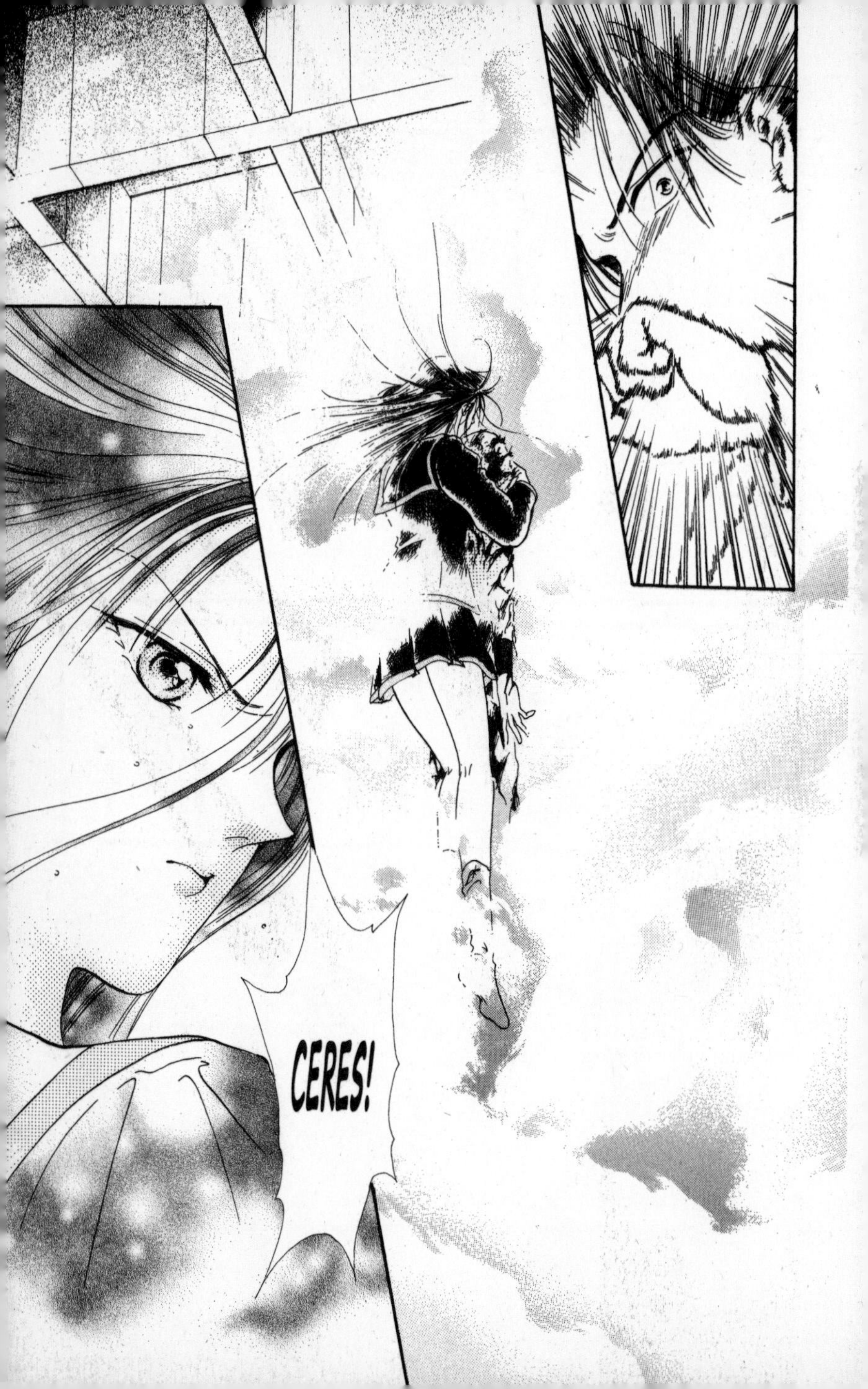
CERES!

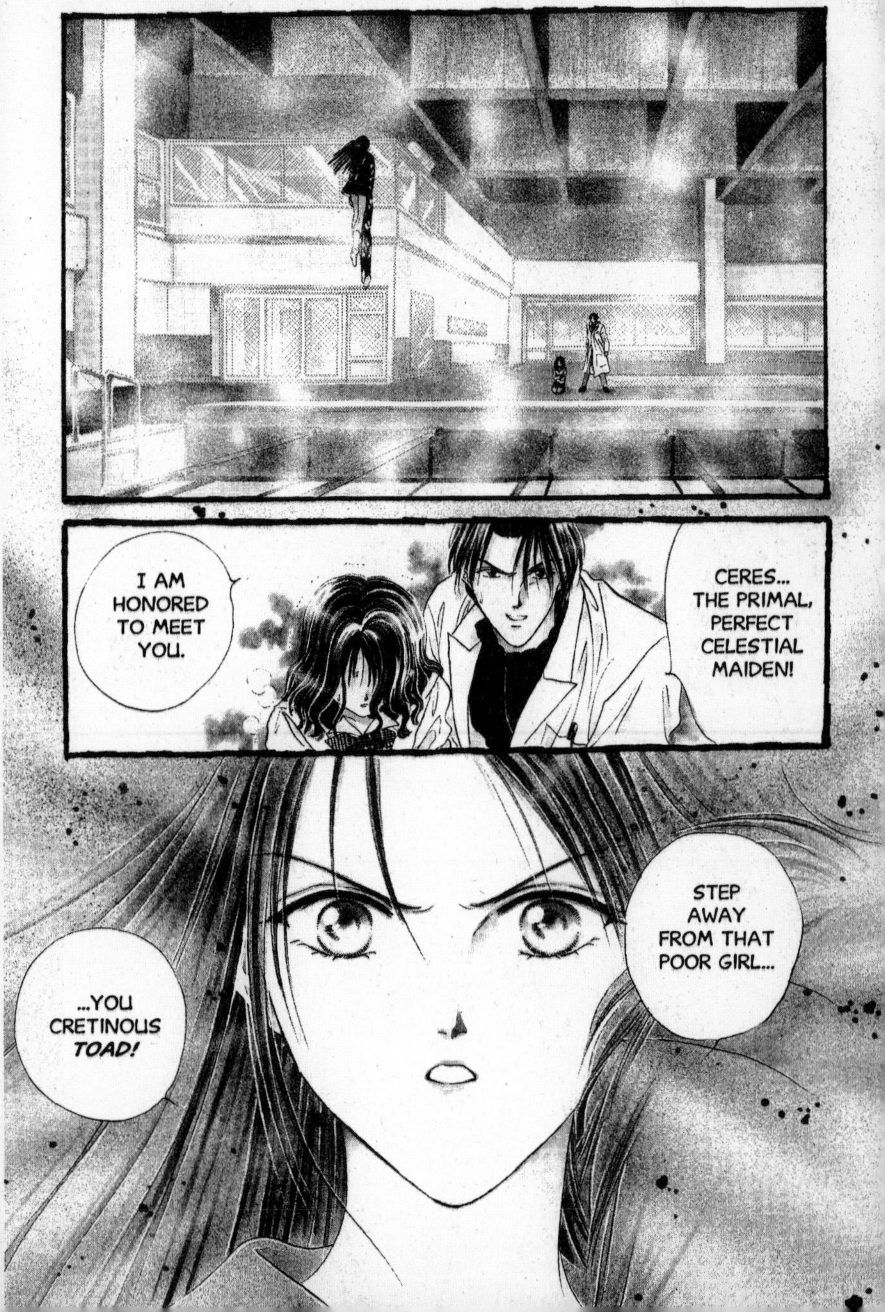
CERES... THE PRIMAL, PERFECT CELESTIAL MAIDEN!
I AM HONORED TO MEET YOU.
STEP AWAY FROM THAT POOR GIRL...
...YOU CRETINOUS *TOAD!*

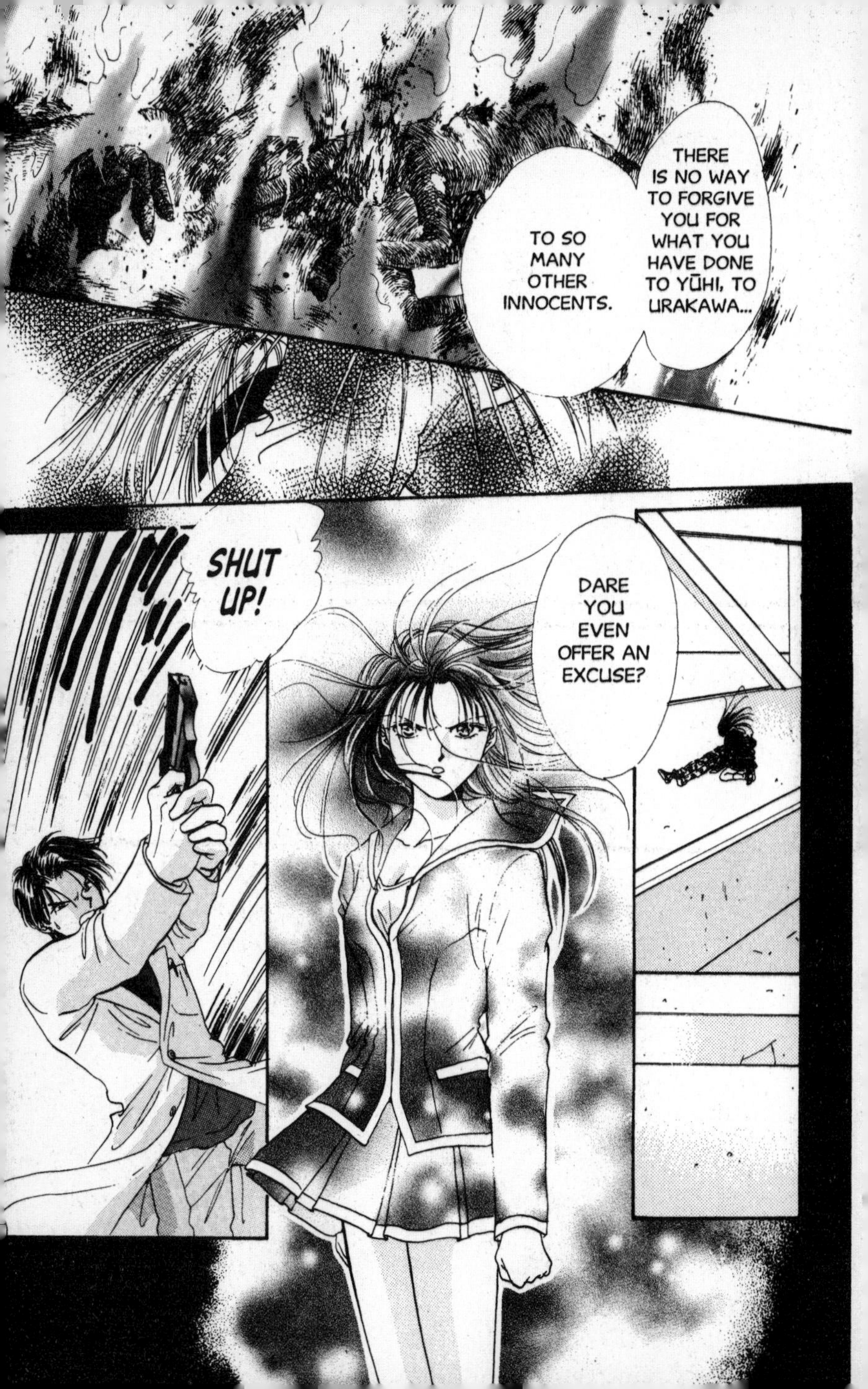
THERE IS NO WAY TO FORGIVE YOU FOR WHAT YOU HAVE DONE TO YŪHI, TO URAKAWA...
TO SO MANY OTHER INNOCENTS.
DARE YOU EVEN OFFER AN EXCUSE?
SHUT UP!

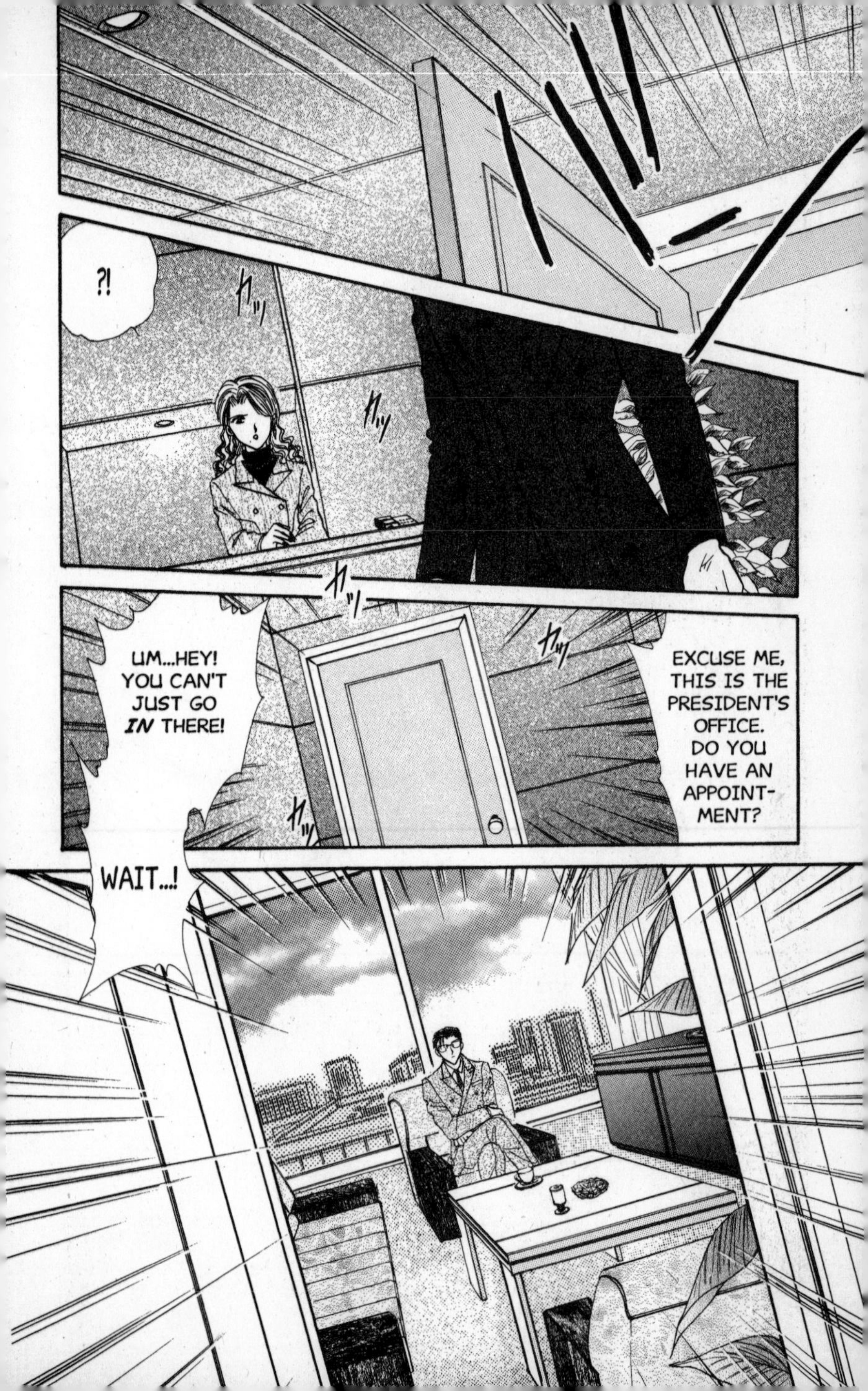
?!
EXCUSE ME, THIS IS THE PRESIDENT'S OFFICE. DO YOU HAVE AN APPOINTMENT?
UM...HEY! YOU CAN'T JUST GO *IN* THERE!
WAIT...!

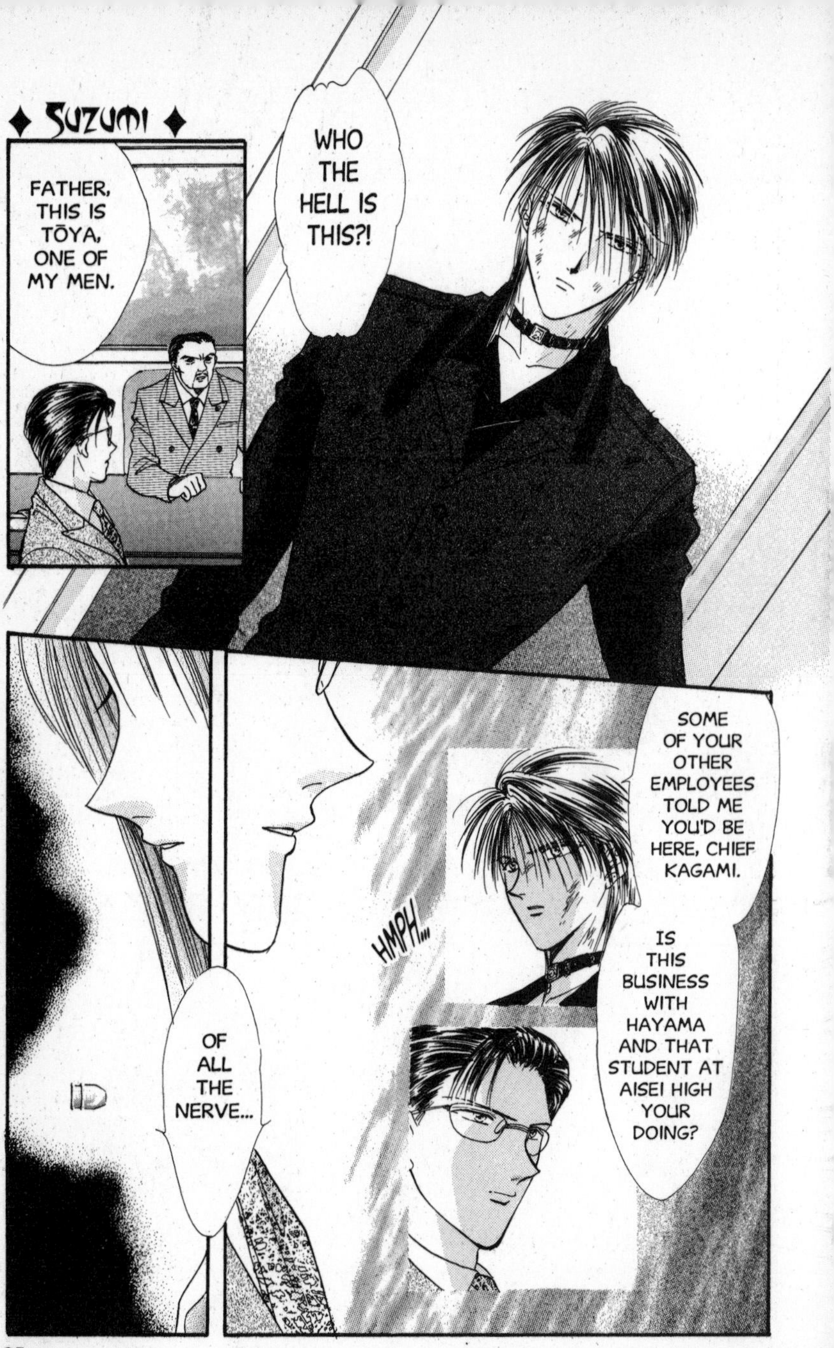
WHO THE HELL IS THIS?!
FATHER, THIS IS TŌYA, ONE OF MY MEN.
SOME OF YOUR OTHER EMPLOYEES TOLD ME YOU'D BE HERE, CHIEF KAGAMI.
HMPH...
IS THIS BUSINESS WITH HAYAMA AND THAT STUDENT AT AISEI HIGH YOUR DOING?
OF ALL THE NERVE...

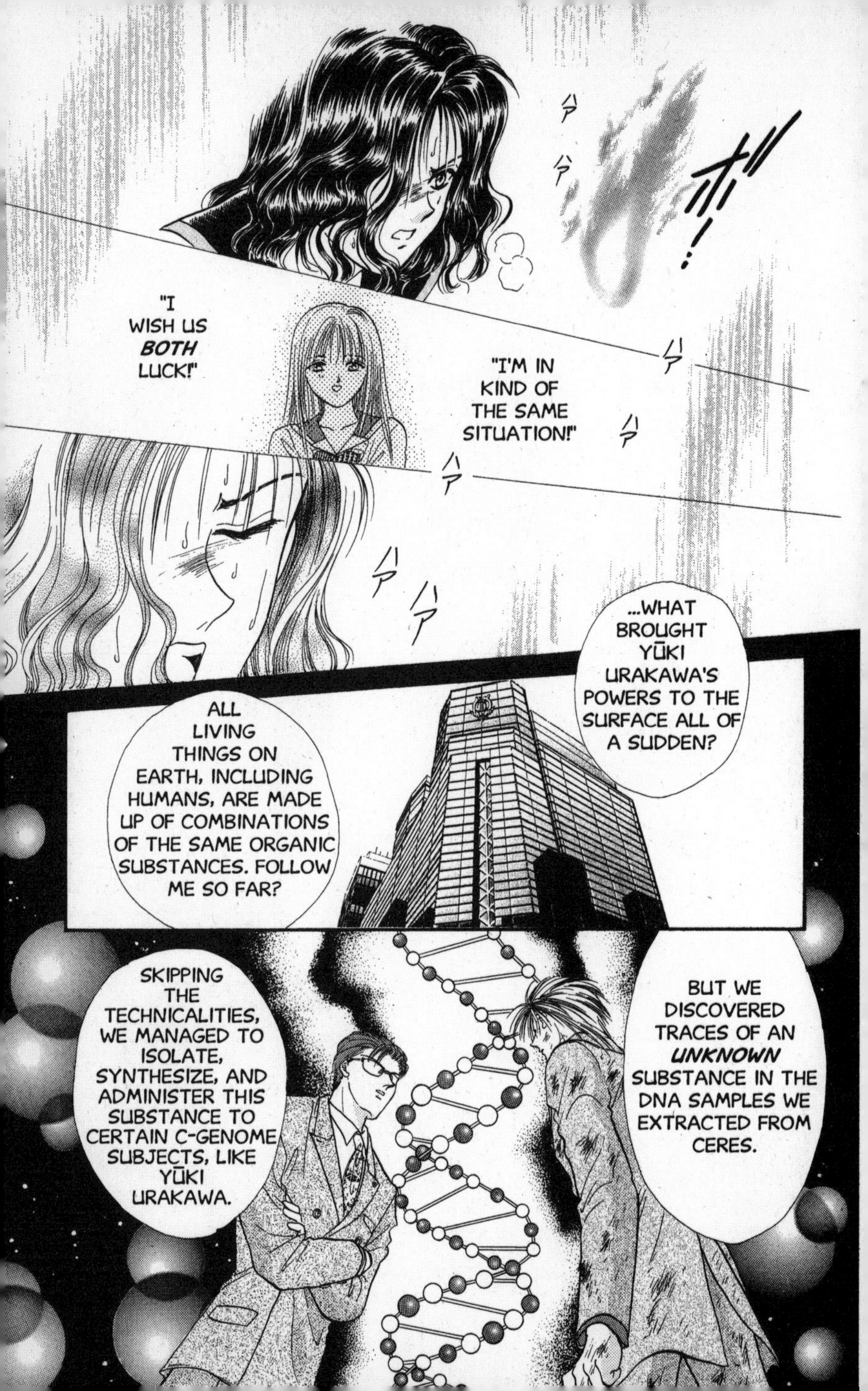
"I'M IN KIND OF THE SAME SITUATION!"
"I WISH US *BOTH* LUCK!"
...WHAT BROUGHT YŪKI URAKAWA'S POWERS TO THE SURFACE ALL OF A SUDDEN?
ALL LIVING THINGS ON EARTH, INCLUDING HUMANS, ARE MADE UP OF COMBINATIONS OF THE SAME ORGANIC SUBSTANCES. FOLLOW ME SO FAR?
BUT WE DISCOVERED TRACES OF AN *UNKNOWN* SUBSTANCE IN THE DNA SAMPLES WE EXTRACTED FROM CERES.
SKIPPING THE TECHNICALITIES, WE MANAGED TO ISOLATE, SYNTHESIZE, AND ADMINISTER THIS SUBSTANCE TO CERTAIN C-GENOME SUBJECTS, LIKE YŪKI URAKAWA.

SO, YOU'RE OUT TO CREATE AND CONTROL BEINGS LIKE CERES...?!

IT'S BEEN SEVERAL THOUSAND YEARS SINCE CERES GAVE "POWER" TO OUR MIKAGE ANCESTORS. THE FAMILY HAS CONTINUED TO THRIVE, AND THIS PROJECT WILL, IF SUCCESSFUL, GIVE US EVEN GREATER POWER.

AS FOR ORDINARY PEOPLE...

...THEY ARE QUITE READY TO ACT FOR US IF PROMISED MONEY AND PRESTIGE.

MR. HAYAMA... I CAN'T DO IT... ANYMORE...

HUFF HUFF HUFF

THE NEW SUBSTANCE STARTS WORKING AS SOON AS IT'S INCORPORATED INTO THE SUBJECT'S CELLS.

AT THAT POINT WE CAN *TRIGGER* WHATEVER CELESTIAL POWERS THE SUBJECT POSSESSES.

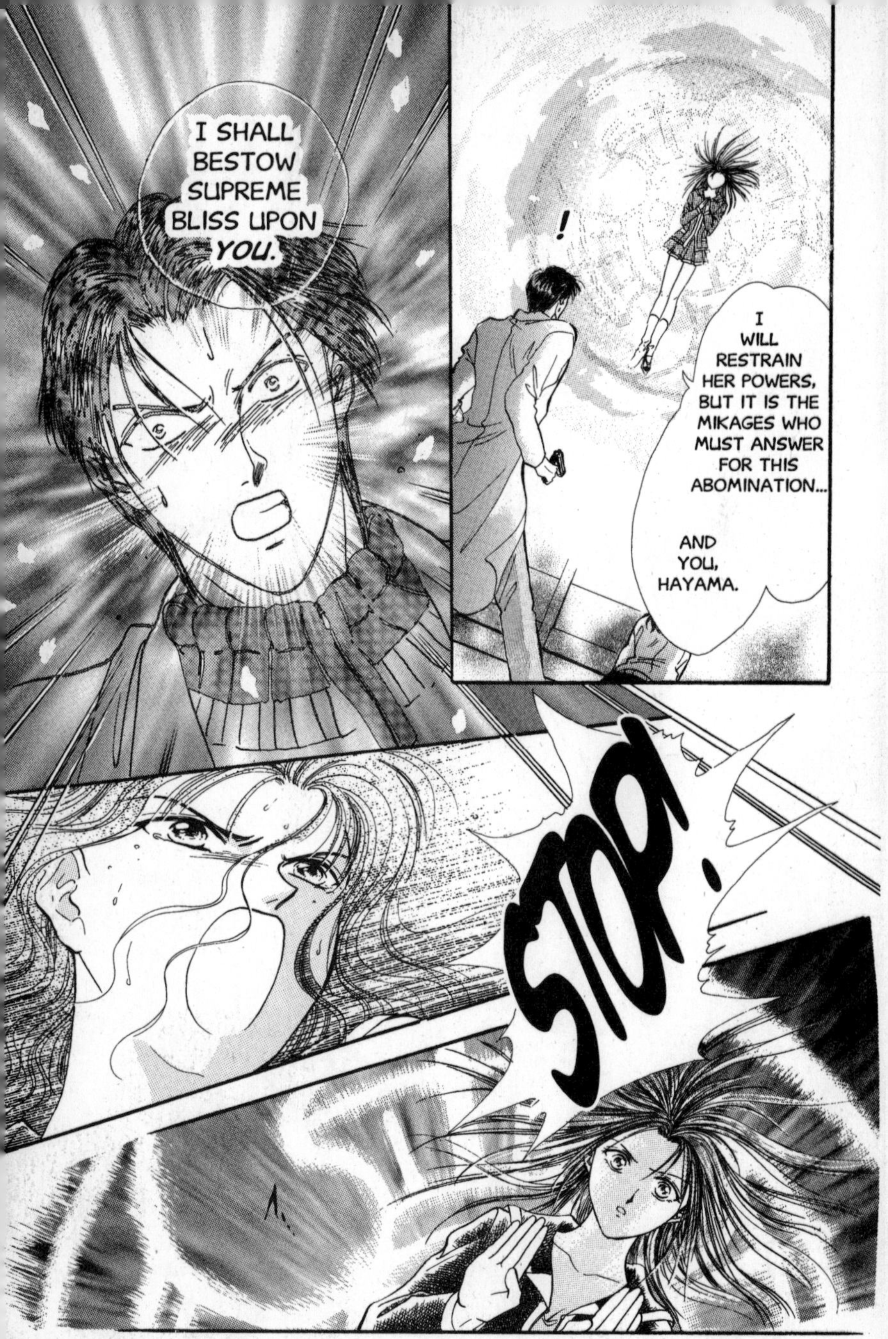
!
I WILL RESTRAIN HER POWERS, BUT IT IS THE MIKAGES WHO MUST ANSWER FOR THIS ABOMINATION...
AND YOU, HAYAMA.
I SHALL BESTOW SUPREME BLISS UPON *YOU*.
STOP!

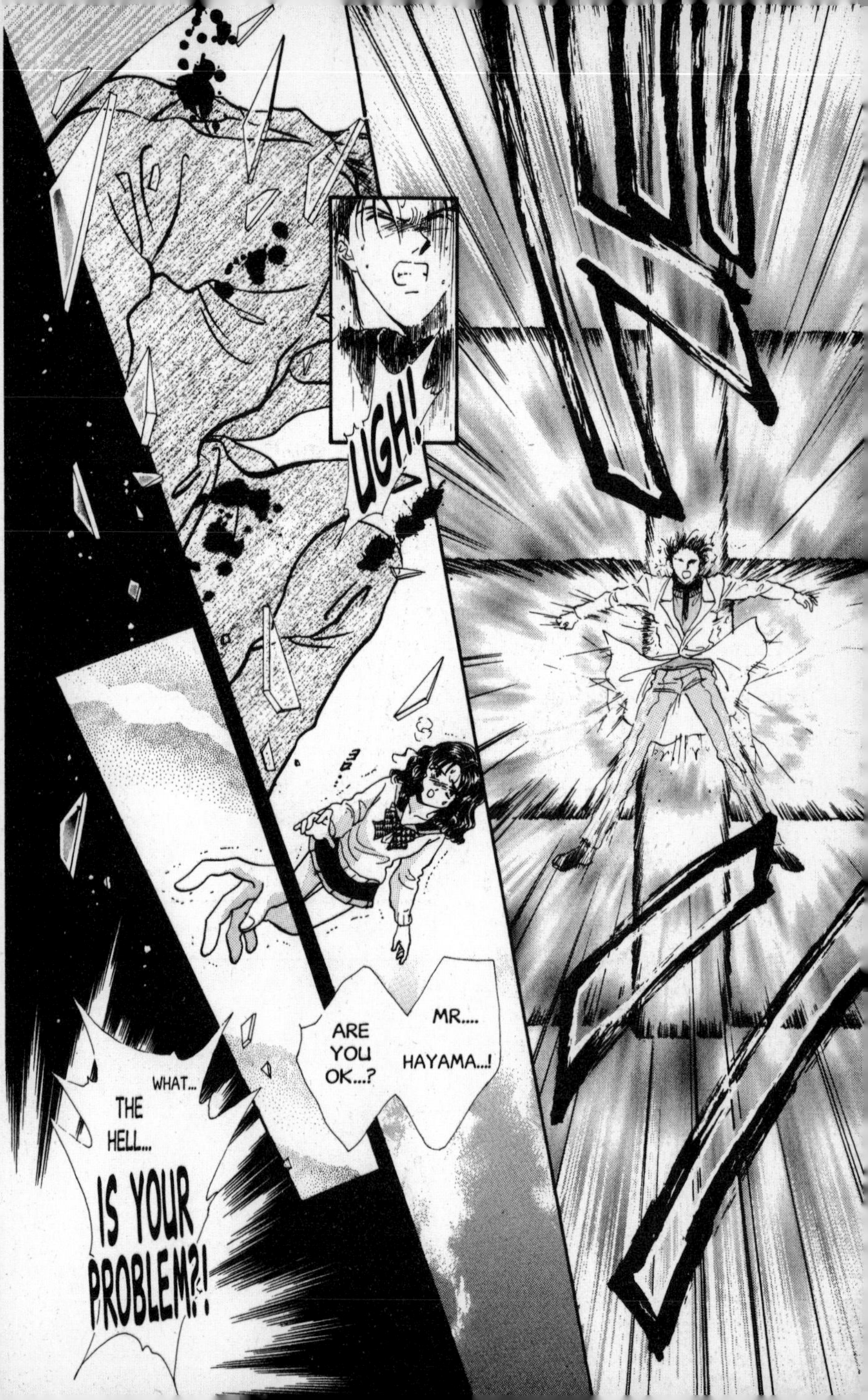
UGH!
MR.... HAYAMA...!
ARE YOU OK...?
WHAT... THE HELL... IS YOUR PROBLEM?!

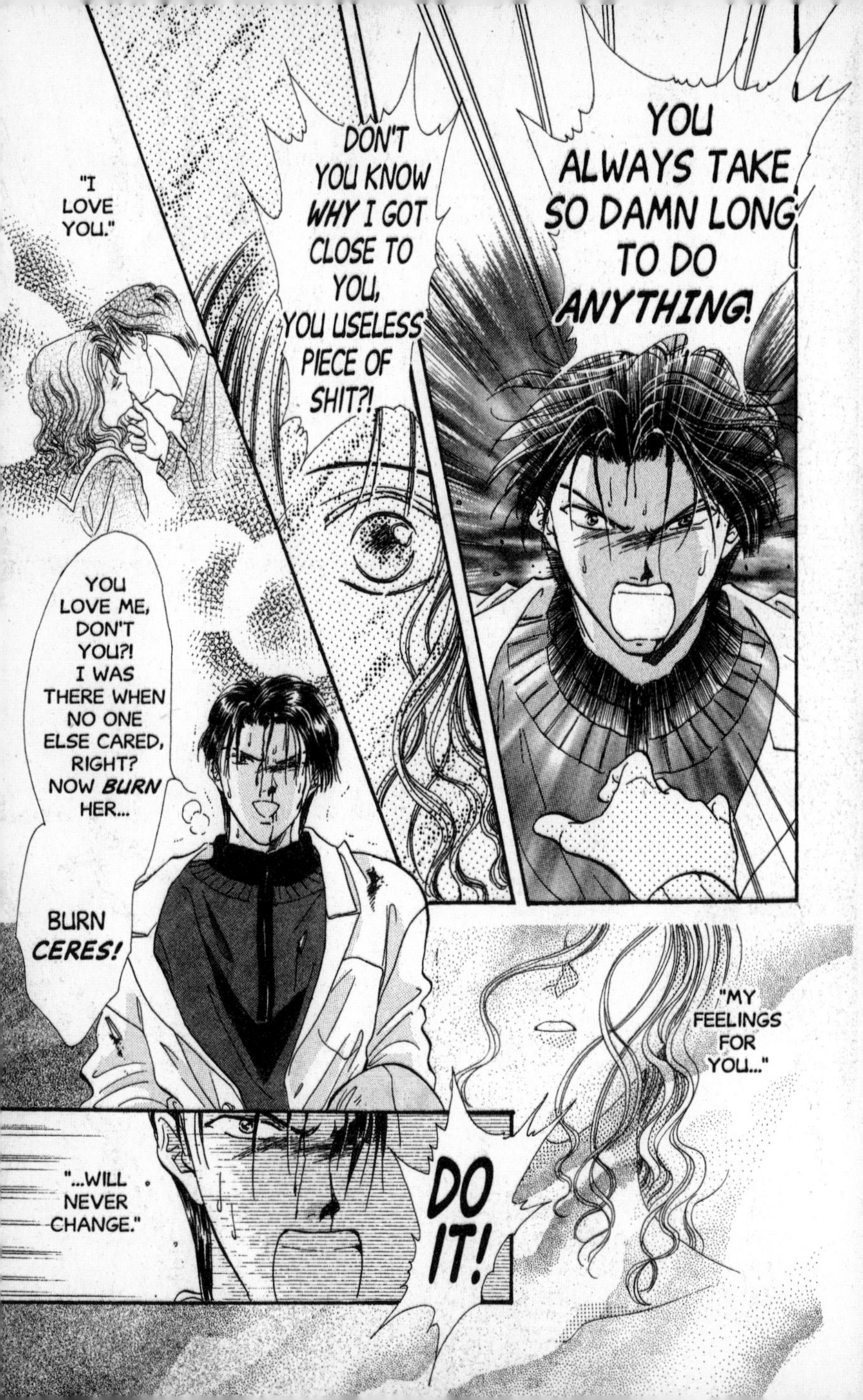
YOU ALWAYS TAKE SO DAMN LONG TO DO *ANYTHING!*
DON'T YOU KNOW *WHY* I GOT CLOSE TO YOU, YOU USELESS PIECE OF SHIT?!
"I LOVE YOU."
YOU LOVE ME, DON'T YOU?! I WAS THERE WHEN NO ONE ELSE CARED, RIGHT? NOW *BURN* HER...
BURN *CERES!*
"MY FEELINGS FOR YOU..."
DO IT!
"...WILL NEVER CHANGE."

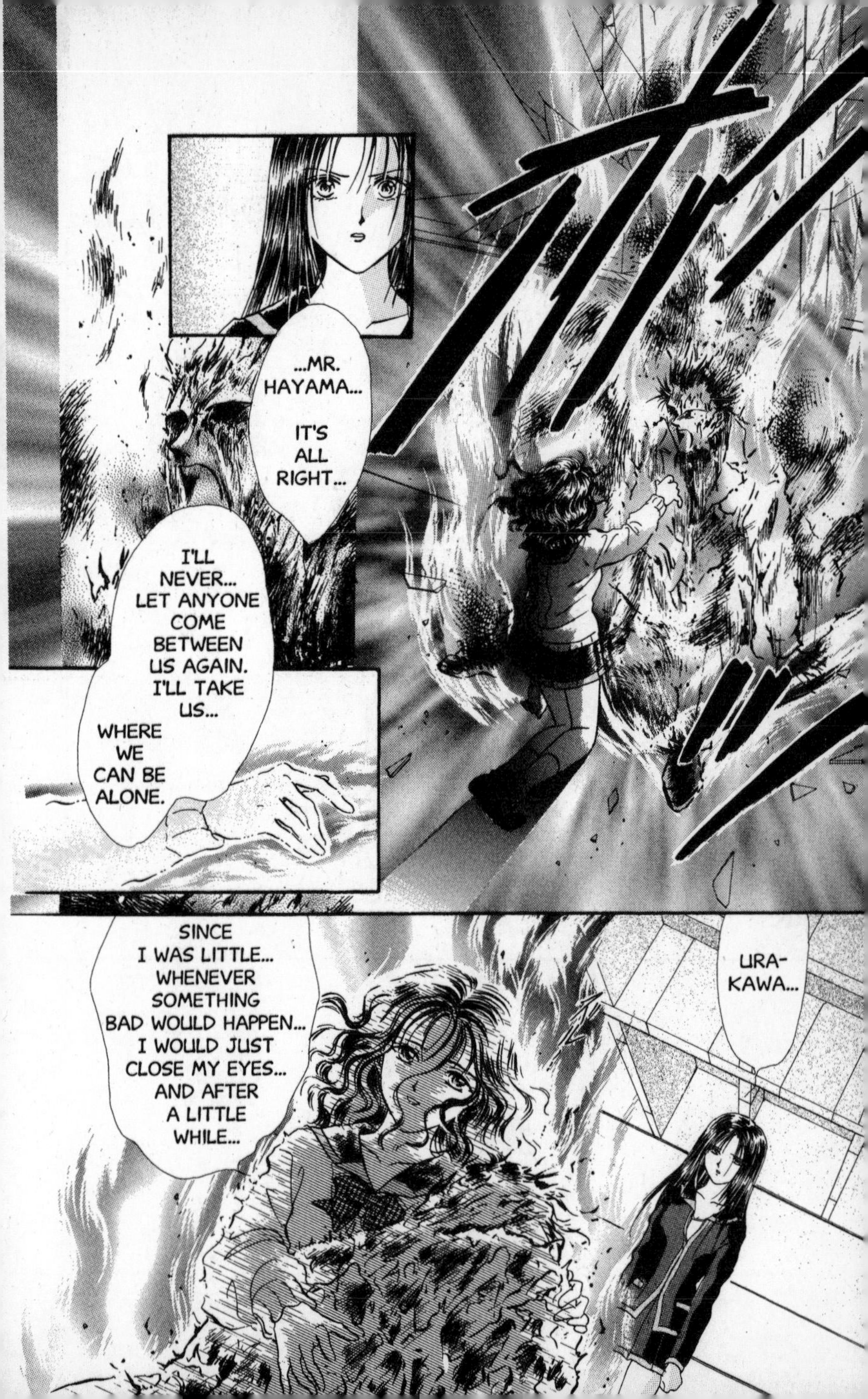
...MR. HAYAMA... IT'S ALL RIGHT...
I'LL NEVER... LET ANYONE COME BETWEEN US AGAIN. I'LL TAKE US... WHERE WE CAN BE ALONE.
URA-KAWA...
SINCE I WAS LITTLE... WHENEVER SOMETHING BAD WOULD HAPPEN... I WOULD JUST CLOSE MY EYES... AND AFTER A LITTLE WHILE...

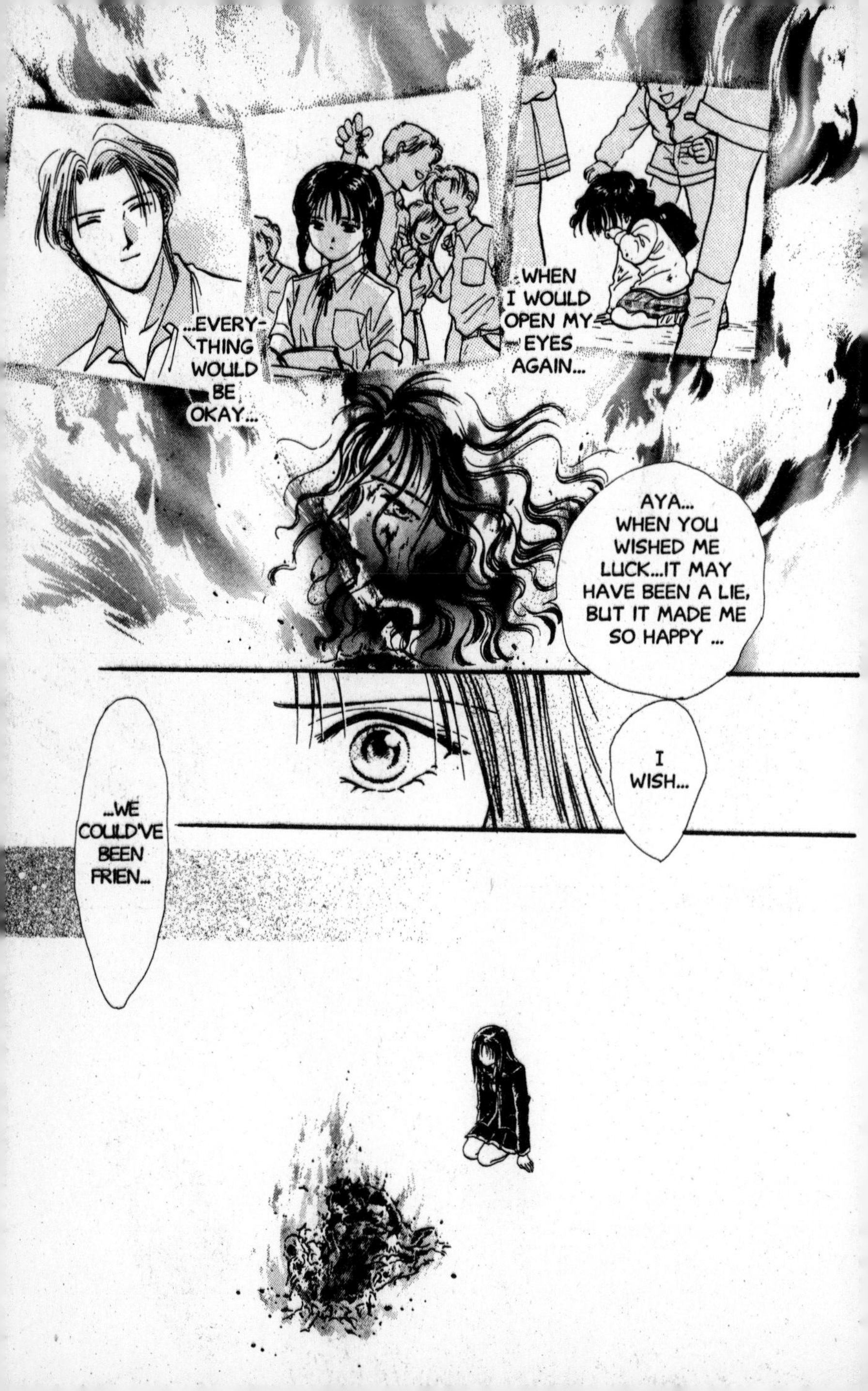
WHEN I WOULD OPEN MY EYES AGAIN...
...EVERY-THING WOULD BE OKAY...
AYA... WHEN YOU WISHED ME LUCK...IT MAY HAVE BEEN A LIE, BUT IT MADE ME SO HAPPY ...
I WISH...
...WE COULD'VE BEEN FRIEN...

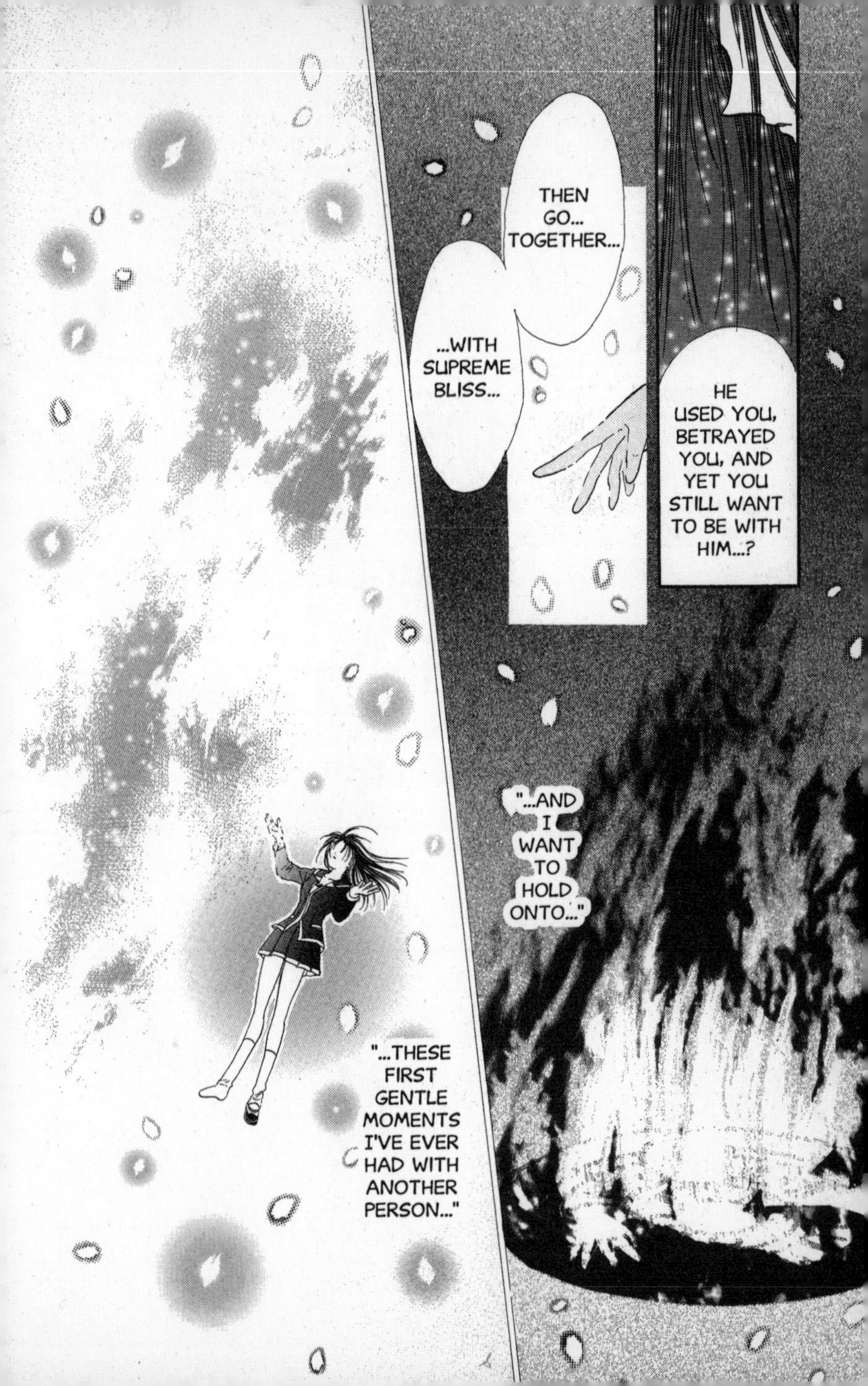
HE USED YOU, BETRAYED YOU, AND YET YOU STILL WANT TO BE WITH HIM...?
THEN GO... TOGETHER...
...WITH SUPREME BLISS...
"...AND I WANT TO HOLD ONTO..."
"...THESE FIRST GENTLE MOMENTS I'VE EVER HAD WITH ANOTHER PERSON..."

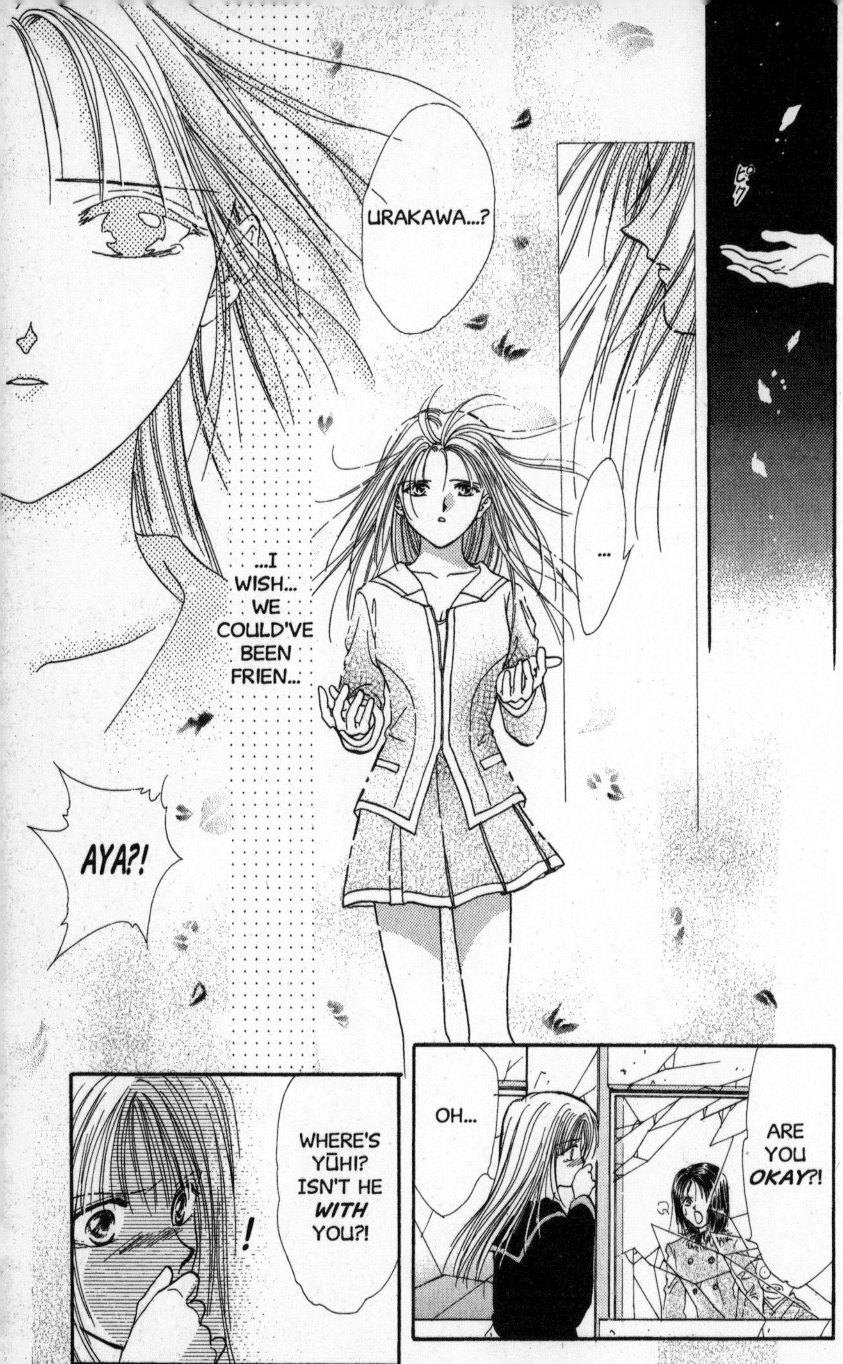
...
URAKAWA...?
...I WISH... WE COULD'VE BEEN FRIEN...
AYA?!
ARE YOU OKAY?!
OH...
WHERE'S YŪHI? ISN'T HE WITH YOU?!
!

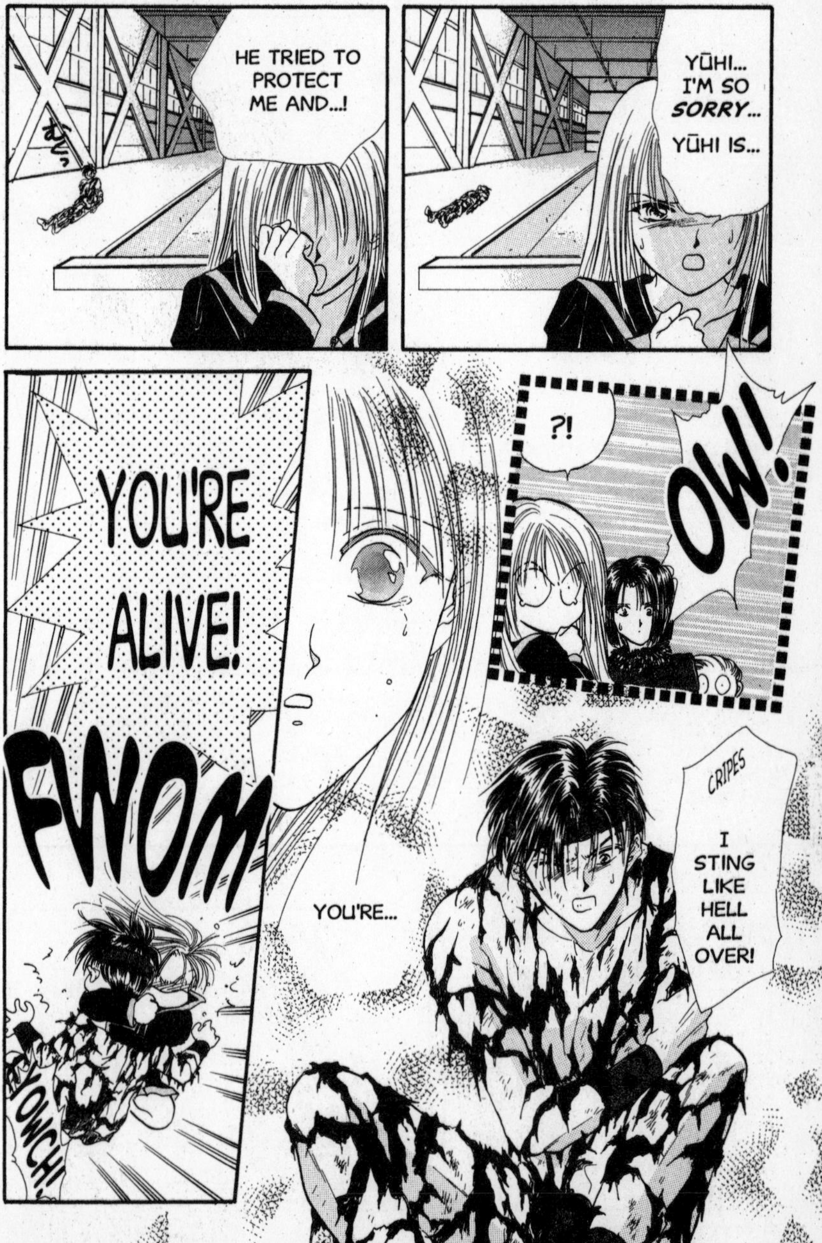
YŪHI... I'M SO SORRY... YŪHI IS...
HE TRIED TO PROTECT ME AND...!
?!
OW!
CRIPES
I STING LIKE HELL ALL OVER!
YOU'RE...
YOU'RE ALIVE!
FWOM
YOWCH!

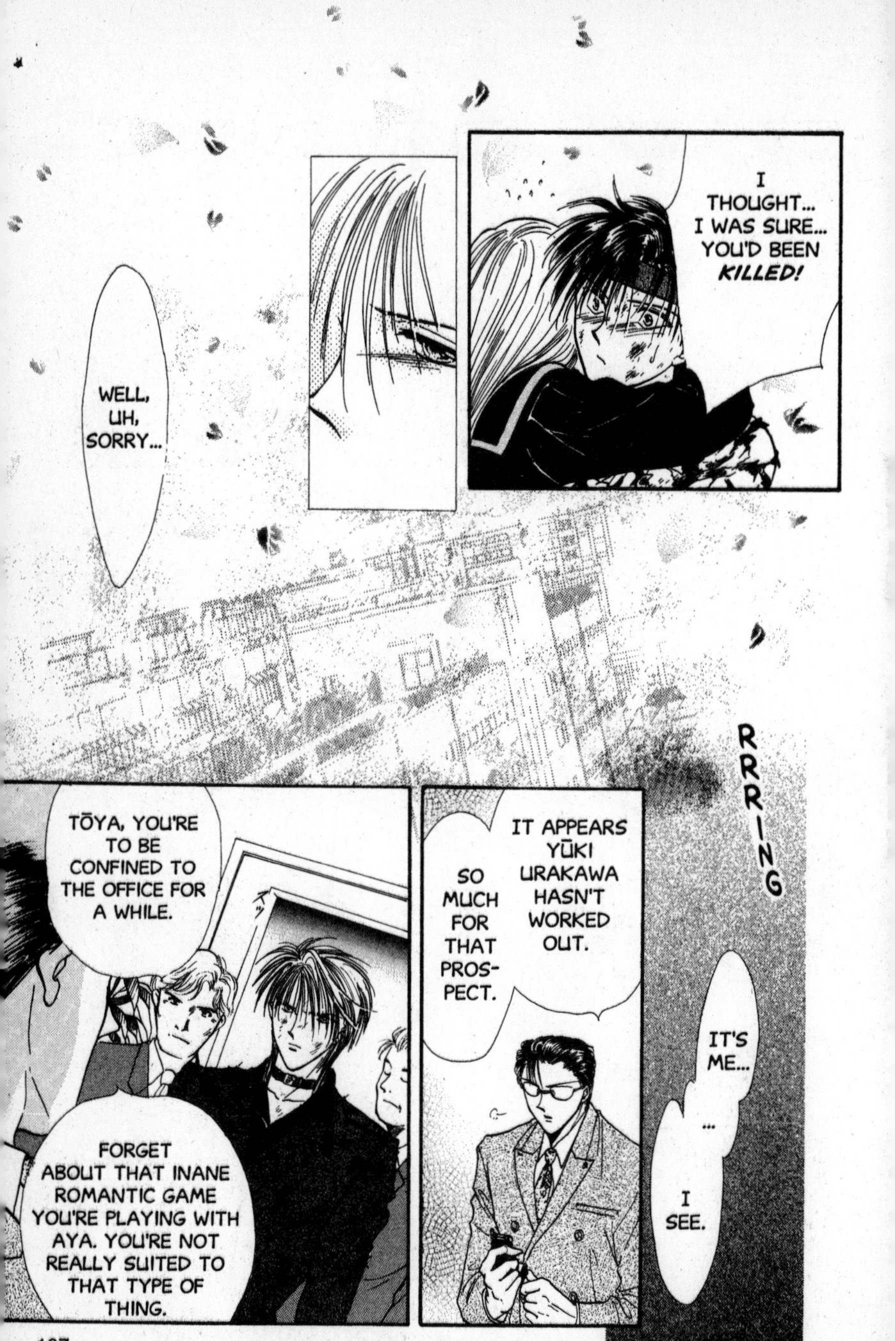
I THOUGHT... I WAS SURE... YOU'D BEEN *KILLED!*
WELL, UH, SORRY...
RRRING
IT'S ME...
...
I SEE.
IT APPEARS YŪKI URAKAWA HASN'T WORKED OUT.
SO MUCH FOR THAT PROSPECT.
TŌYA, YOU'RE TO BE CONFINED TO THE OFFICE FOR A WHILE.
FORGET ABOUT THAT INANE ROMANTIC GAME YOU'RE PLAYING WITH AYA. YOU'RE NOT REALLY SUITED TO THAT TYPE OF THING.

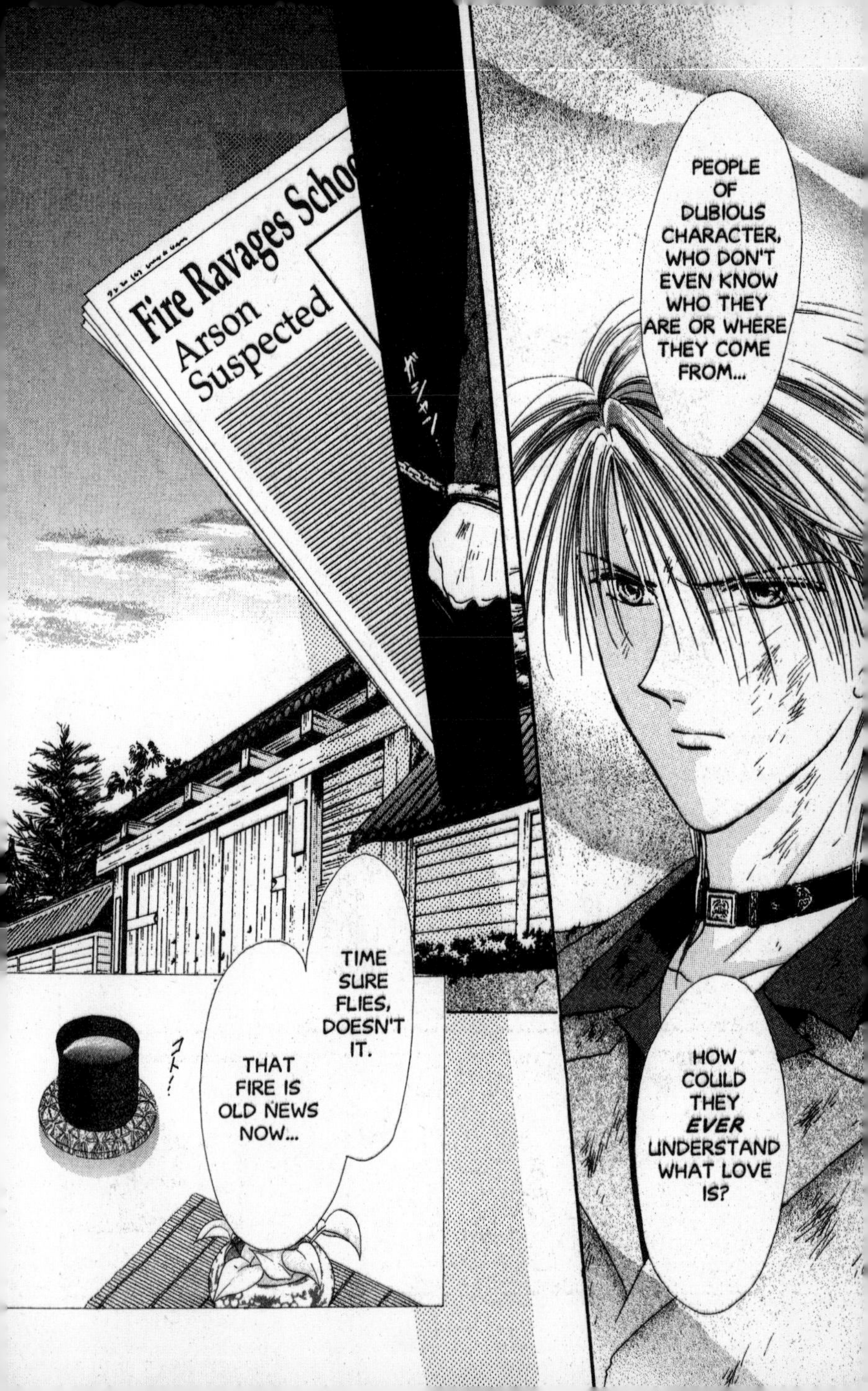
PEOPLE OF DUBIOUS CHARACTER, WHO DON'T EVEN KNOW WHO THEY ARE OR WHERE THEY COME FROM...
HOW COULD THEY *EVER* UNDERSTAND WHAT LOVE IS?
Fire Ravages Schoo
Arson Suspected
TIME SURE FLIES, DOESN'T IT.
THAT FIRE IS OLD NEWS NOW...
コト!!

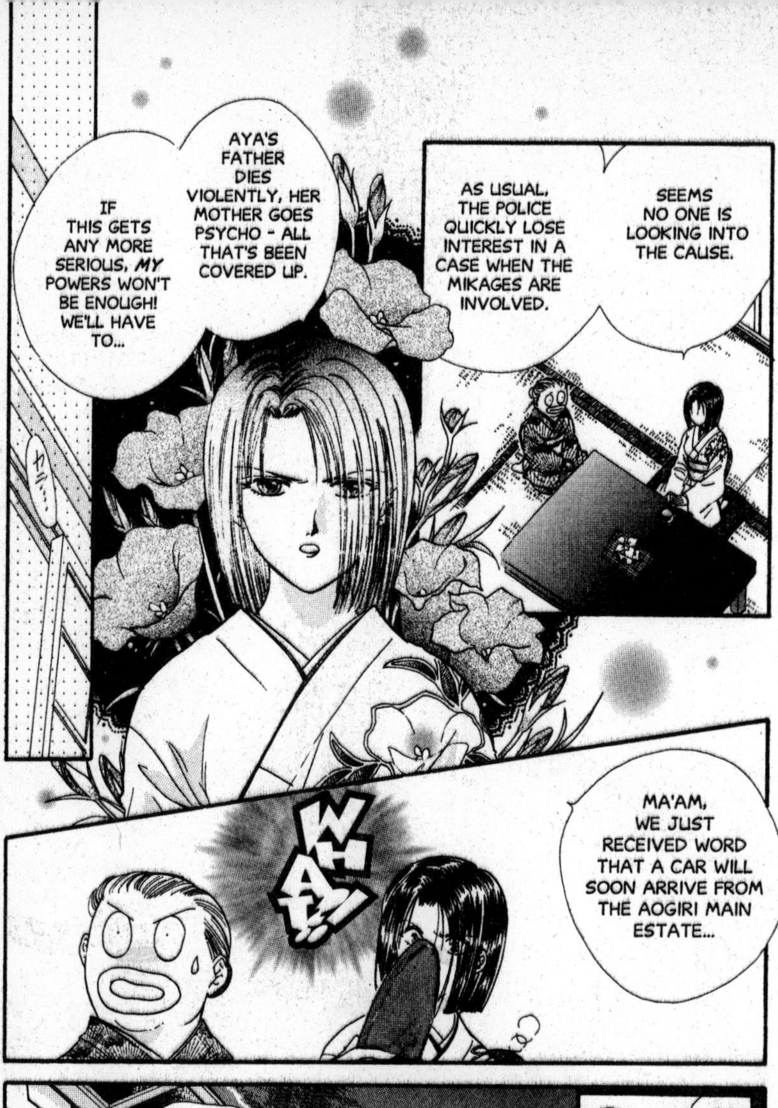
SEEMS NO ONE IS LOOKING INTO THE CAUSE.
AS USUAL, THE POLICE QUICKLY LOSE INTEREST IN A CASE WHEN THE MIKAGES ARE INVOLVED.
AYA'S FATHER DIES VIOLENTLY, HER MOTHER GOES PSYCHO - ALL THAT'S BEEN COVERED UP.
IF THIS GETS ANY MORE SERIOUS, *MY* POWERS WON'T BE ENOUGH! WE'LL HAVE TO...
MA'AM, WE JUST RECEIVED WORD THAT A CAR WILL SOON ARRIVE FROM THE AOGIRI MAIN ESTATE...
WHAT!
THE READERS CAN'T SEE MY FACE!
SORRY!
I'M *BORED!*

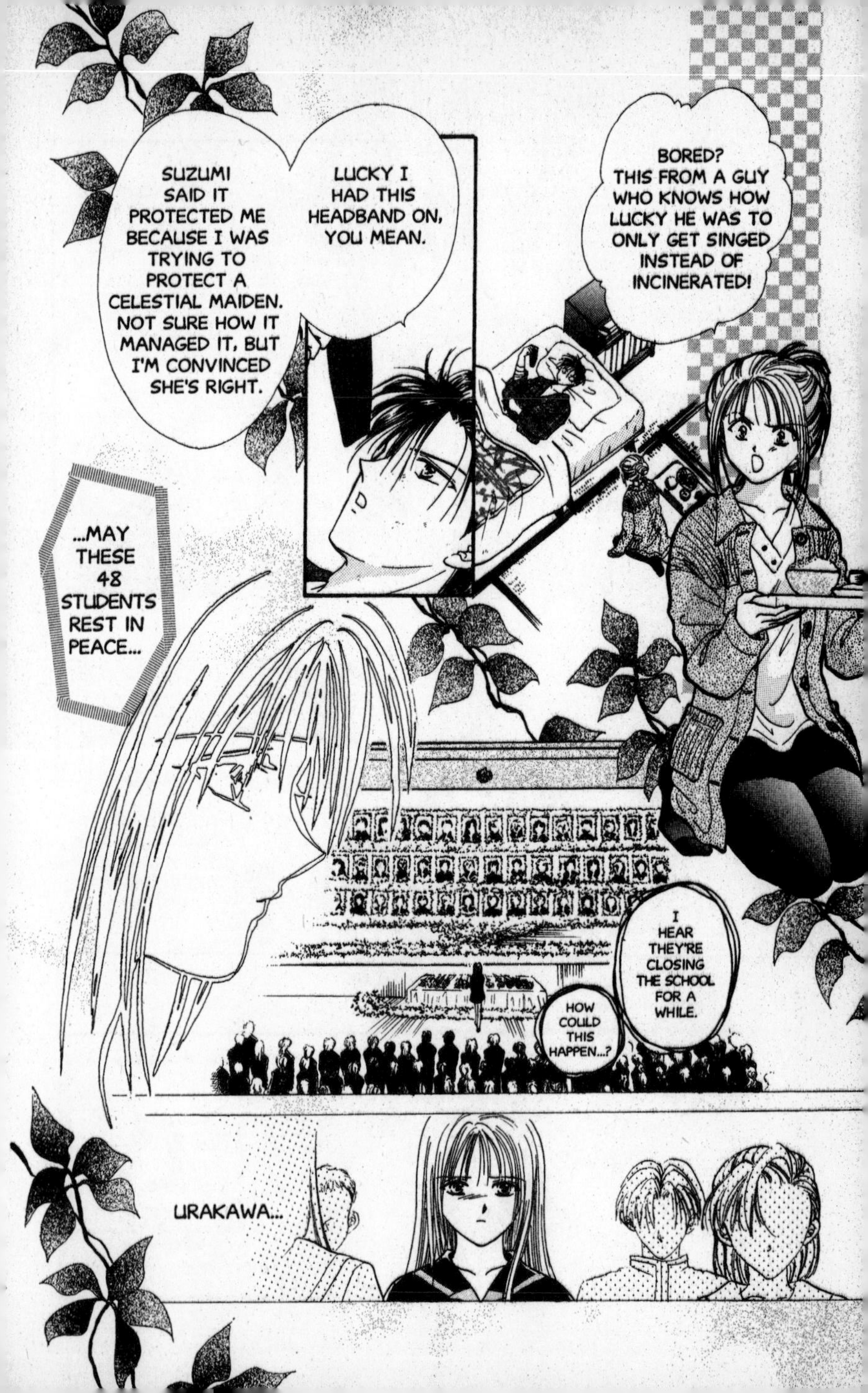
BORED? THIS FROM A GUY WHO KNOWS HOW LUCKY HE WAS TO ONLY GET SINGED INSTEAD OF INCINERATED!
LUCKY I HAD THIS HEADBAND ON, YOU MEAN.
SUZUMI SAID IT PROTECTED ME BECAUSE I WAS TRYING TO PROTECT A CELESTIAL MAIDEN. NOT SURE HOW IT MANAGED IT, BUT I'M CONVINCED SHE'S RIGHT.
I HEAR THEY'RE CLOSING THE SCHOOL FOR A WHILE.
HOW COULD THIS HAPPEN...?
...MAY THESE 48 STUDENTS REST IN PEACE...
URAKAWA...

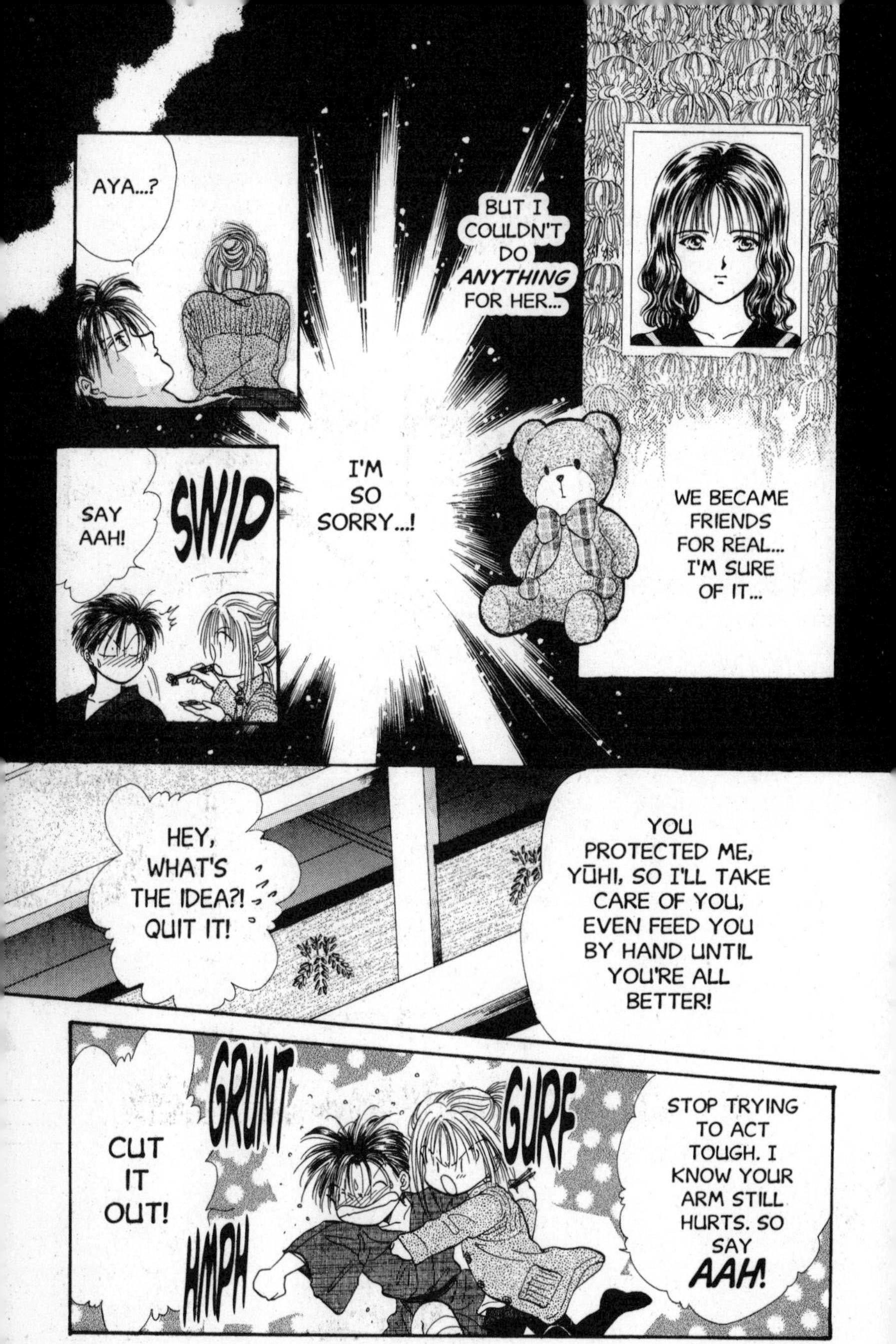

WE BECAME FRIENDS FOR REAL... I'M SURE OF IT...
BUT I COULDN'T DO *ANYTHING* FOR HER...
I'M SO SORRY...!
AYA...?
SAY AAH!
SWIP
YOU PROTECTED ME, YŪHI, SO I'LL TAKE CARE OF YOU, EVEN FEED YOU BY HAND UNTIL YOU'RE ALL BETTER!
HEY, WHAT'S THE IDEA?! QUIT IT!
STOP TRYING TO ACT TOUGH. I KNOW YOUR ARM STILL HURTS. SO SAY **AAH!**
GURF
GRUNT
CUT IT OUT!
HMPH

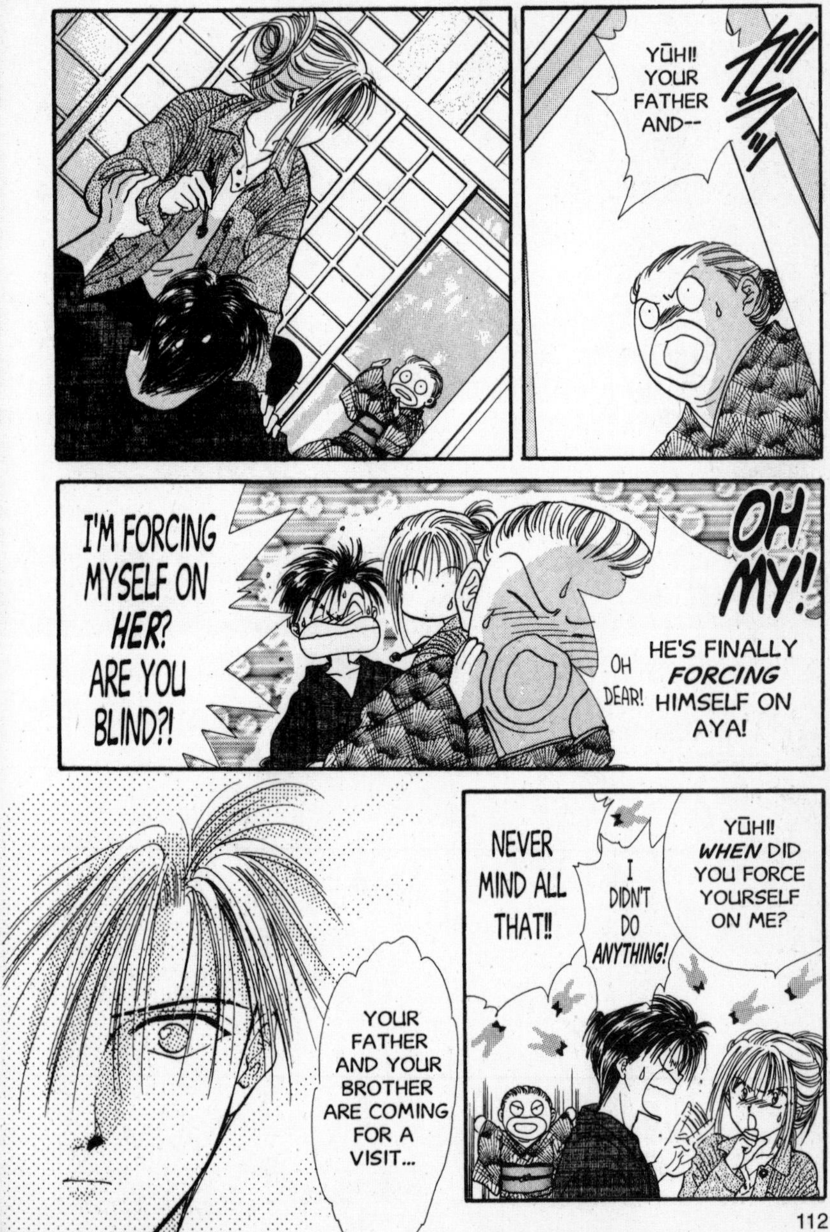
YŪHI! YOUR FATHER AND--
OH MY!
HE'S FINALLY *FORCING* HIMSELF ON AYA!
OH DEAR!
I'M FORCING MYSELF ON *HER*? ARE YOU BLIND?!
YŪHI! *WHEN* DID YOU FORCE YOURSELF ON ME?
I DIDN'T DO *ANYTHING!*
NEVER MIND ALL THAT!!
YOUR FATHER AND YOUR BROTHER ARE COMING FOR A VISIT...

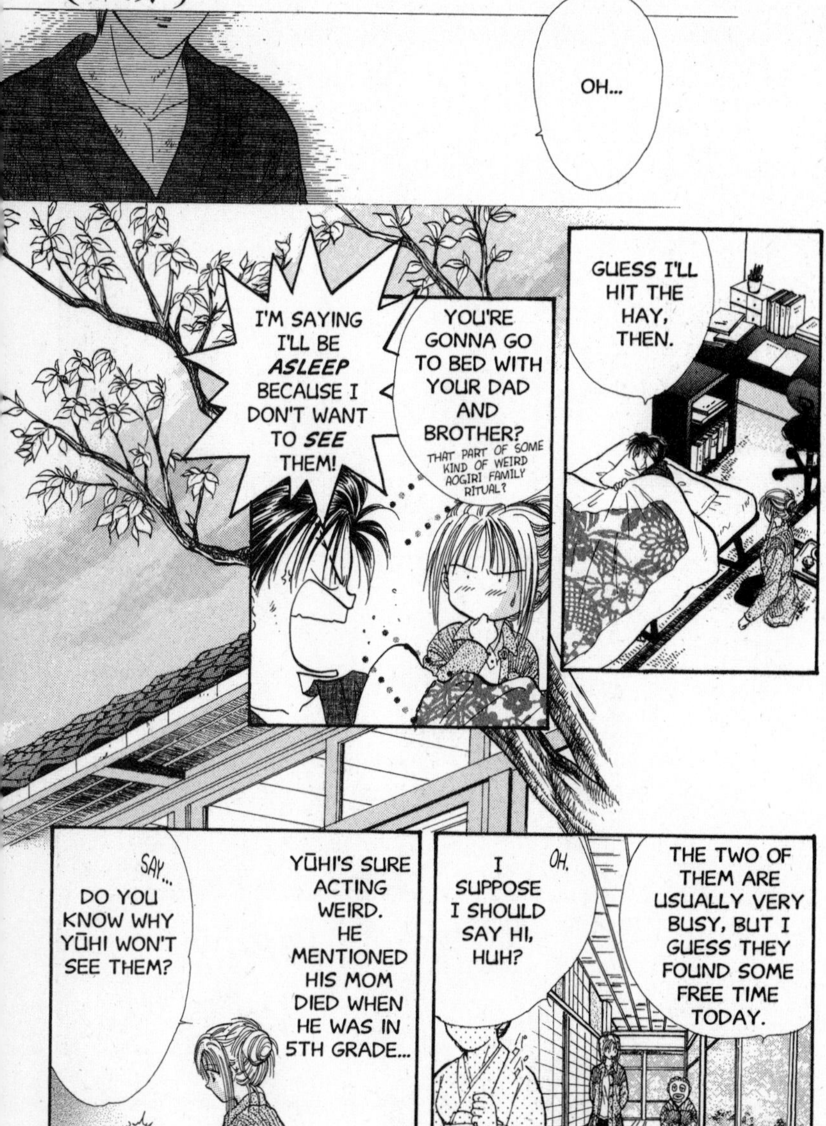
OH...
GUESS I'LL HIT THE HAY, THEN.
YOU'RE GONNA GO TO BED WITH YOUR DAD AND BROTHER?
THAT PART OF SOME KIND OF WEIRD AOGIRI FAMILY RITUAL?
I'M SAYING I'LL BE *ASLEEP* BECAUSE I DON'T WANT TO *SEE* THEM!
THE TWO OF THEM ARE USUALLY VERY BUSY, BUT I GUESS THEY FOUND SOME FREE TIME TODAY.
OH.
I SUPPOSE I SHOULD SAY HI, HUH?
YŪHI'S SURE ACTING WEIRD. HE MENTIONED HIS MOM DIED WHEN HE WAS IN 5TH GRADE...
SAY...
DO YOU KNOW WHY YŪHI WON'T SEE THEM?

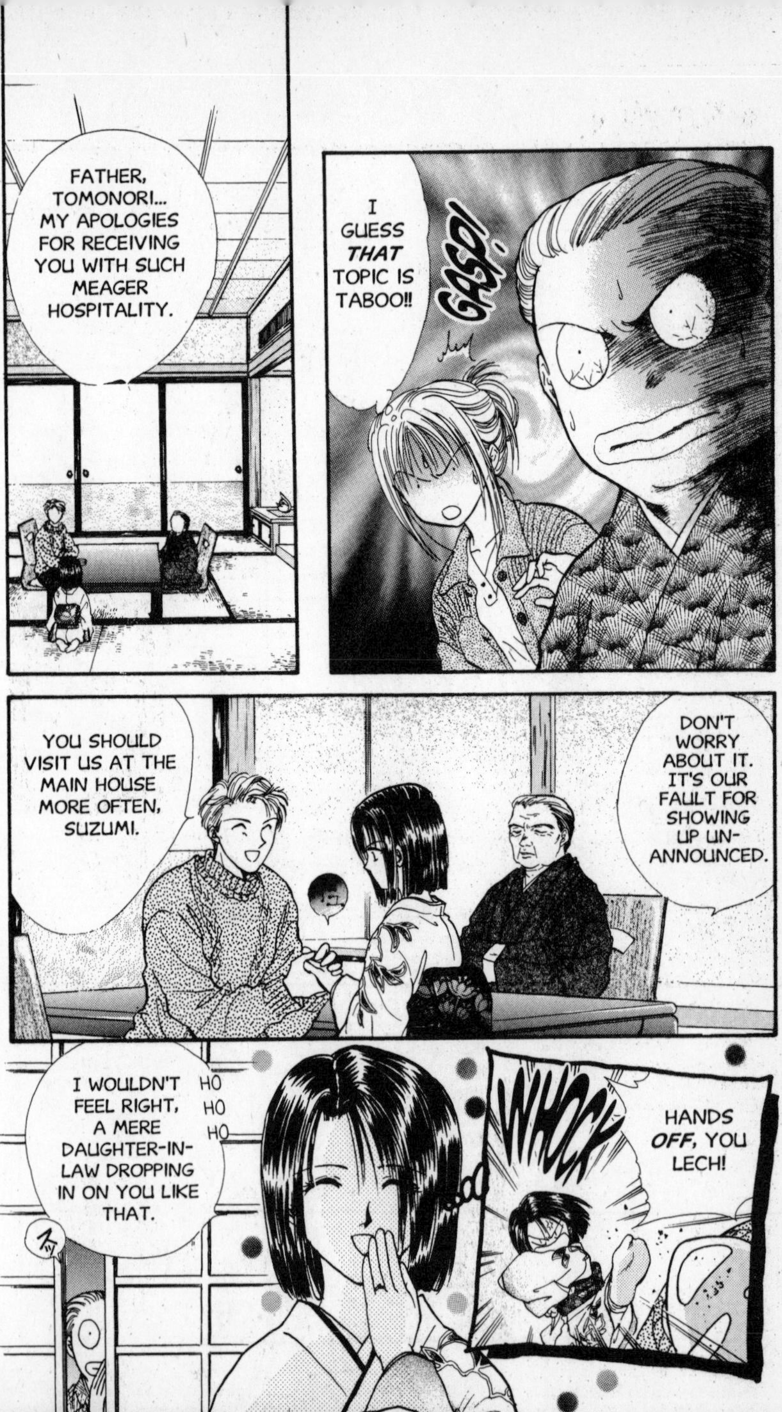
I GUESS *THAT* TOPIC IS TABOO!!
GASP!
FATHER, TOMONORI... MY APOLOGIES FOR RECEIVING YOU WITH SUCH MEAGER HOSPITALITY.
DON'T WORRY ABOUT IT. IT'S OUR FAULT FOR SHOWING UP UN-ANNOUNCED.
YOU SHOULD VISIT US AT THE MAIN HOUSE MORE OFTEN, SUZUMI.
WHACK
HANDS *OFF*, YOU LECH!
I WOULDN'T FEEL RIGHT, A MERE DAUGHTER-IN-LAW DROPPING IN ON YOU LIKE THAT.
HO HO HO

Although I only have a superficial understanding, maybe I can do a simple explanation of all the scientific terms when the tankōbon comes out. (Do I know enough to do that?) Hmmm....

As for those clones I mentioned in the last sidebar, "monkey clones" came up on the news the other day. It's a huge controversy and people are protesting and saying, "Stop this now! Wouldn't it be terrible if they did this kind of research on humans!?"

So I asked the people at the laboratory about it, and they said, "It's like having your identical twin get born later." That wasn't how I had imagined it to be so I was surprised. ⑧

A clone is "a copy," in other words, kind of like the robots in **Perman**, a manga by Fujiko Fujio where kids have robots that look exactly like them so that they can go off to save the world while their look-a-like robots attend school for them (What kind of example is that?). You take one of your cells, and artificially create your clone from it... You know, it's like in old manga stories where they always show a person with an exact duplicate of themselves. But when you think about it, you realize it's not possible... ⑥⑥

When I get real busy, I complain that I need a clone of myself. But the life that would begin with that single cell has to start over from infancy. And furthermore, the cell would be as old as I am, so it's been used for 20-odd years and a little aged (cells die, and genes get worn out) so that's the kind of baby you'd get...

Well, it would look just like any other baby though.

MRS. Q! WHERE'S YŪHI?

EXCUSE ME.

WELL... HE SAID HE'S NOT FEELING WELL AND ISN'T REALLY READY FOR VISITORS...

WELL, AS LONG AS HE'S ON THE MEND.

...

ANYWAY, WE'VE PAID SUZUMI OUR RESPECTS, SO PERHAPS WE SHOULD BE ON OUR WAY...

WHAT'S EMBARRASSING TO US IS HOW HIS NAME IS ALL OVER THE NEWSPAPERS.

WE HEAR HIS BURNS AREN'T SERIOUS, AND HE'S TOO STUBBORN TO DIE FROM SOMETHING LIKE THIS ANYWAY.

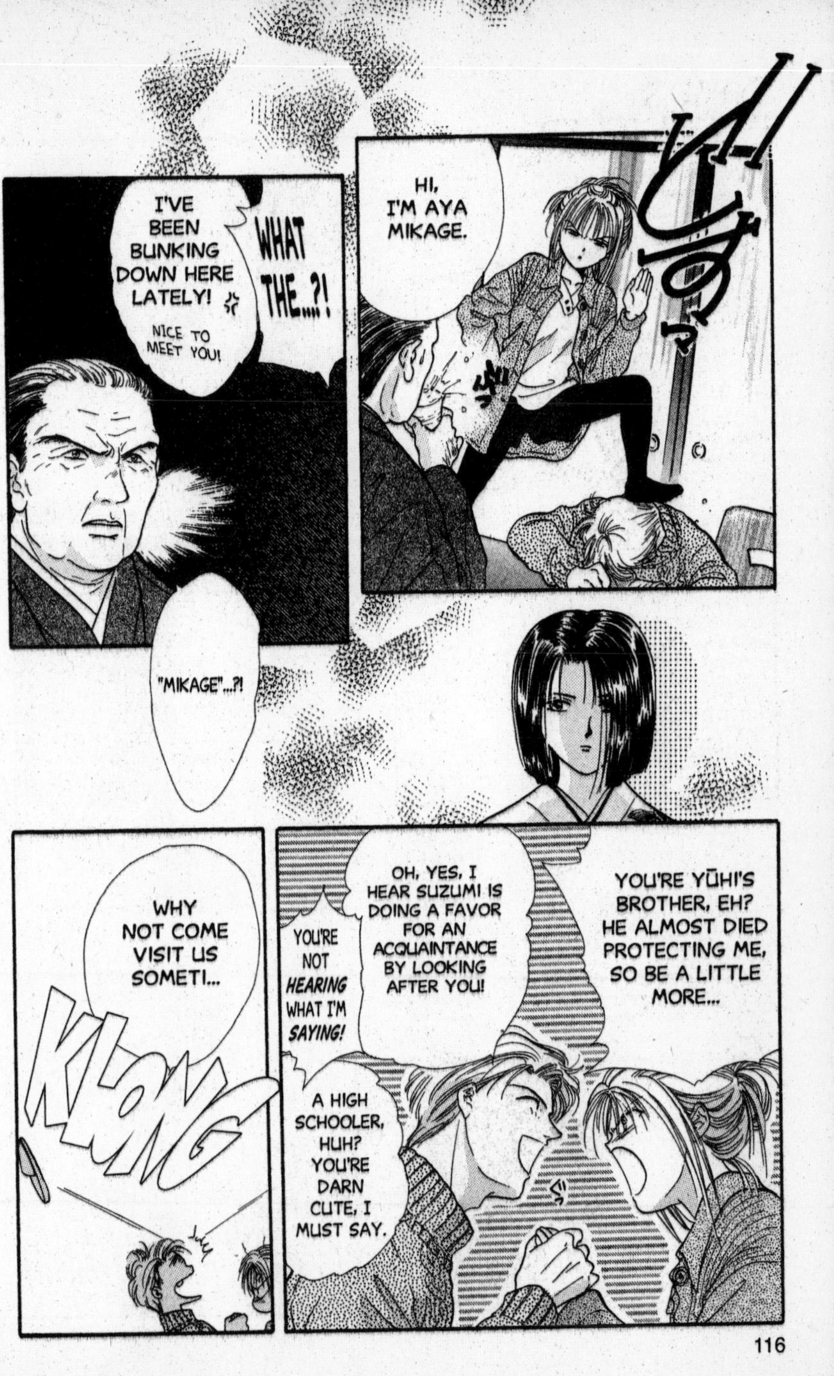
HI, I'M AYA MIKAGE.
I'VE BEEN BUNKING DOWN HERE LATELY!
NICE TO MEET YOU!
WHAT THE..?!
"MIKAGE"...?!
YOU'RE YŪHI'S BROTHER, EH? HE ALMOST DIED PROTECTING ME, SO BE A LITTLE MORE...
OH, YES, I HEAR SUZUMI IS DOING A FAVOR FOR AN ACQUAINTANCE BY LOOKING AFTER YOU!
YOU'RE NOT *HEARING* WHAT I'M *SAYING!*
A HIGH SCHOOLER, HUH? YOU'RE DARN CUTE, I MUST SAY.
WHY NOT COME VISIT US SOMETI...
KLONG

Ceres: 3

AS LECHEROUS AS EVER, I SEE, DROOLING AFTER EVERY PRETTY GIRL WHO WALKS BY.

YŪHI!!

DON'T *TOUCH* HER!

LOOK WHO'S TALKING PROPRIETY, THE GUY WHO'S PLASTERED HIS NAME AS "THE THIRD SON OF THE AOGIRIS" ALL OVER THE PAPERS.

HMPH!

FINE, THANKS. VERY NICE OF YOU TO FIND THE TIME TO STOP BY AND INQUIRE AFTER MY HEALTH.

AHEM... HOW'RE YOU DOING, YŪHI?

THAT'S BECAUSE *SOMEBODY* MAKES LARGE DONATIONS TO AISEI HIGH SCHOOL.

117

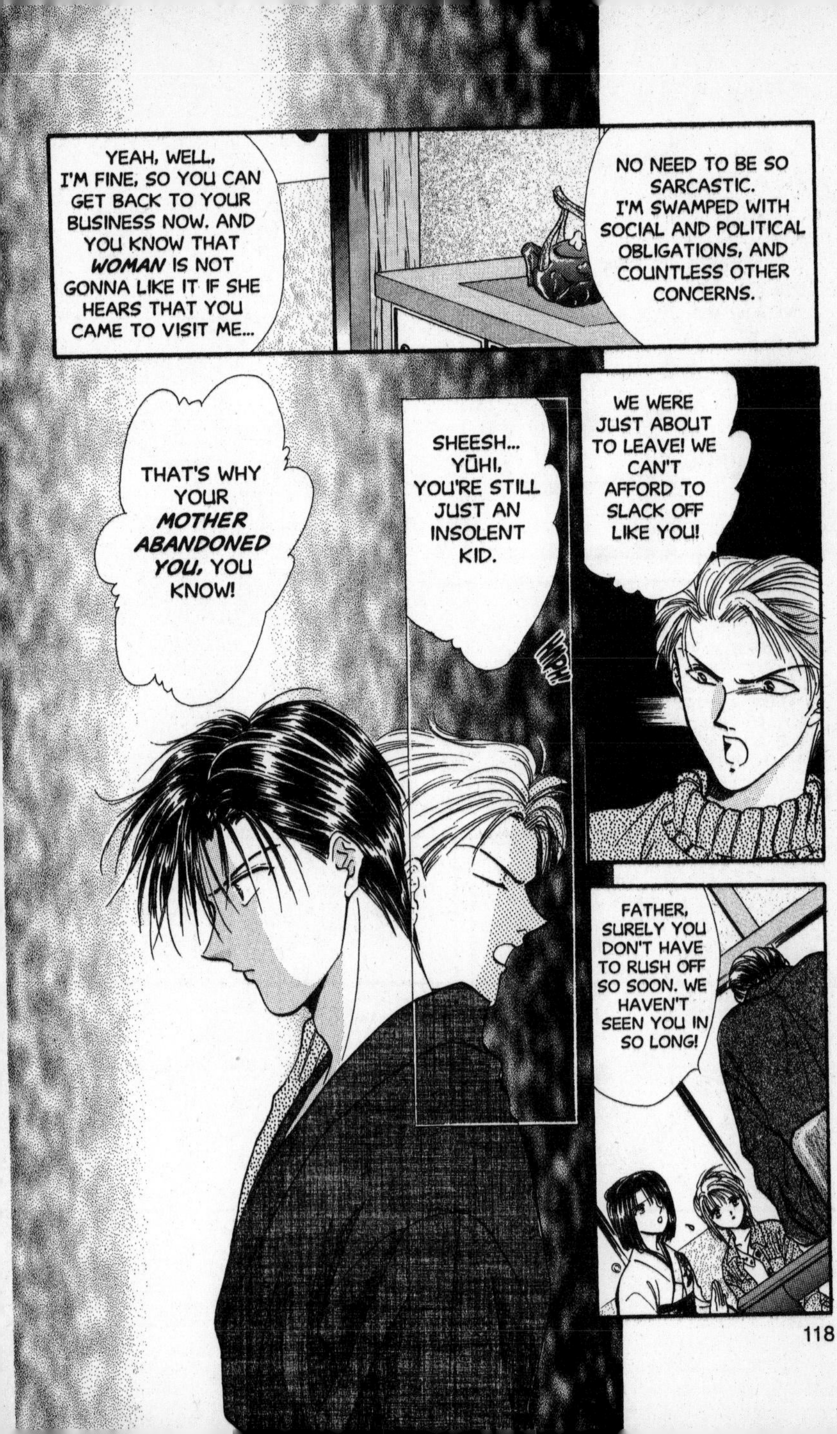
NO NEED TO BE SO SARCASTIC. I'M SWAMPED WITH SOCIAL AND POLITICAL OBLIGATIONS, AND COUNTLESS OTHER CONCERNS.
YEAH, WELL, I'M FINE, SO YOU CAN GET BACK TO YOUR BUSINESS NOW. AND YOU KNOW THAT *WOMAN* IS NOT GONNA LIKE IT IF SHE HEARS THAT YOU CAME TO VISIT ME...
WE WERE JUST ABOUT TO LEAVE! WE CAN'T AFFORD TO SLACK OFF LIKE YOU!
FATHER, SURELY YOU DON'T HAVE TO RUSH OFF SO SOON. WE HAVEN'T SEEN YOU IN SO LONG!
SHEESH... YŪHI, YOU'RE STILL JUST AN INSOLENT KID.
THAT'S WHY YOUR *MOTHER ABANDONED YOU,* YOU KNOW!

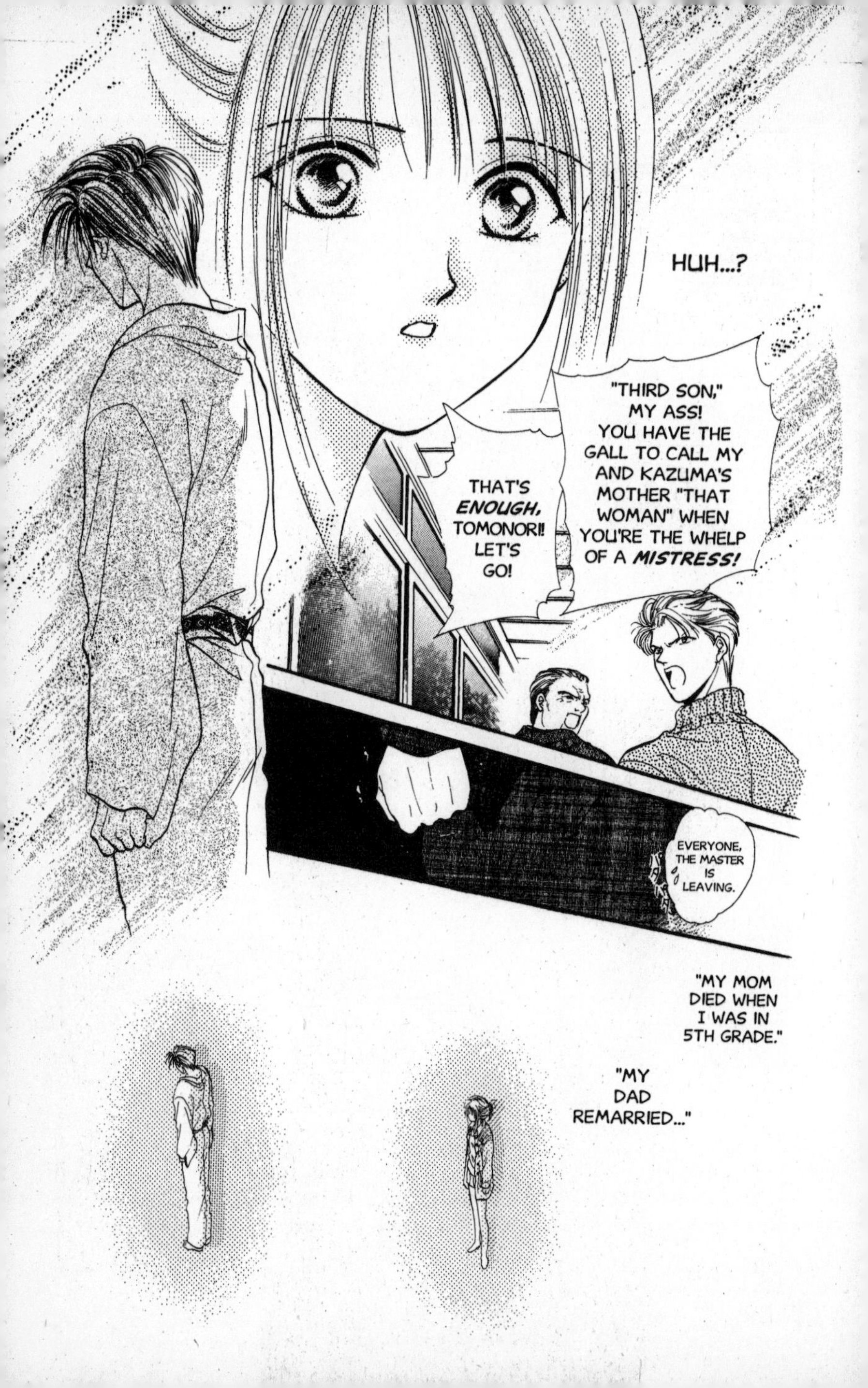
HUH...?
"THIRD SON," MY ASS! YOU HAVE THE GALL TO CALL MY AND KAZUMA'S MOTHER "THAT WOMAN" WHEN YOU'RE THE WHELP OF A *MISTRESS!*
THAT'S *ENOUGH,* TOMONORI!! LET'S GO!
EVERYONE, THE MASTER IS LEAVING.
"MY MOM DIED WHEN I WAS IN 5TH GRADE."
"MY DAD REMARRIED..."

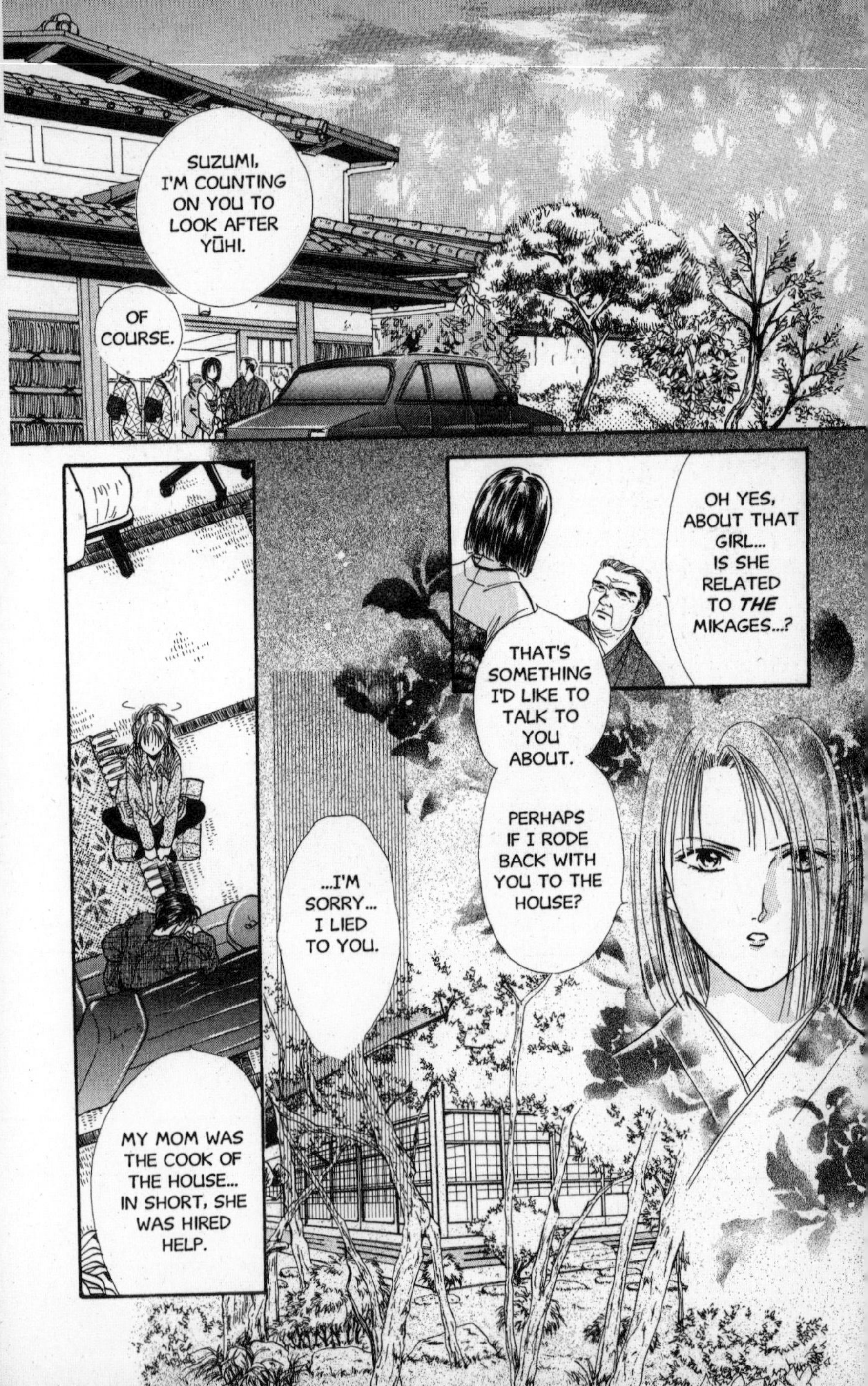
SUZUMI, I'M COUNTING ON YOU TO LOOK AFTER YŪHI.
OF COURSE.
OH YES, ABOUT THAT GIRL... IS SHE RELATED TO *THE* MIKAGES...?
THAT'S SOMETHING I'D LIKE TO TALK TO YOU ABOUT.
PERHAPS IF I RODE BACK WITH YOU TO THE HOUSE?
...I'M SORRY... I LIED TO YOU.
MY MOM WAS THE COOK OF THE HOUSE... IN SHORT, SHE WAS HIRED HELP.

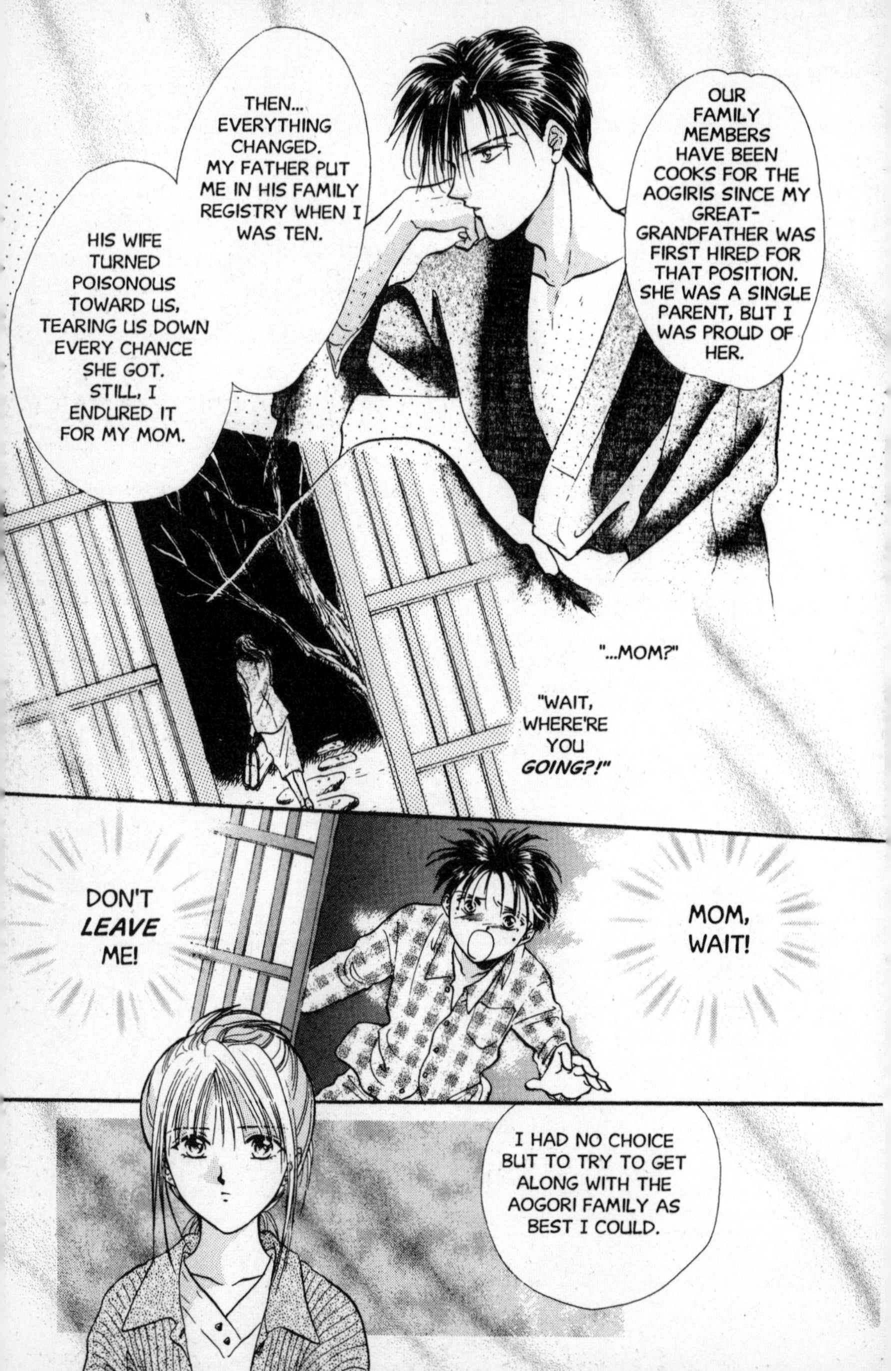
OUR FAMILY MEMBERS HAVE BEEN COOKS FOR THE AOGIRIS SINCE MY GREAT-GRANDFATHER WAS FIRST HIRED FOR THAT POSITION. SHE WAS A SINGLE PARENT, BUT I WAS PROUD OF HER.
THEN... EVERYTHING CHANGED. MY FATHER PUT ME IN HIS FAMILY REGISTRY WHEN I WAS TEN.
HIS WIFE TURNED POISONOUS TOWARD US, TEARING US DOWN EVERY CHANCE SHE GOT. STILL, I ENDURED IT FOR MY MOM.
"...MOM?"
"WAIT, WHERE'RE YOU *GOING?!*"
MOM, WAIT!
DON'T *LEAVE* ME!
I HAD NO CHOICE BUT TO TRY TO GET ALONG WITH THE AOGORI FAMILY AS BEST I COULD.

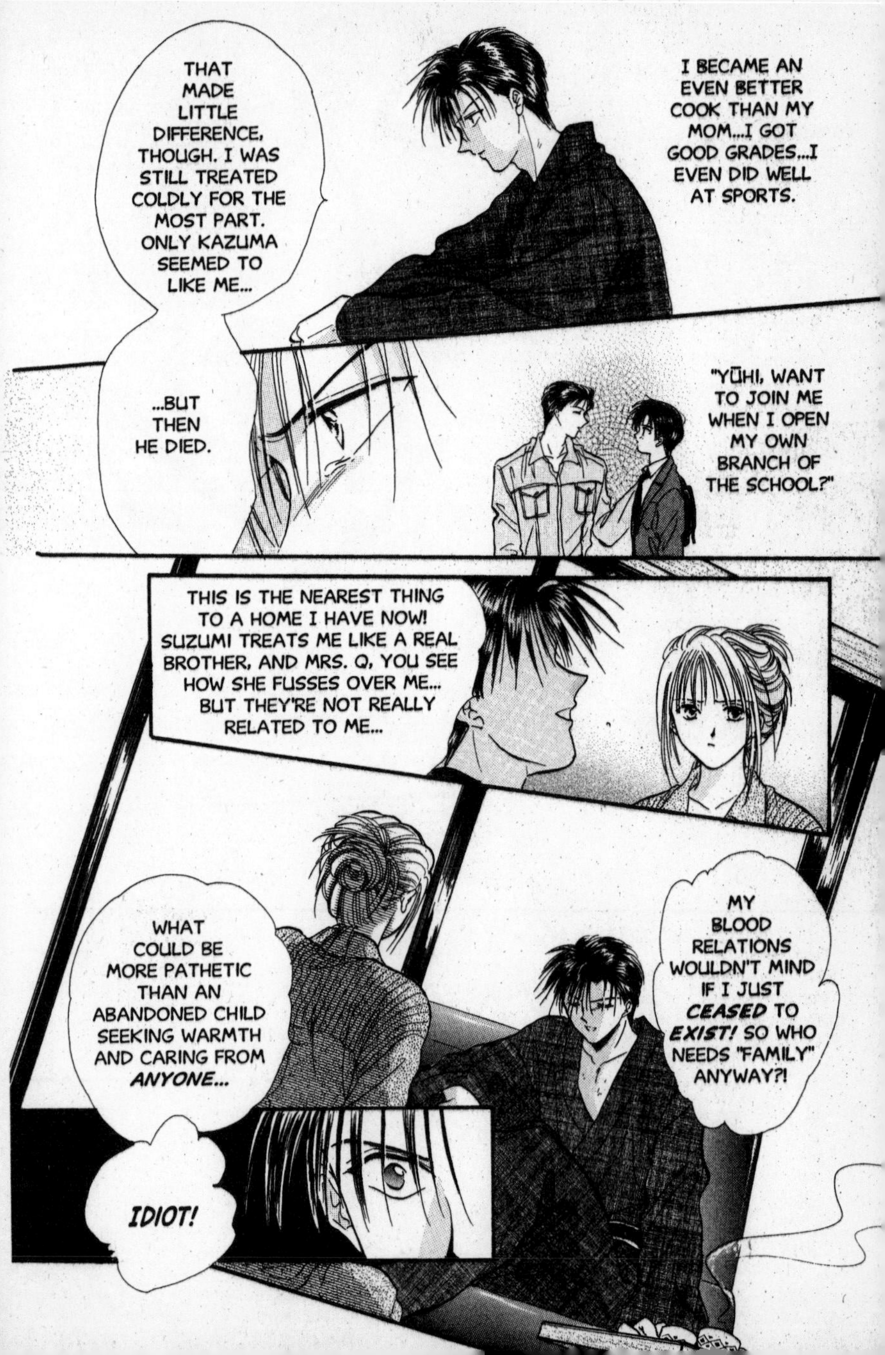
I BECAME AN EVEN BETTER COOK THAN MY MOM...I GOT GOOD GRADES...I EVEN DID WELL AT SPORTS.
THAT MADE LITTLE DIFFERENCE, THOUGH. I WAS STILL TREATED COLDLY FOR THE MOST PART. ONLY KAZUMA SEEMED TO LIKE ME...
"YŪHI, WANT TO JOIN ME WHEN I OPEN MY OWN BRANCH OF THE SCHOOL?"
...BUT THEN HE DIED.
THIS IS THE NEAREST THING TO A HOME I HAVE NOW! SUZUMI TREATS ME LIKE A REAL BROTHER, AND MRS. Q, YOU SEE HOW SHE FUSSES OVER ME... BUT THEY'RE NOT REALLY RELATED TO ME...
MY BLOOD RELATIONS WOULDN'T MIND IF I JUST ***CEASED*** TO ***EXIST!*** SO WHO NEEDS "FAMILY" ANYWAY?!
WHAT COULD BE MORE PATHETIC THAN AN ABANDONED CHILD SEEKING WARMTH AND CARING FROM ***ANYONE...***
IDIOT!

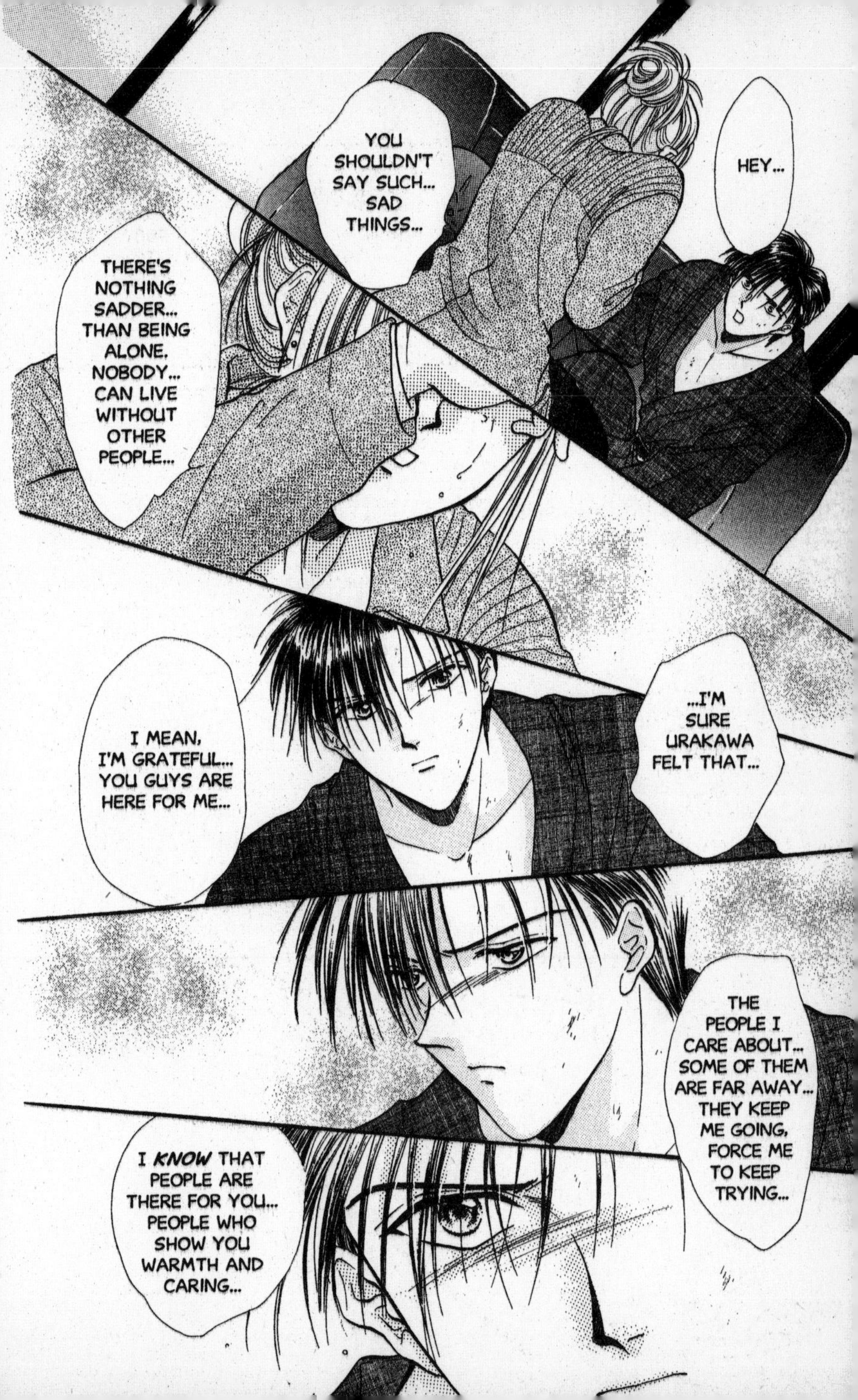
HEY...
YOU SHOULDN'T SAY SUCH... SAD THINGS...
THERE'S NOTHING SADDER... THAN BEING ALONE. NOBODY... CAN LIVE WITHOUT OTHER PEOPLE...
...I'M SURE URAKAWA FELT THAT...
I MEAN, I'M GRATEFUL... YOU GUYS ARE HERE FOR ME...
THE PEOPLE I CARE ABOUT... SOME OF THEM ARE FAR AWAY... THEY KEEP ME GOING, FORCE ME TO KEEP TRYING...
I *KNOW* THAT PEOPLE ARE THERE FOR YOU... PEOPLE WHO SHOW YOU WARMTH AND CARING...

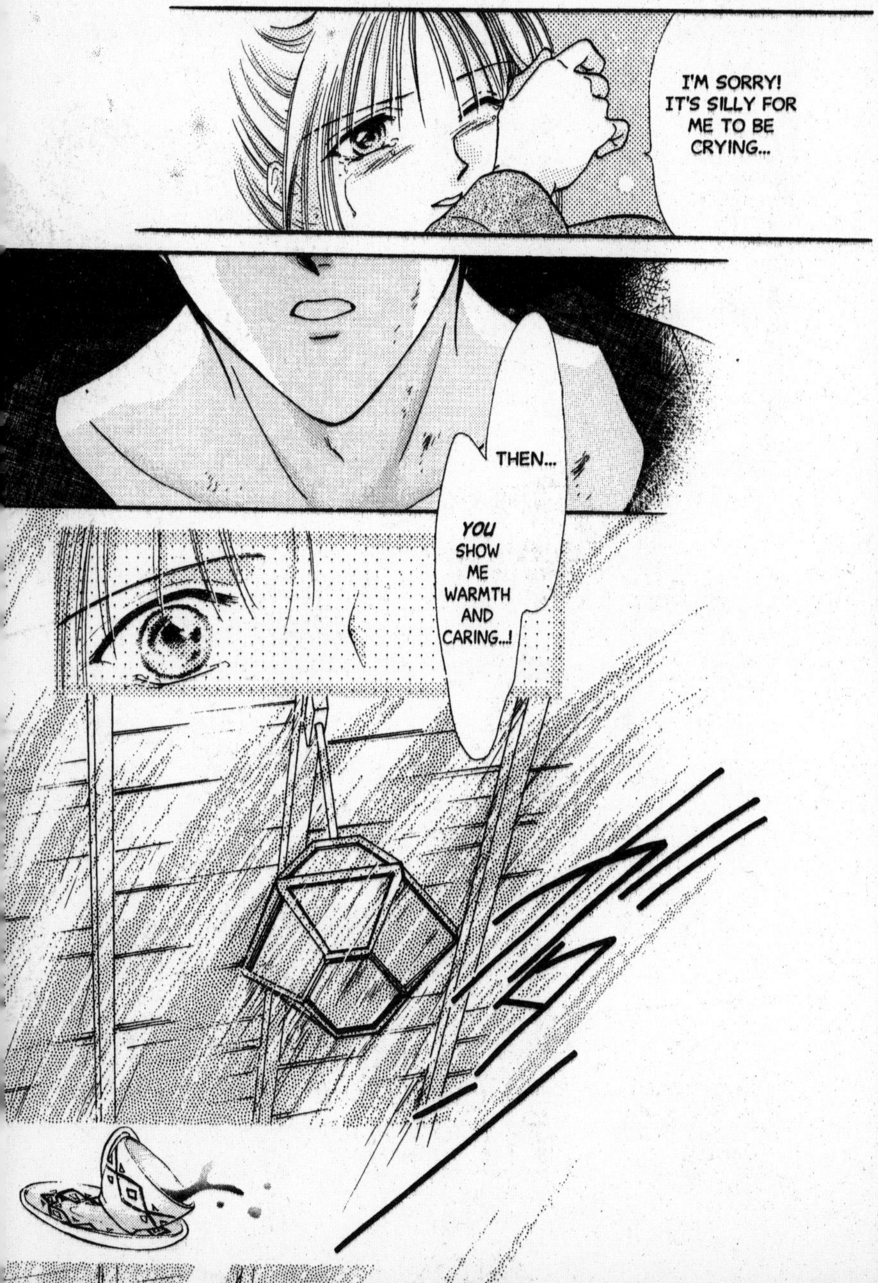
I'M SORRY! IT'S SILLY FOR ME TO BE CRYING...
THEN...
YOU SHOW ME WARMTH AND CARING...!

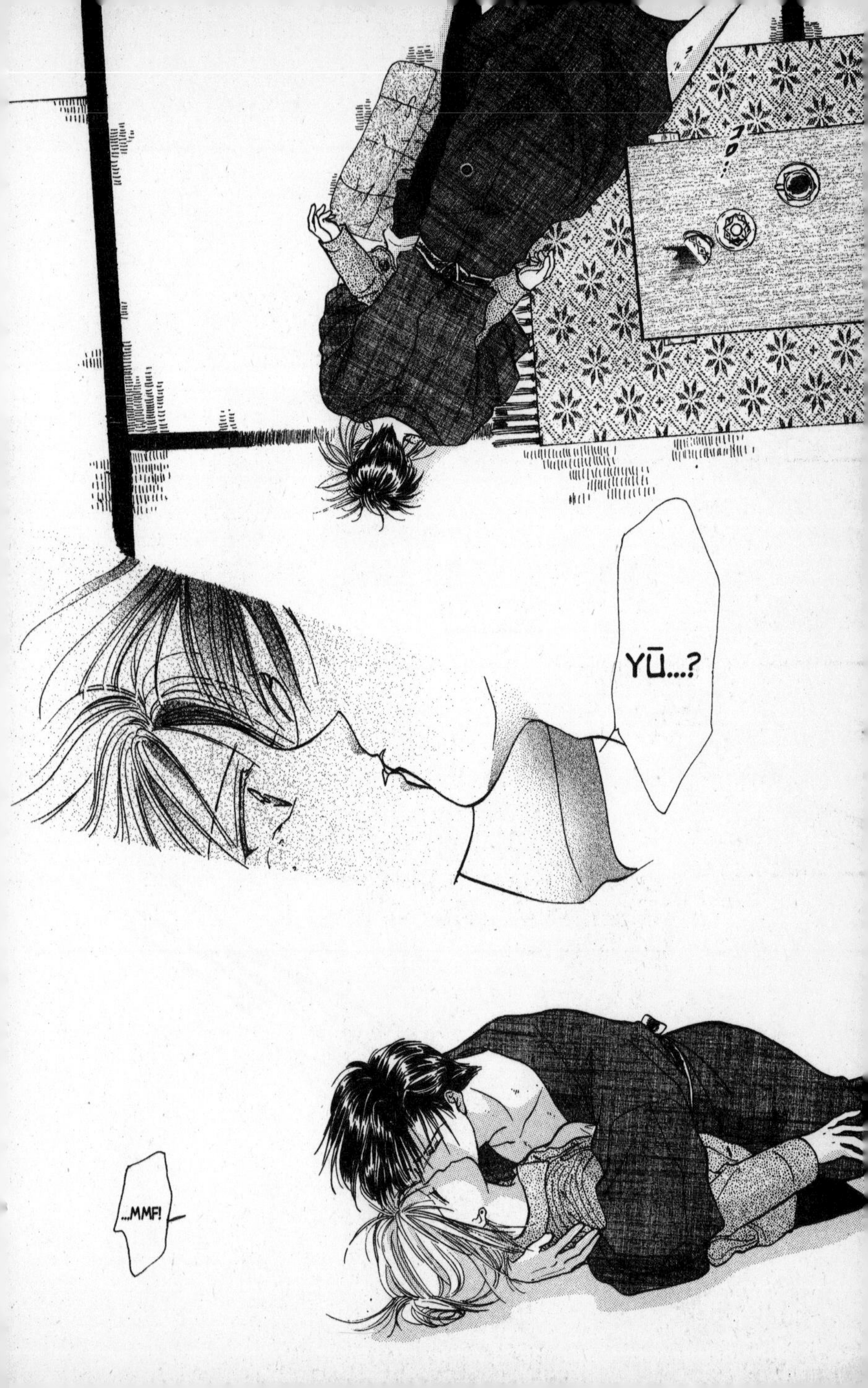
YŪ...?
...MMF!

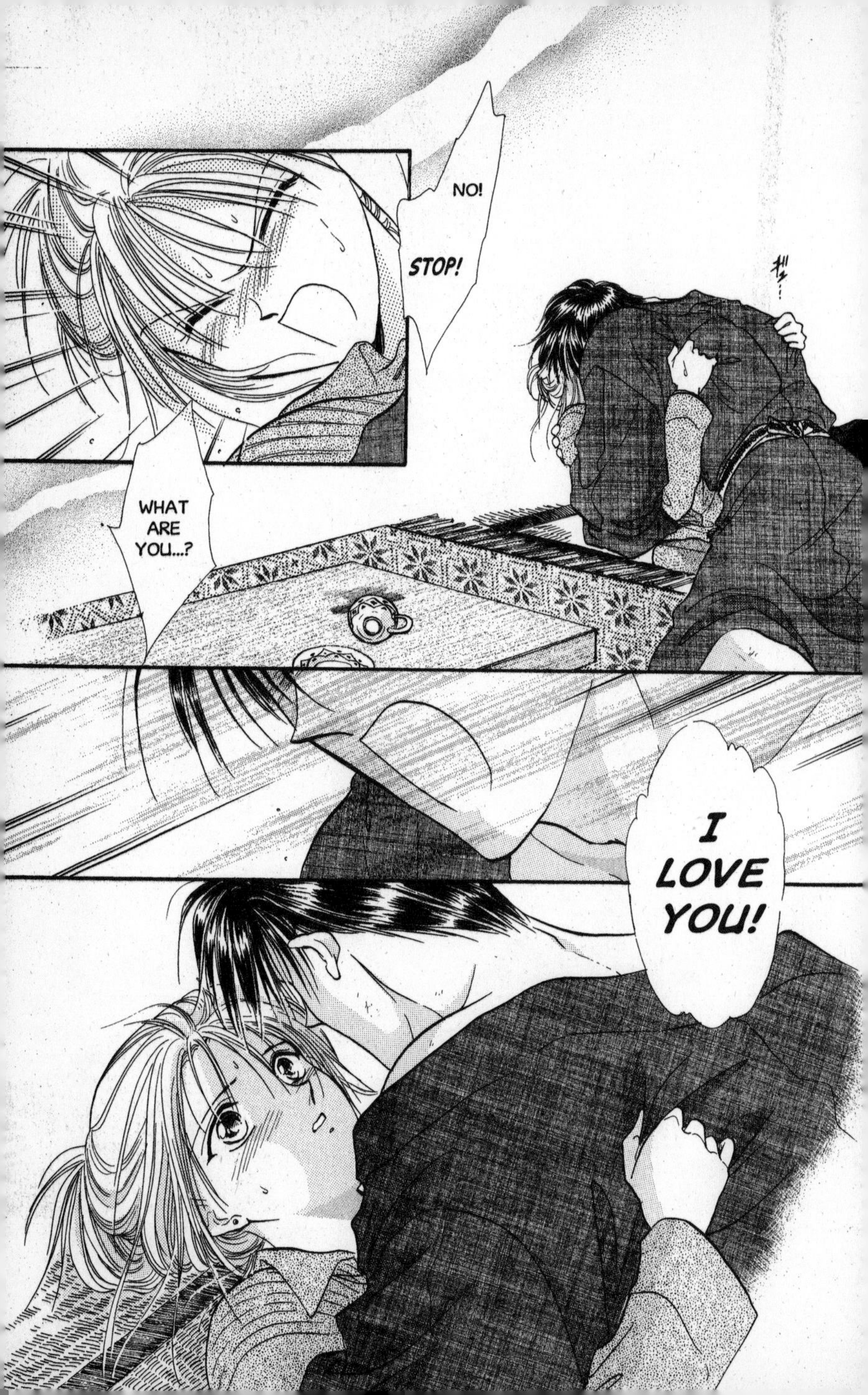
WHAT ARE YOU...?
NO!
STOP!
I LOVE YOU!

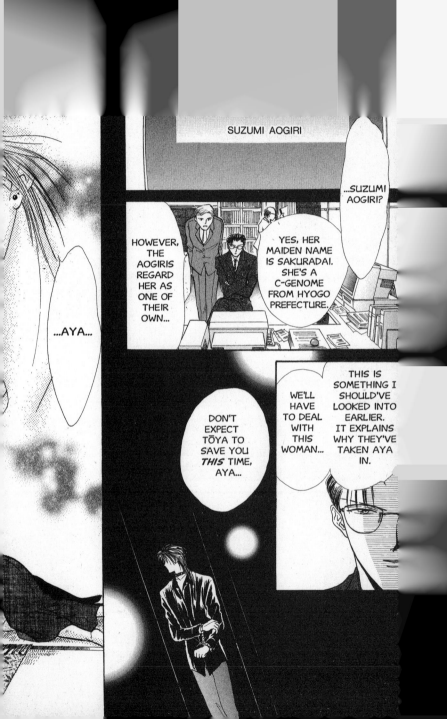

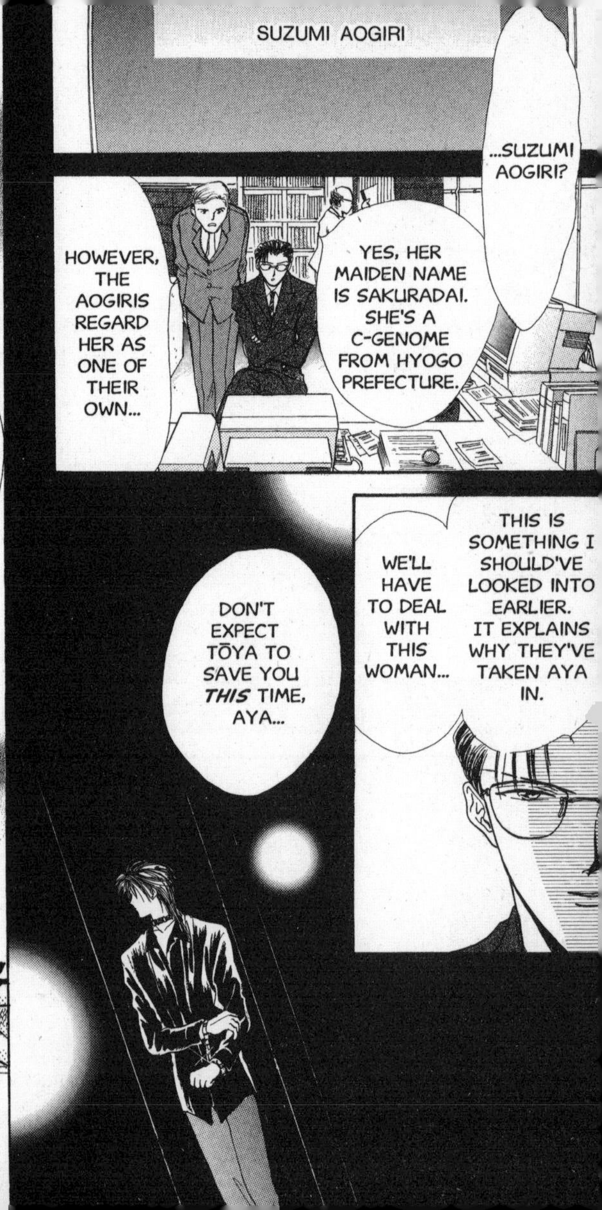
SUZUMI AOGIRI
...SUZUMI AOGIRI?
YES, HER MAIDEN NAME IS SAKURADAI. SHE'S A C-GENOME FROM HYOGO PREFECTURE.
HOWEVER, THE AOGIRIS REGARD HER AS ONE OF THEIR OWN...
THIS IS SOMETHING I SHOULD'VE LOOKED INTO EARLIER. IT EXPLAINS WHY THEY'VE TAKEN AYA IN.
WE'LL HAVE TO DEAL WITH THIS WOMAN...
DON'T EXPECT TŌYA TO SAVE YOU *THIS* TIME, AYA...
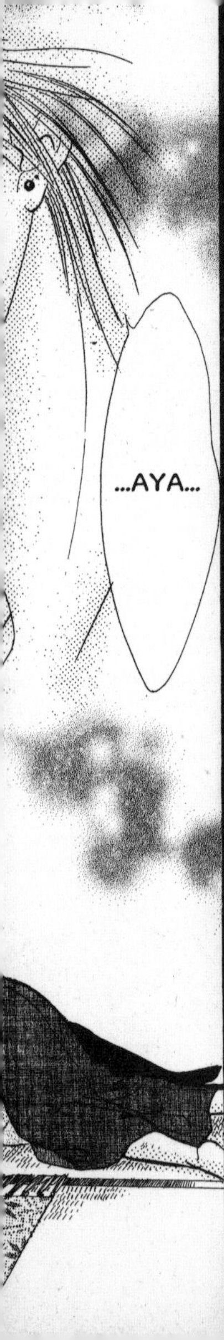
...AYA...

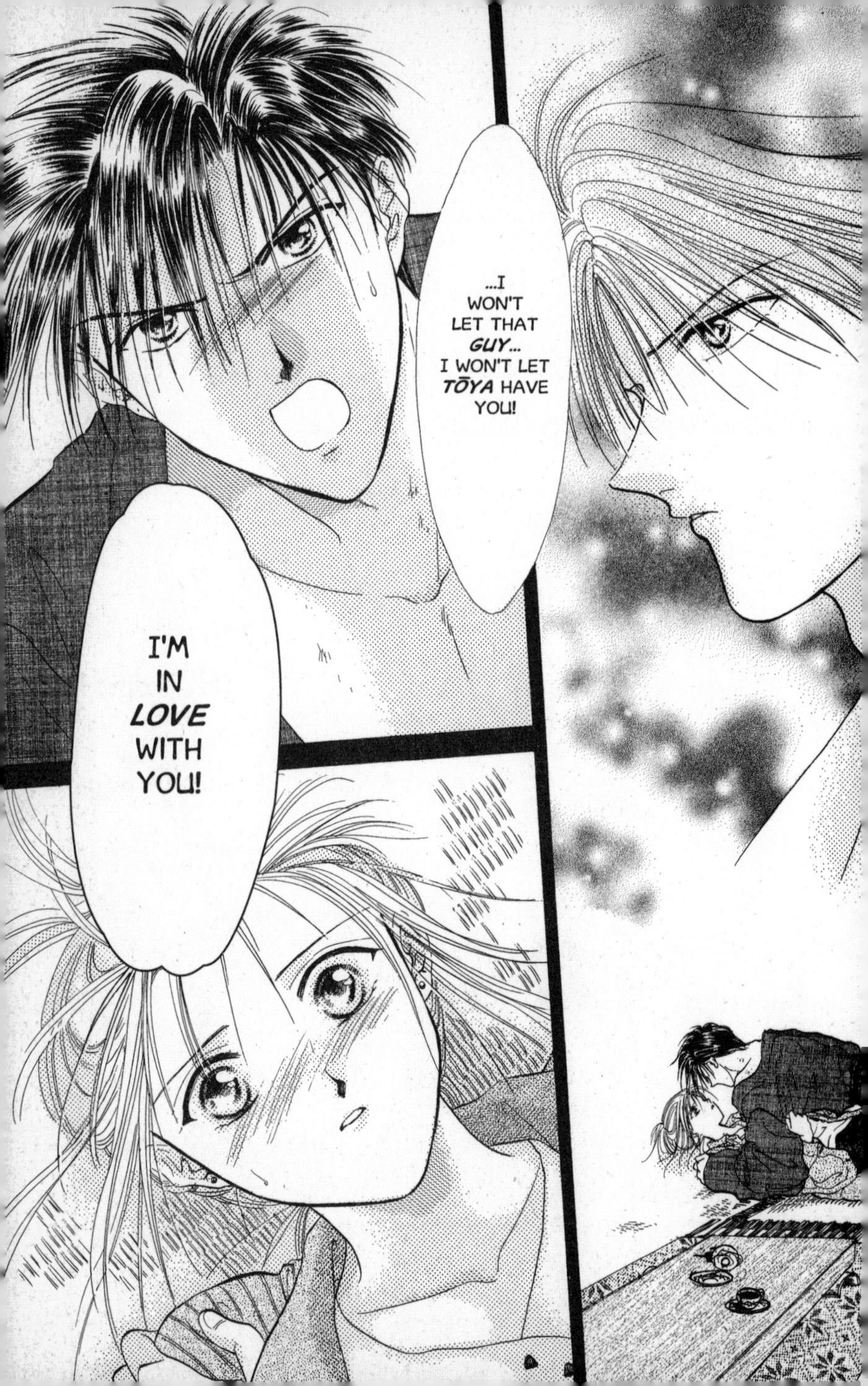
...I WON'T LET THAT *GUY*... I WON'T LET *TŌYA* HAVE YOU!
I'M IN *LOVE* WITH YOU!

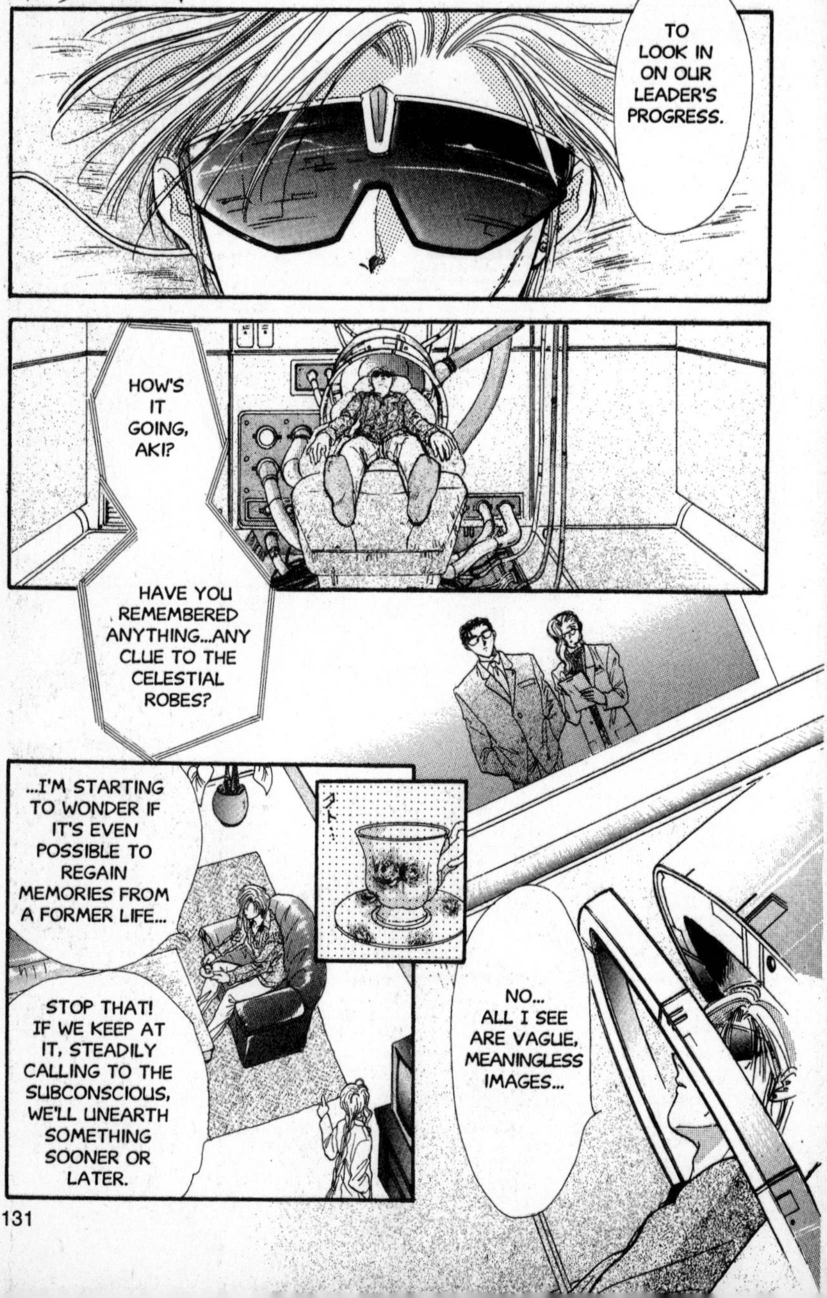
TO LOOK IN ON OUR LEADER'S PROGRESS.
HOW'S IT GOING, AKI?
HAVE YOU REMEMBERED ANYTHING...ANY CLUE TO THE CELESTIAL ROBES?
NO... ALL I SEE ARE VAGUE, MEANINGLESS IMAGES...
...I'M STARTING TO WONDER IF IT'S EVEN POSSIBLE TO REGAIN MEMORIES FROM A FORMER LIFE...
STOP THAT! IF WE KEEP AT IT, STEADILY CALLING TO THE SUBCONSCIOUS, WE'LL UNEARTH SOMETHING SOONER OR LATER.

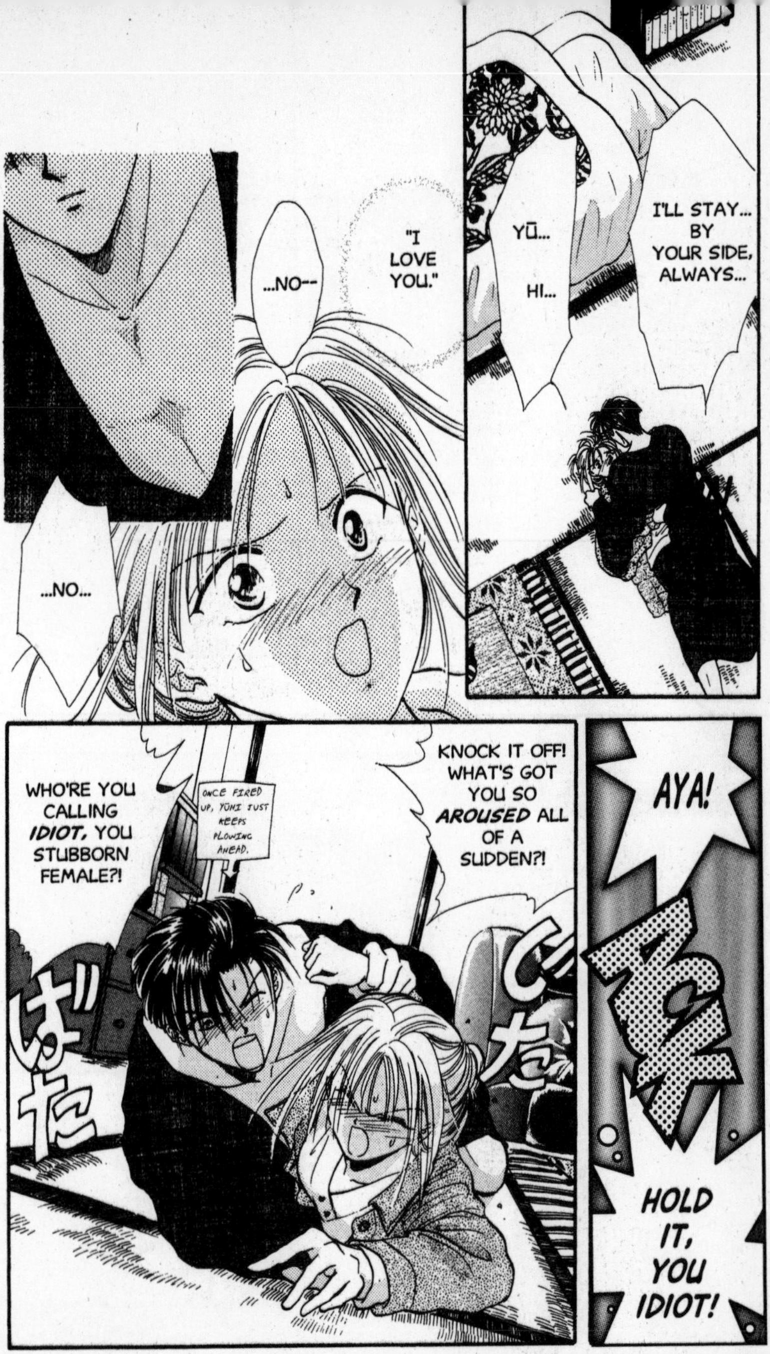

I'LL STAY... BY YOUR SIDE, ALWAYS...
YŪ... HI...
"I LOVE YOU."
...NO--
...NO...
AYA!
HOLD IT, YOU IDIOT!
KNOCK IT OFF! WHAT'S GOT YOU SO AROUSED ALL OF A SUDDEN?!
ONCE FIRED UP, YŪHI JUST KEEPS PLOWING AHEAD.
WHO'RE YOU CALLING IDIOT, YOU STUBBORN FEMALE?!
じた
ばた

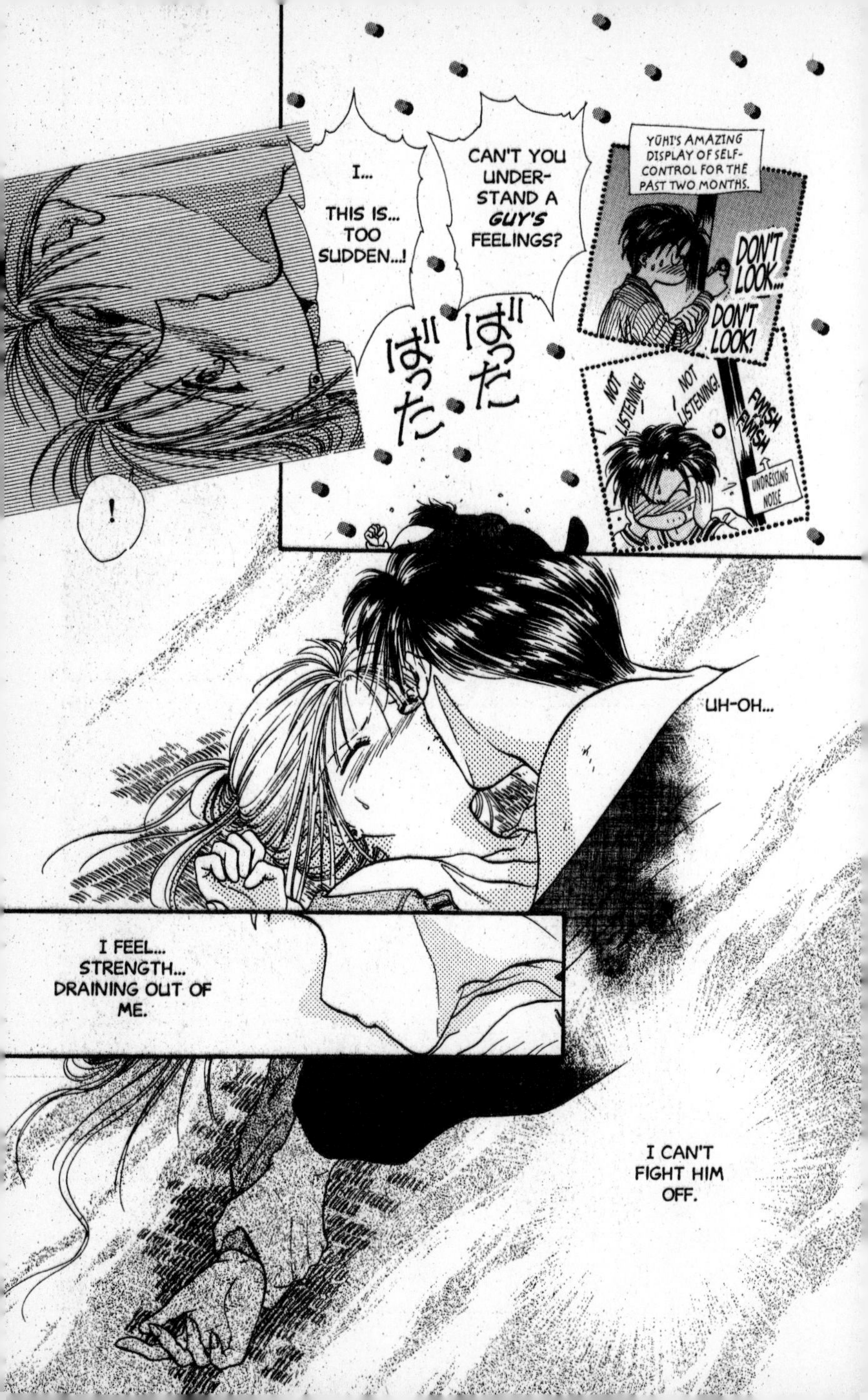

YŪHI'S AMAZING DISPLAY OF SELF-CONTROL FOR THE PAST TWO MONTHS.
DON'T LOOK... DON'T LOOK!
CAN'T YOU UNDER-STAND A *GUY'S* FEELINGS?
I... THIS IS... TOO SUDDEN...!
ばったばった
NOT LISTENING! NOT LISTENING!
FWISH FWISH
UNDRESSING NOISE
!
UH-OH...
I FEEL... STRENGTH... DRAINING OUT OF ME.
I CAN'T FIGHT HIM OFF.

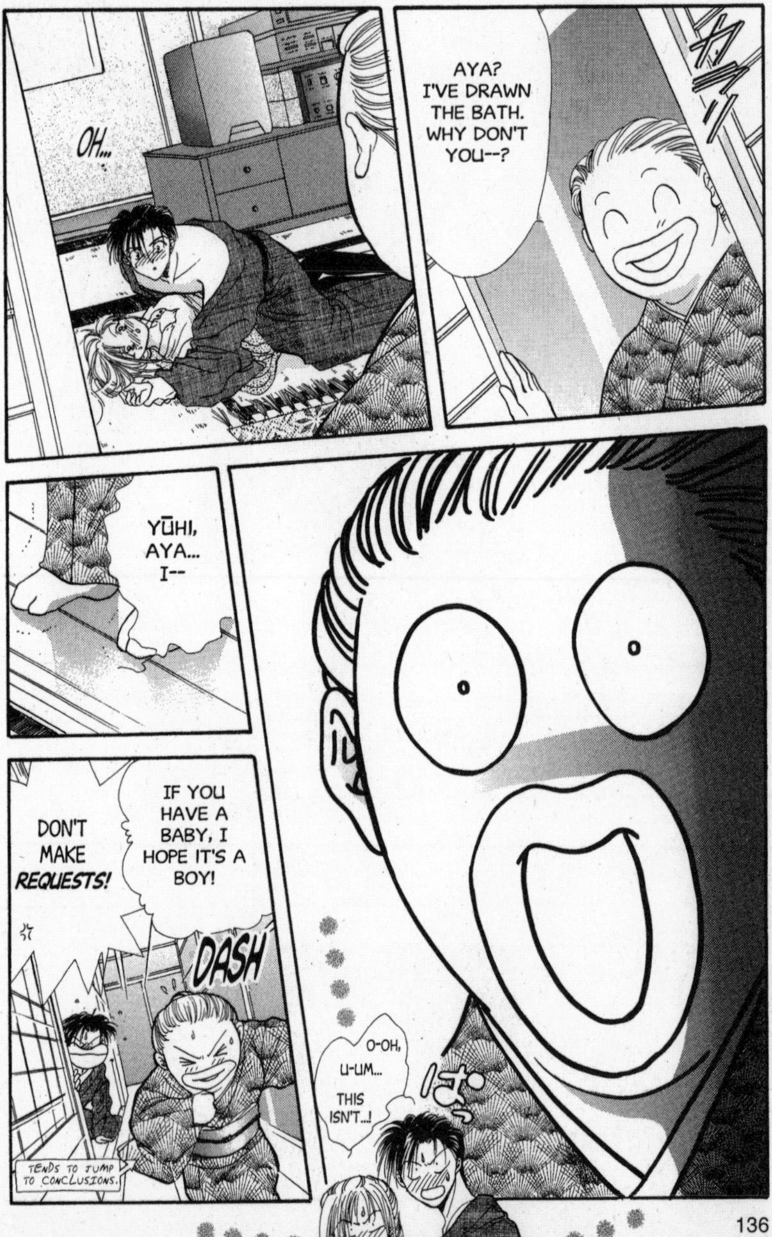
AYA? I'VE DRAWN THE BATH. WHY DON'T YOU--?
OH...
O-OH, U-UM... THIS ISN'T...!
YŪHI, AYA... I--
IF YOU HAVE A BABY, I HOPE IT'S A BOY!
DON'T MAKE REQUESTS!
DASH
TENDS TO JUMP TO CONCLUSIONS.

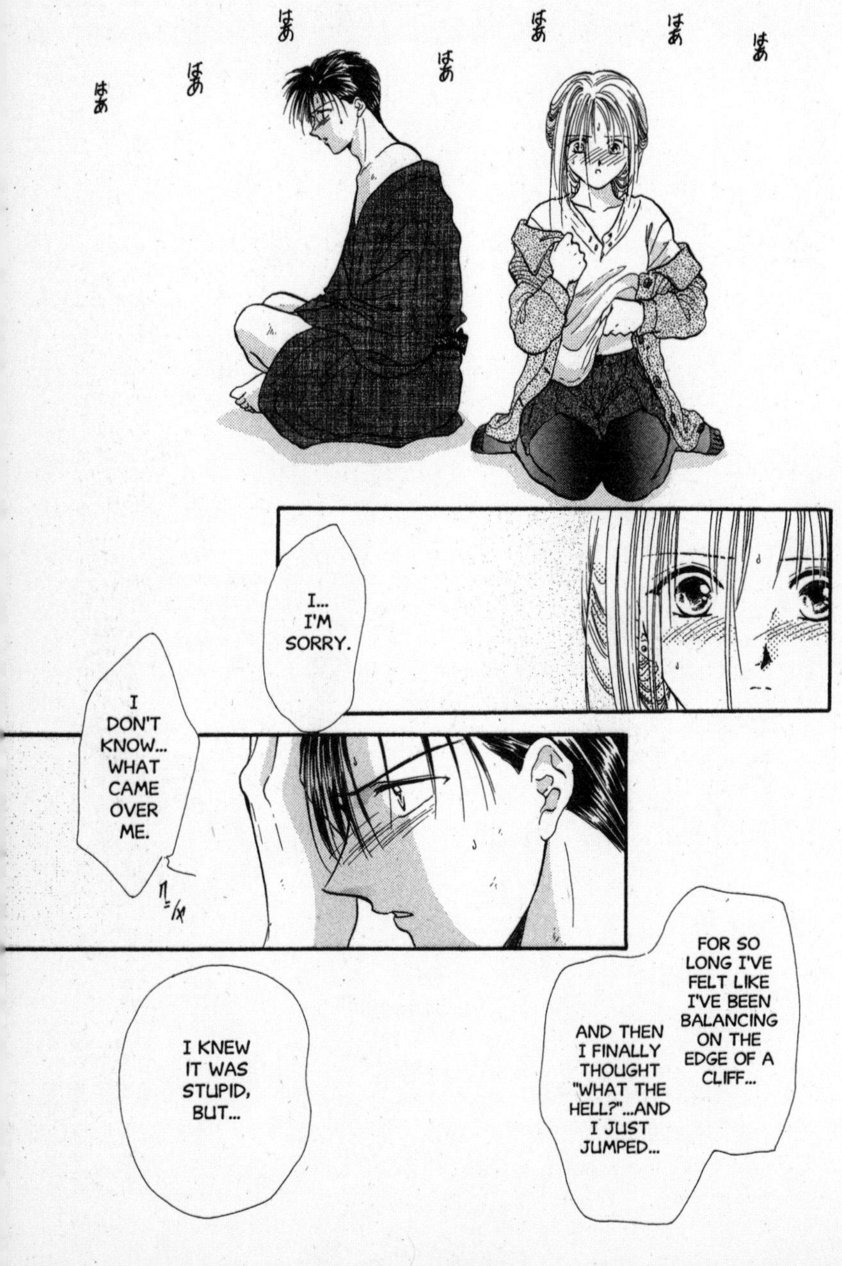
はぁ
はぁ
はぁ
はぁ
はぁ
はぁ
はぁ
I... I'M SORRY.
I DON'T KNOW... WHAT CAME OVER ME.
FOR SO LONG I'VE FELT LIKE I'VE BEEN BALANCING ON THE EDGE OF A CLIFF...
AND THEN I FINALLY THOUGHT "WHAT THE HELL?"...AND I JUST JUMPED...
I KNEW IT WAS STUPID, BUT...

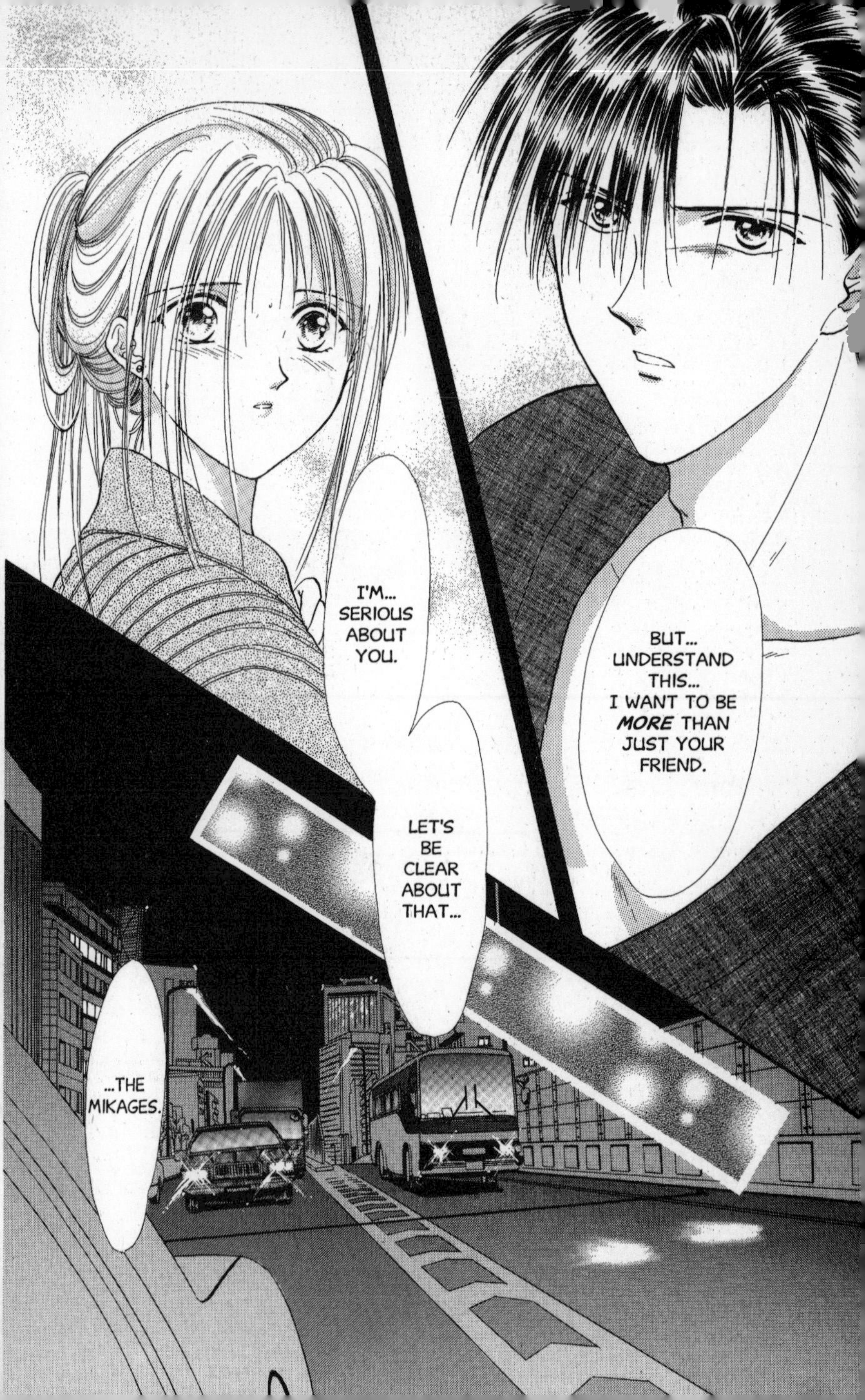
BUT... UNDERSTAND THIS... I WANT TO BE *MORE* THAN JUST YOUR FRIEND.
I'M... SERIOUS ABOUT YOU.
LET'S BE CLEAR ABOUT THAT...
...THE MIKAGES.

Ceres: 3

-CONTINUED

So, I've been told that humans have a maximum life span of 120 years, no matter what!! Even if you're the picture of health until then, you'll just kick the bucket when you hit 120! ...That means, if I get to live 90-odd more years, since my cloned baby's cells are already aged 20-odd years, she would only live to be 90-odd years old as well...

HMM...

"...But what about kidneys?" I asked the laboratory people. I've heard that if you have a bad kidney, it's really difficult to get a transplant. I once saw a special on TV where they said, "Your own cloned kidney would be a perfect match! You wouldn't have any problems with rejection! Whee!" But wouldn't a clone made from your **current cells** still get bad kidneys? And one day while you're waiting for the cloned baby to grow up, you could just croak! And then the clone would also have bad kidneys, and the clone would croak. Then at the end you'd be like, "What was all that for?" RIGHT?

And in my case, if I made a clone of myself and tried to make her do my work for me, the clone would be an individual too, so the research technician told me, "Even if she had the talent to draw manga, she might not want to." ...In other words, I would have to train her. ☺

And even if she's my clone, as long as she has her own persona, she would probably protest and say, "Manga? Yeah, right!" And her personality might not be the same depending on the environment she grows up in. She would just look exactly like me...

So the conclusion was that "There's not much point in cloning people"... Seriously! IT WOULD JUST INCREASE THE POPULATION! WELL, I GUESS THERE MIGHT BE SOME OTHER REASONS TO CLONE PEOPLE!

139

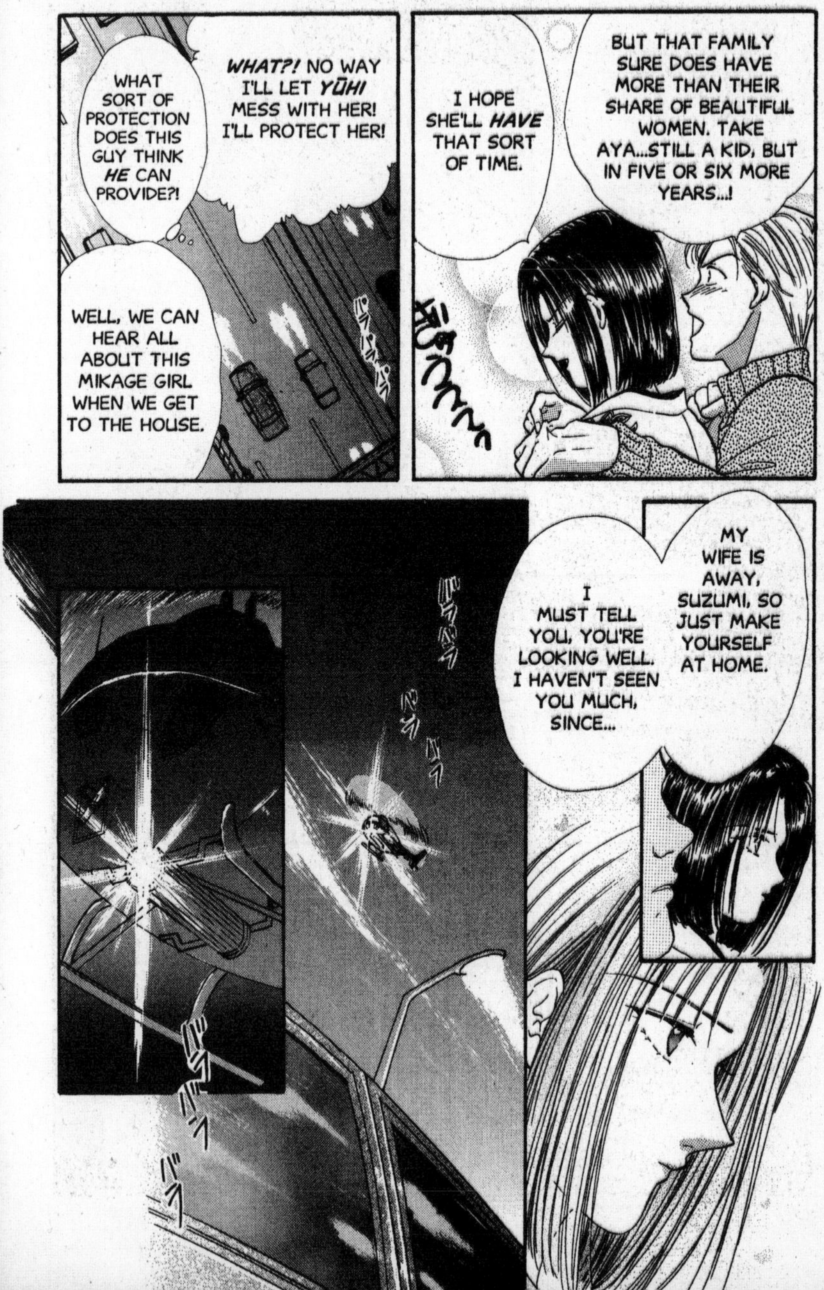
BUT THAT FAMILY SURE DOES HAVE MORE THAN THEIR SHARE OF BEAUTIFUL WOMEN. TAKE AYA...STILL A KID, BUT IN FIVE OR SIX MORE YEARS...!
I HOPE SHE'LL *HAVE* THAT SORT OF TIME.
WHAT?! NO WAY I'LL LET *YŪHI* MESS WITH HER! I'LL PROTECT HER!
WHAT SORT OF PROTECTION DOES THIS GUY THINK *HE* CAN PROVIDE?!
WELL, WE CAN HEAR ALL ABOUT THIS MIKAGE GIRL WHEN WE GET TO THE HOUSE.
MY WIFE IS AWAY, SUZUMI, SO JUST MAKE YOURSELF AT HOME.
I MUST TELL YOU, YOU'RE LOOKING WELL. I HAVEN'T SEEN YOU MUCH, SINCE...

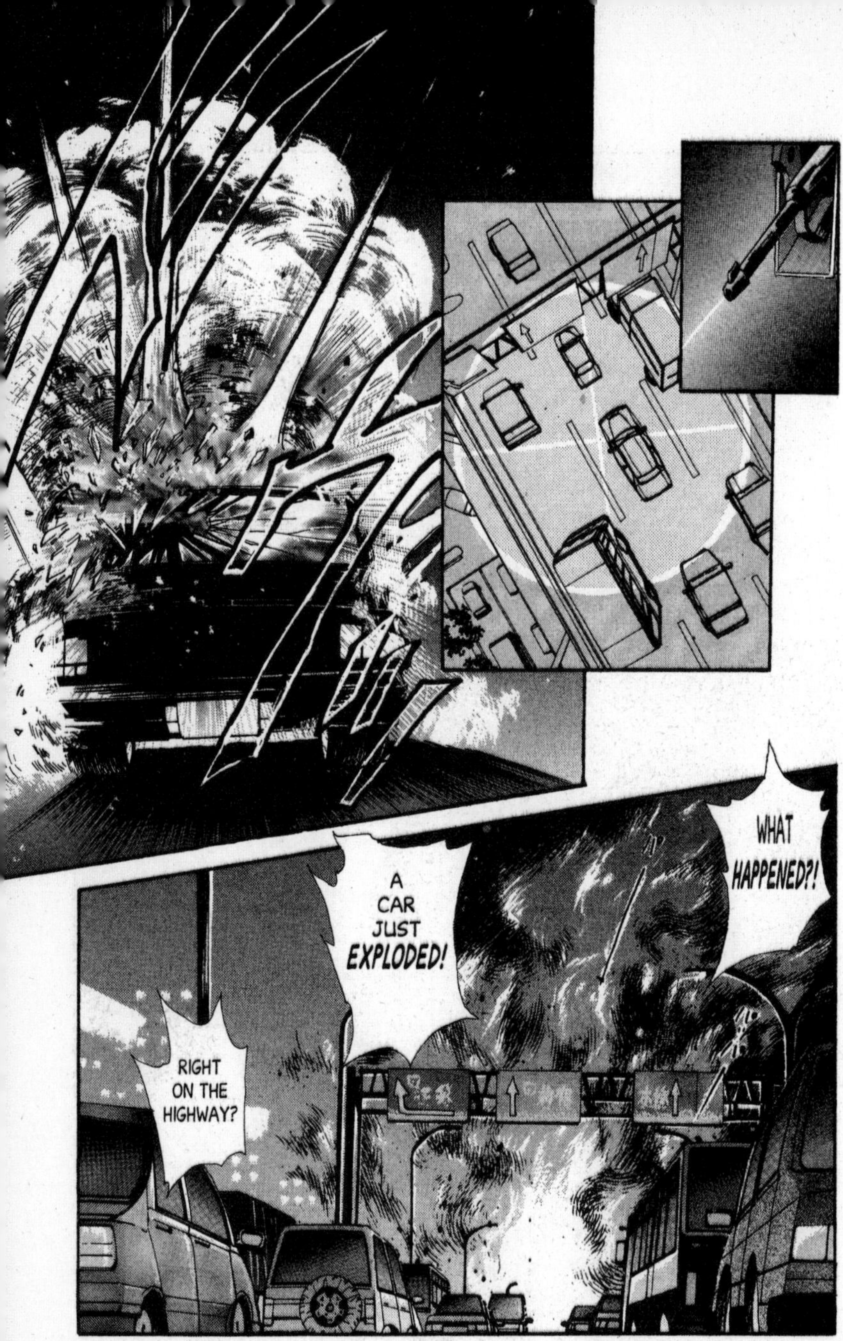
WHAT HAPPENED?!
A CAR JUST EXPLODED!
RIGHT ON THE HIGHWAY?

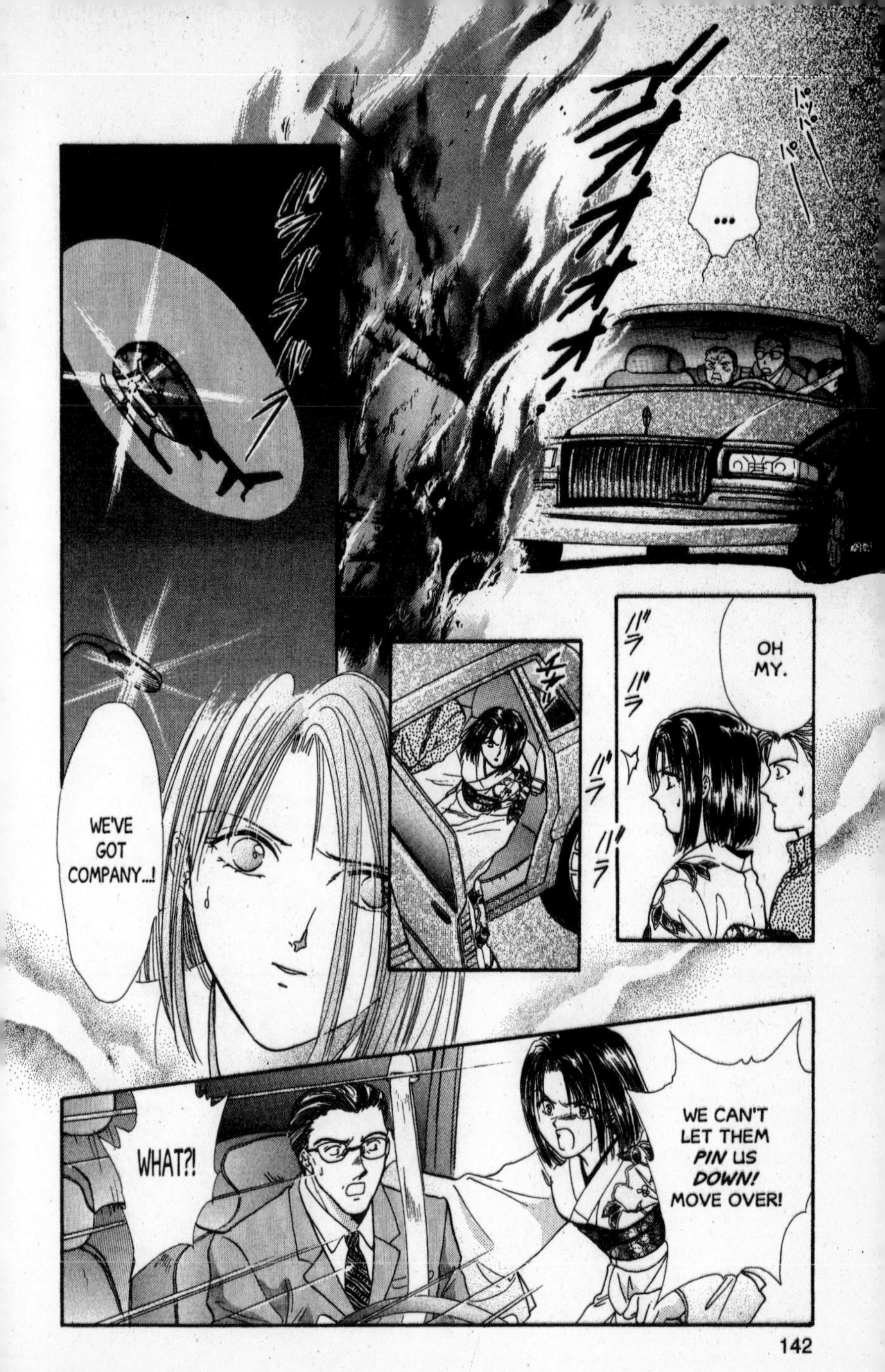
...
OH MY.
WE'VE GOT COMPANY...!
WE CAN'T LET THEM *PIN* US *DOWN!* MOVE OVER!
WHAT?!

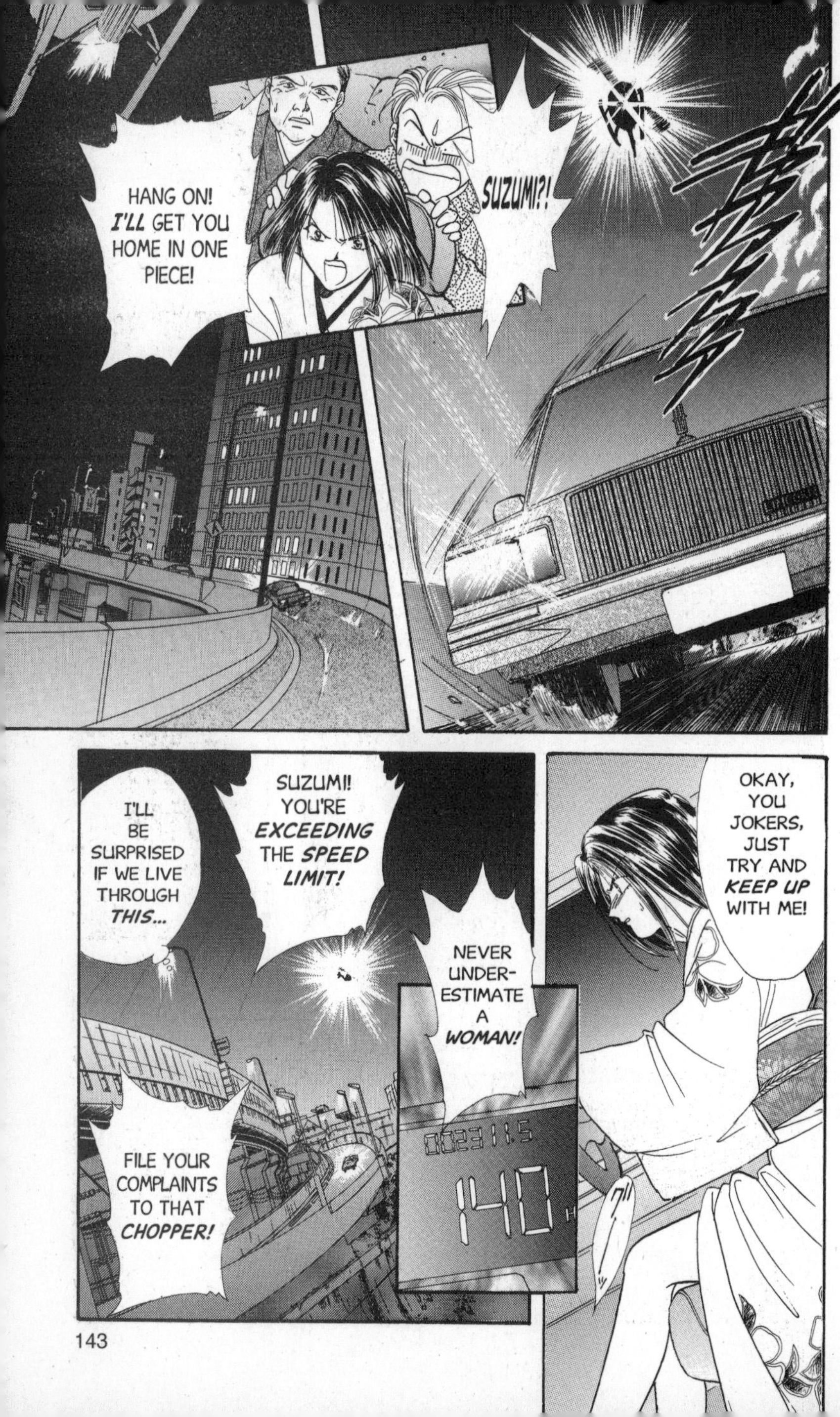
SUZUMI?!
HANG ON! I'LL GET YOU HOME IN ONE PIECE!
OKAY, YOU JOKERS, JUST TRY AND KEEP UP WITH ME!
SUZUMI! YOU'RE EXCEEDING THE SPEED LIMIT!
I'LL BE SURPRISED IF WE LIVE THROUGH THIS...
NEVER UNDER-ESTIMATE A WOMAN!
0023 11.5
140
FILE YOUR COMPLAINTS TO THAT CHOPPER!

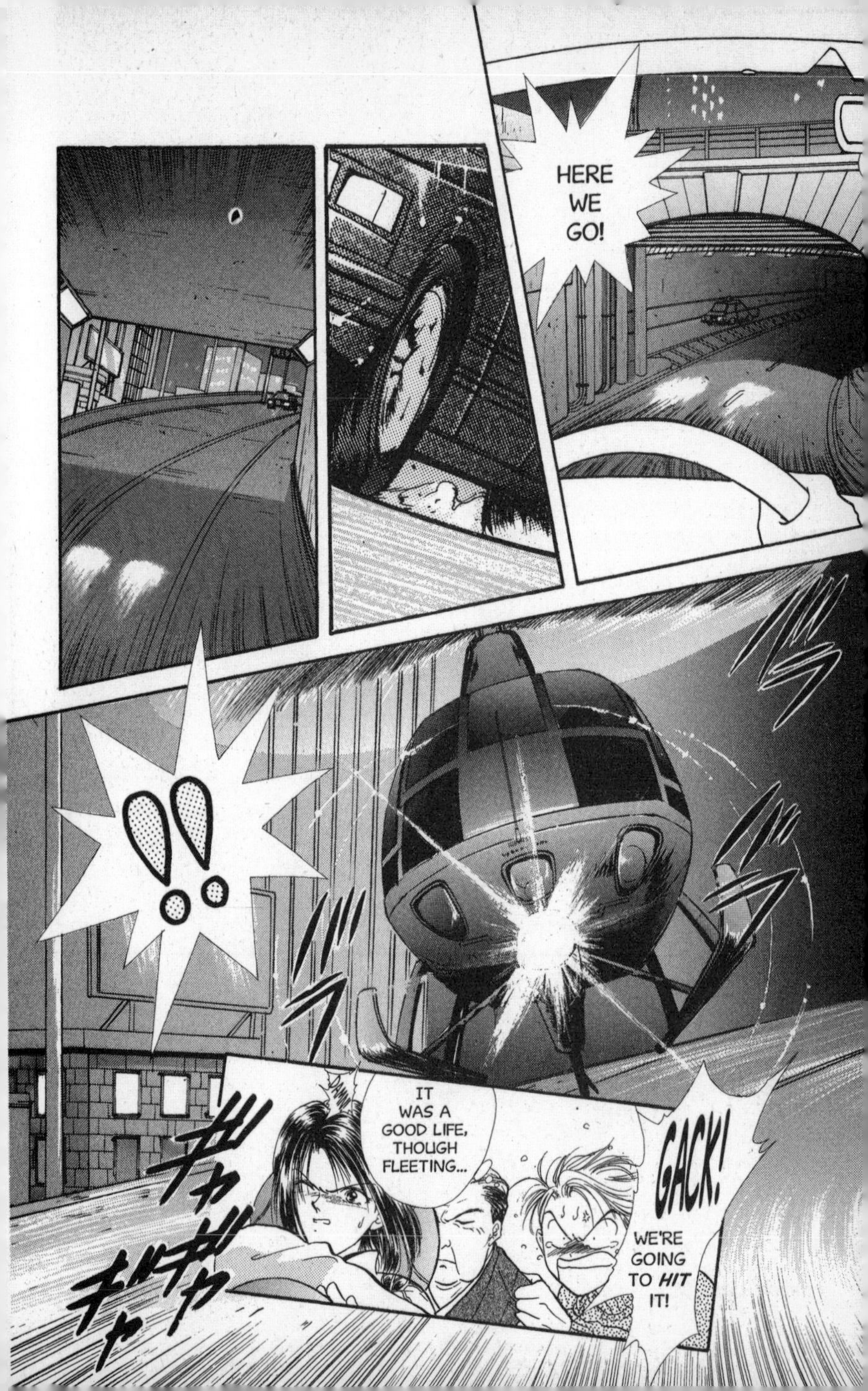
HERE WE GO!
!!
GACK!
WE'RE GOING TO *HIT* IT!
IT WAS A GOOD LIFE, THOUGH FLEETING...

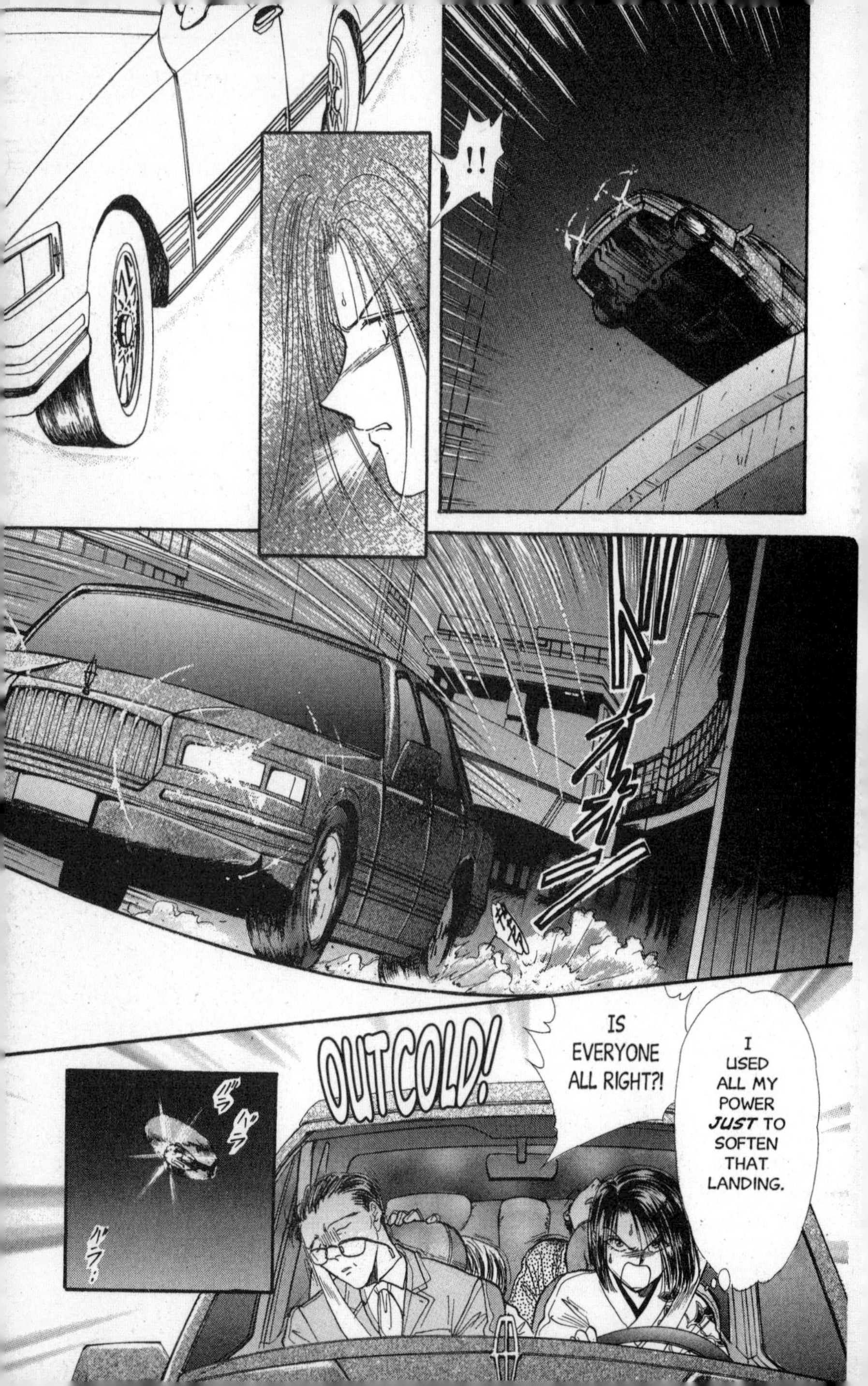
!!
I USED ALL MY POWER *JUST* TO SOFTEN THAT LANDING.
IS EVERYONE ALL RIGHT?!
OUTCOLD!

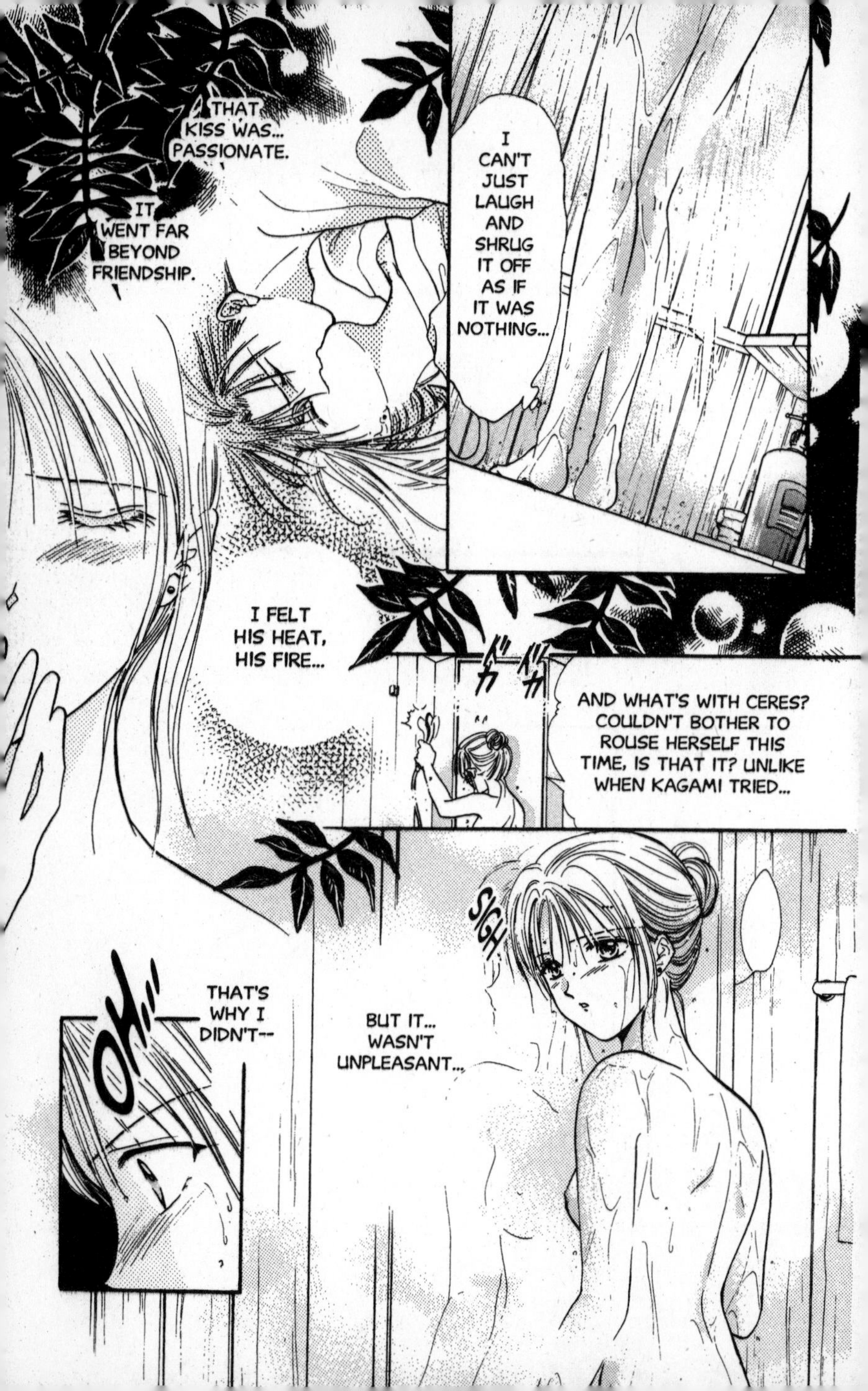
I CAN'T JUST LAUGH AND SHRUG IT OFF AS IF IT WAS NOTHING...
THAT KISS WAS... PASSIONATE.
IT WENT FAR BEYOND FRIENDSHIP.
I FELT HIS HEAT, HIS FIRE...
AND WHAT'S WITH CERES? COULDN'T BOTHER TO ROUSE HERSELF THIS TIME, IS THAT IT? UNLIKE WHEN KAGAMI TRIED...
SIGH
BUT IT... WASN'T UNPLEASANT...
THAT'S WHY I DIDN'T--
OH...!

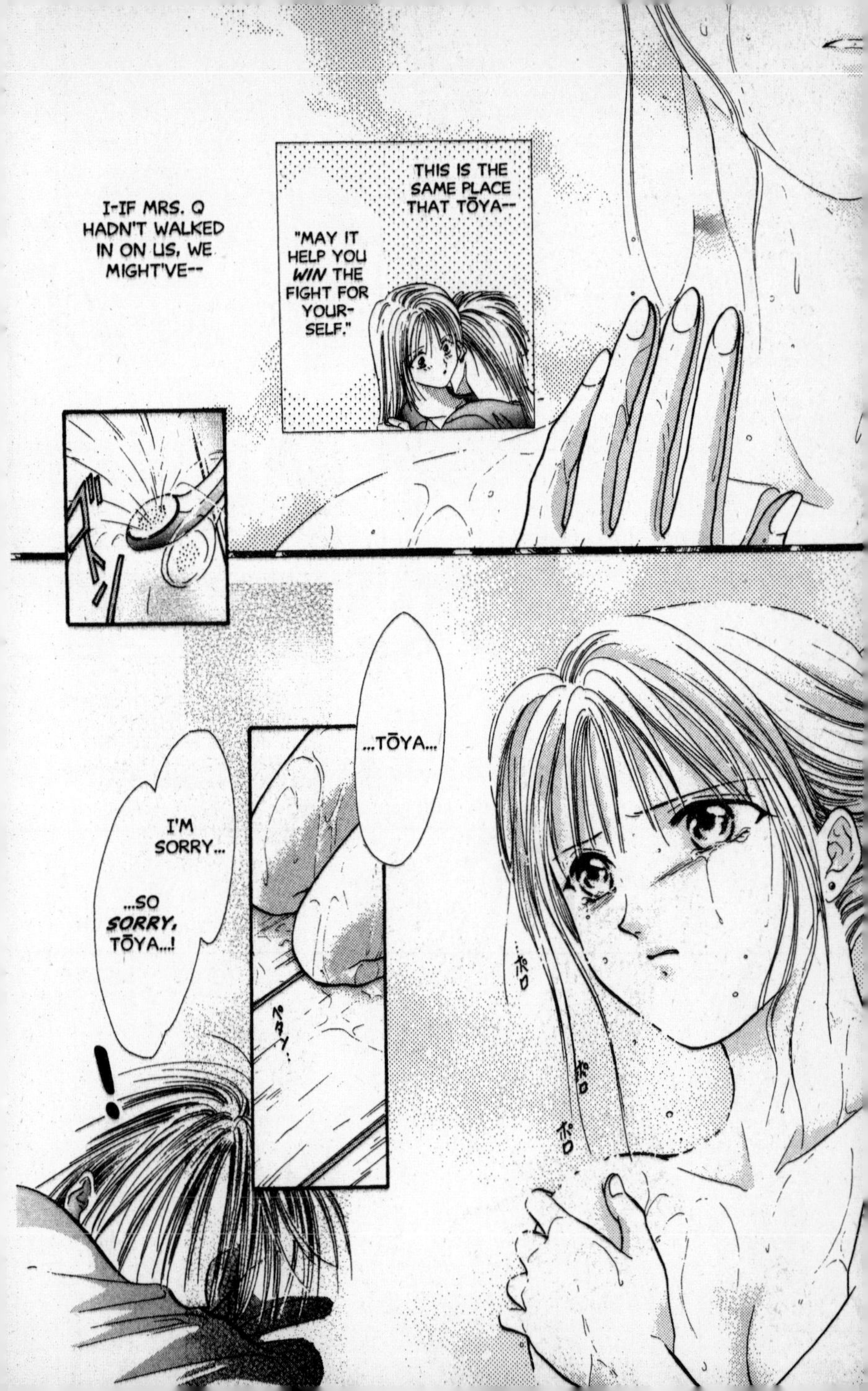
THIS IS THE SAME PLACE THAT TŌYA--
"MAY IT HELP YOU *WIN* THE FIGHT FOR YOURSELF."
I-IF MRS. Q HADN'T WALKED IN ON US, WE MIGHT'VE--
...ポロ
ポロ
ポロ
...TŌYA...
I'M SORRY...
...SO *SORRY,* TŌYA...!
!

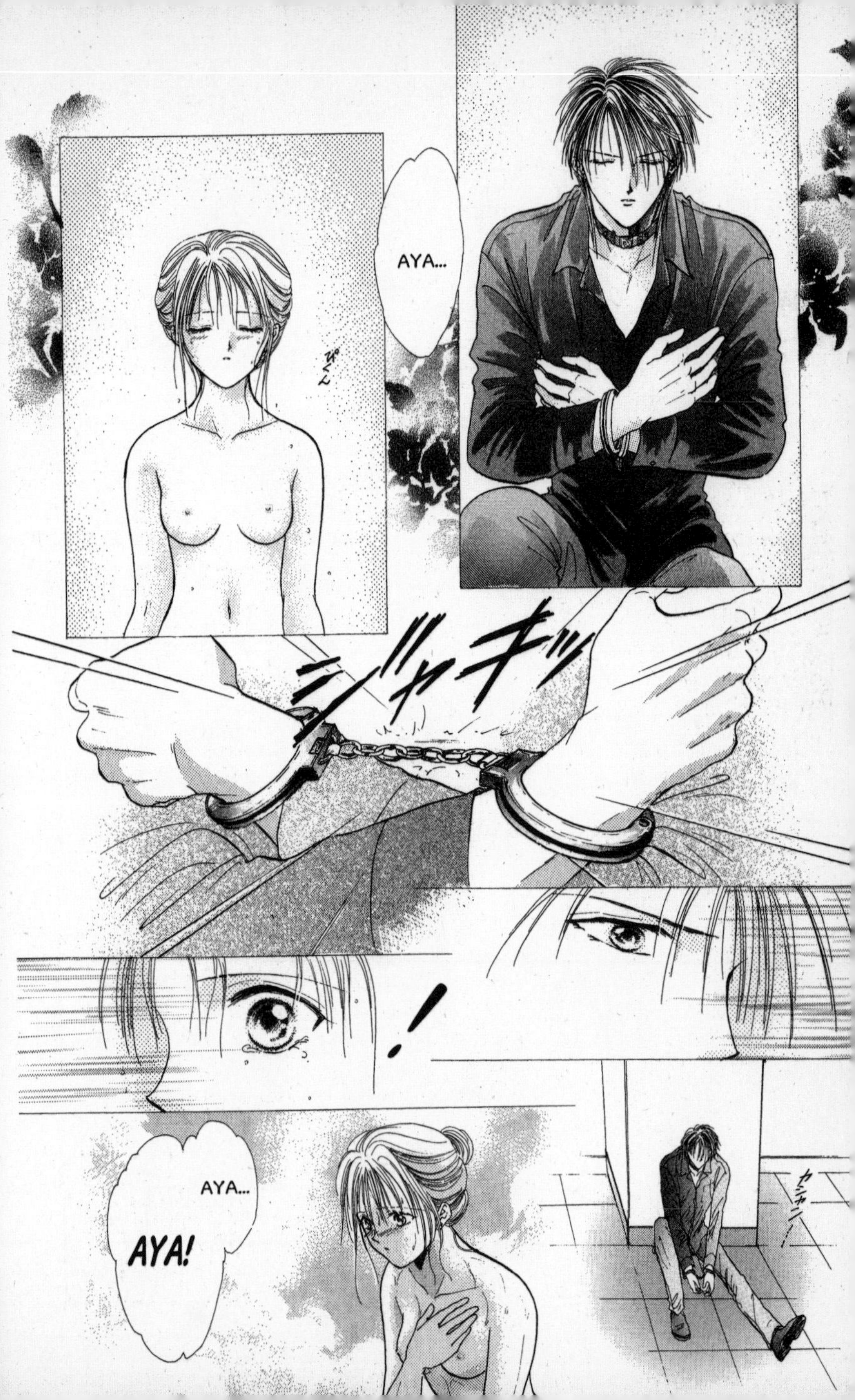
AYA...
ぴくん
ジャキッ
!
カシャン
AYA...
AYA!

153

YOU STILL DON'T GET IT, DO YOU? YOUR DESTINY IS WITH US, AND NOTHING CAN CHANGE THAT.

IF YOU'RE JUST AFTER *ME*...AFTER CERES, YOU *KNOW* WHERE TO FIND ME!

YOUR PEOPLE CAUSED URAKAWA'S DEATH! WHY? WHAT *PURPOSE* DID IT SERVE?!

OH, MY OH ME... OH MY...

AND JUST SO YOU FULLY UNDERSTAND *THAT,* SOMEONE VERY CLOSE TO YOU WILL SOON SET AN EVEN MORE VIVID EXAMPLE.

YOU SEALED HER FATE!

WE CAUSED URAKAWA'S DEATH? HARDLY.

THE UNKNOWN SUBSTANCE THAT WAS FOUND IN *YOUR* BODY AWAKENED HER POWERS.

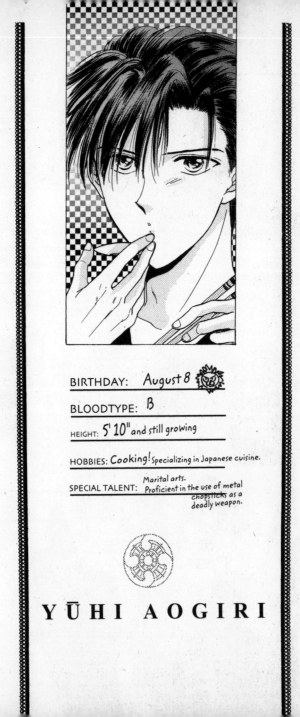

BIRTHDAY: August 8

BLOODTYPE: B

HEIGHT: 5' 10" and still growing

HOBBIES: Cooking! Specializing in Japanese cuisine.

SPECIAL TALENT: Marital arts.
Proficient in the use of metal chopsticks as a deadly weapon.

YŪHI AOGIRI

RIPRRINNGG

WOMEN WITH CELESTIAL BLOOD ARE REALLY HOT.

VERY NICE... HER PICTURE DOESN'T DO HER JUSTICE.

!!

I'LL CHECK INSIDE HER KIMONO. HEH HEH...

RIPRRINNGG

A CELL PHONE! THAT GAVE ME A START. IS IT TUCKED IN HER OBI?

SUZUMI AOGIRI...

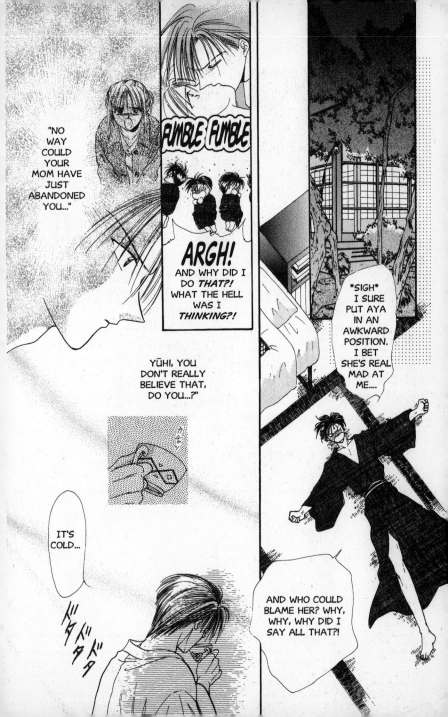

"NO WAY COULD YOUR MOM HAVE JUST ABANDONED YOU..."

FUMBLE FUMBLE

ARGH! AND WHY DID I DO *THAT*?! WHAT THE HELL WAS I *THINKING*?!

YŪHI, YOU DON'T REALLY BELIEVE THAT, DO YOU...?"

SIGH I SURE PUT AYA IN AN AWKWARD POSITION. I BET SHE'S REAL MAD AT ME....

IT'S COLD...

AND WHO COULD BLAME HER? WHY, WHY, WHY DID I SAY ALL THAT?!

IT'S BEEN SO LONG...

...AND I'VE MISSED YOU SO MUCH...

I HOPE WE'RE IN TIME. I HATE TO THINK WHAT THEY MIGHT DO TO HER...

イライラ
イラ イラ

SHE'S OVERCOME THE *MOST AWFUL THINGS,* BELIEVE ME...

SUZUMI WOULDN'T GIVE THEM THE CHANCE!

THESE PEOPLE ZERO RIGHT IN ON YOUR BIGGEST WEAKNESSES AND EXPLOIT THEM...

I KNOW...

WE'RE ALMOST THERE!

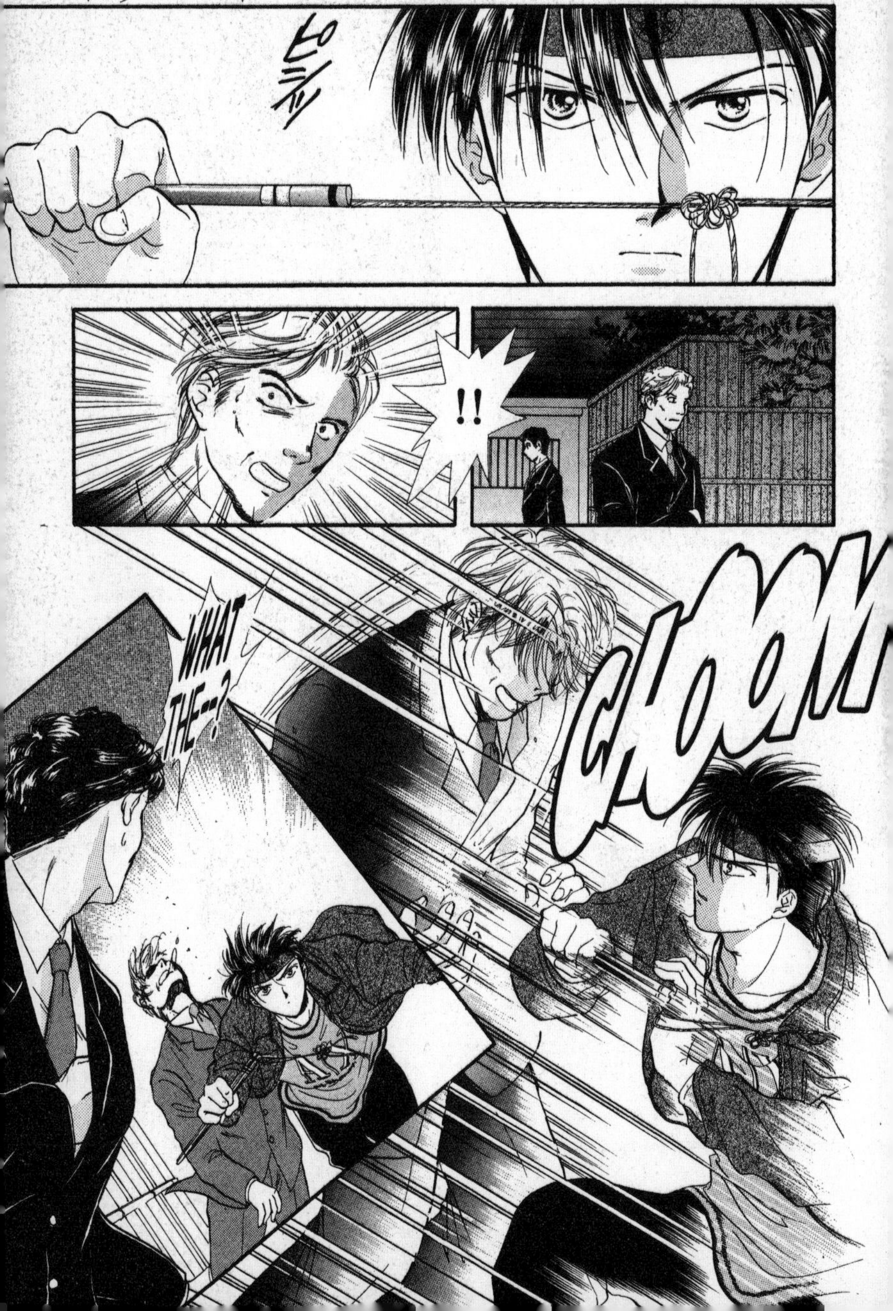
ピシッ
!!
CLOOM
WHAT THE--?

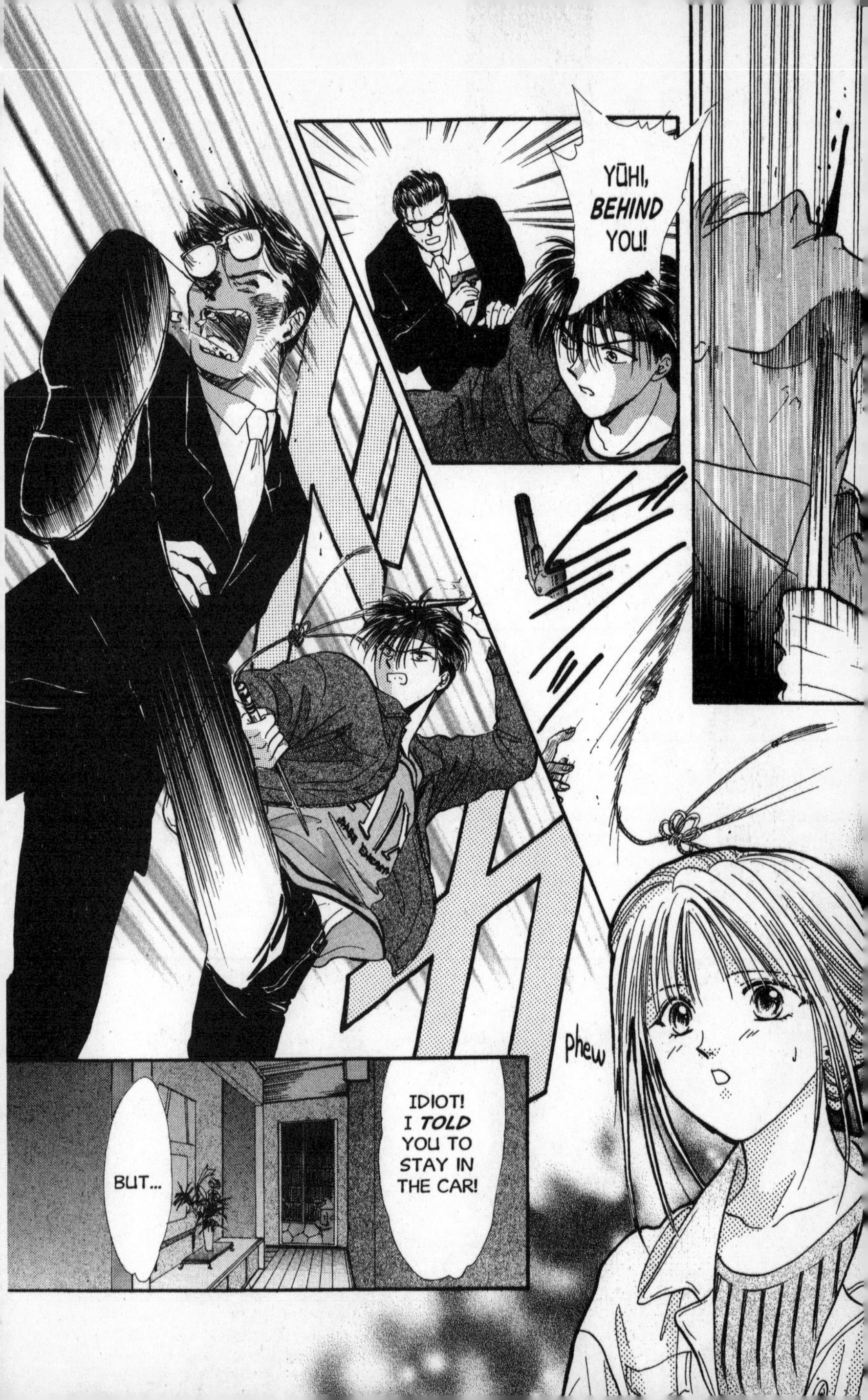
YŪHI, BEHIND YOU!
phew
IDIOT! I TOLD YOU TO STAY IN THE CAR!
BUT...

Ceres: 3

STOP RIGHT THERE!

...I'M NOT GOING TO LET YOU FACE THIS BY YOURSELF.

UNLESS YOU DON'T CARE WHAT HAPPENS TO YOUR FAMILY!

SUZUMI?!

FATHER...!

YŪHI...

STAY BACK...

...KAZUMA...

SHE'S IN "DREAMLAND" RIGHT NOW. WE CAN'T GIVE HER THE VECTOR MEDICATION...

...UNTIL SHE'S COMPLETELY OPEN TO THE POWER OF SUGGESTION.

IS IT TRUE...? YOU REALLY DIDN'T DIE...?

...BELIEVE IT... I'M ALIVE.

KAZUMA...?

YOU'RE MAKING HER SEE VISIONS OF MY *DEAD BROTHER?!*

176

◆ SUZUMI ◆

Last time I wrote about genes wearing out...and it's true! It wears all the way down and then you die. And you know how people always tell you to "Read lots of books in your teens" and "Do your homework"? That's because that's when the brain is the most active, and has the best capacity for memory.

Once you're over 20, a hundred million brain cells die each and every day (I **think** that's the right number), so your memory gets worse and worse. And alcohol! If you drink too much, it kills even more of your brain cells, so you become even more stupid than the average person. It's hard to believe people still drink. I didn't like to study when I was younger. My parents didn't force me to do my homework, but they told me, "If you don't study now, **you're** the one who's going to regret it later." ...At the time, I just said, "Yeah, right!" and stuck my tongue out at them, but let me tell you – I **do** regret not studying. ☺ Trust me, read lots of books. Especially if you want to be a writer or a manga artist. Do your homework. You **will** have a tough time if you're not well-read. Textbooks are written so that everybody can understand them. I should've read them more. I wish I could go back to school again. ☺ Students really have it easy. ☺

Hmm, this volume's columns turned out pretty educational. (Really?) Hopefully bio class won't be so intimidating anymore. Come to think of it, Mikage's company is so mysterious. The full picture isn't clear. The official name of the company is "Mikage International." But people will probably be more concerned about whether Aya ends up with Toya or Yûhi. It's no wonder she's wavering, especially under the current circumstances...

See you in the next volume!

178

179

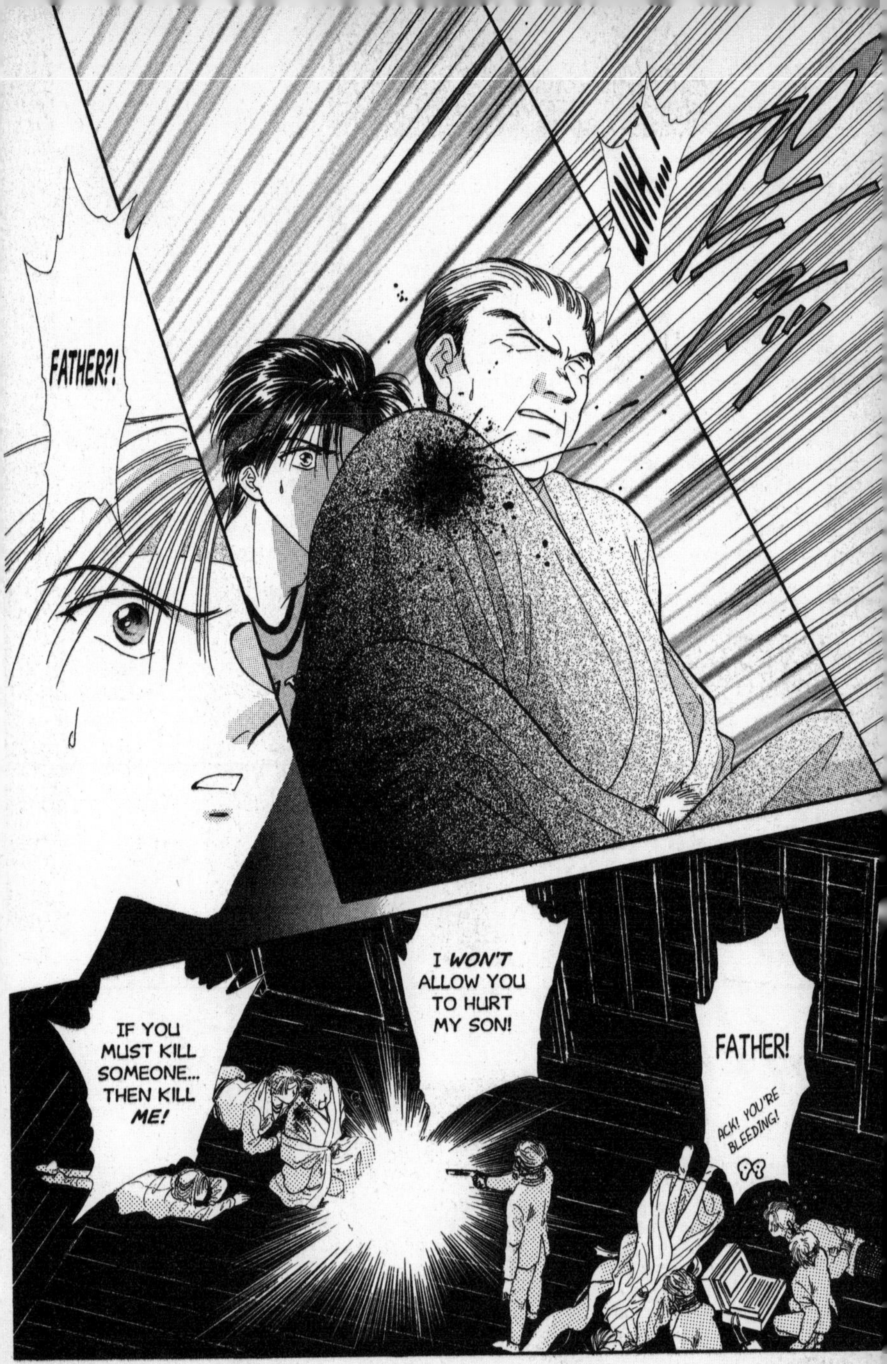
UNH...!
FATHER?!
FATHER!
ACK! YOU'RE BLEEDING!
I WON'T ALLOW YOU TO HURT MY SON!
IF YOU MUST KILL SOMEONE... THEN KILL ME!

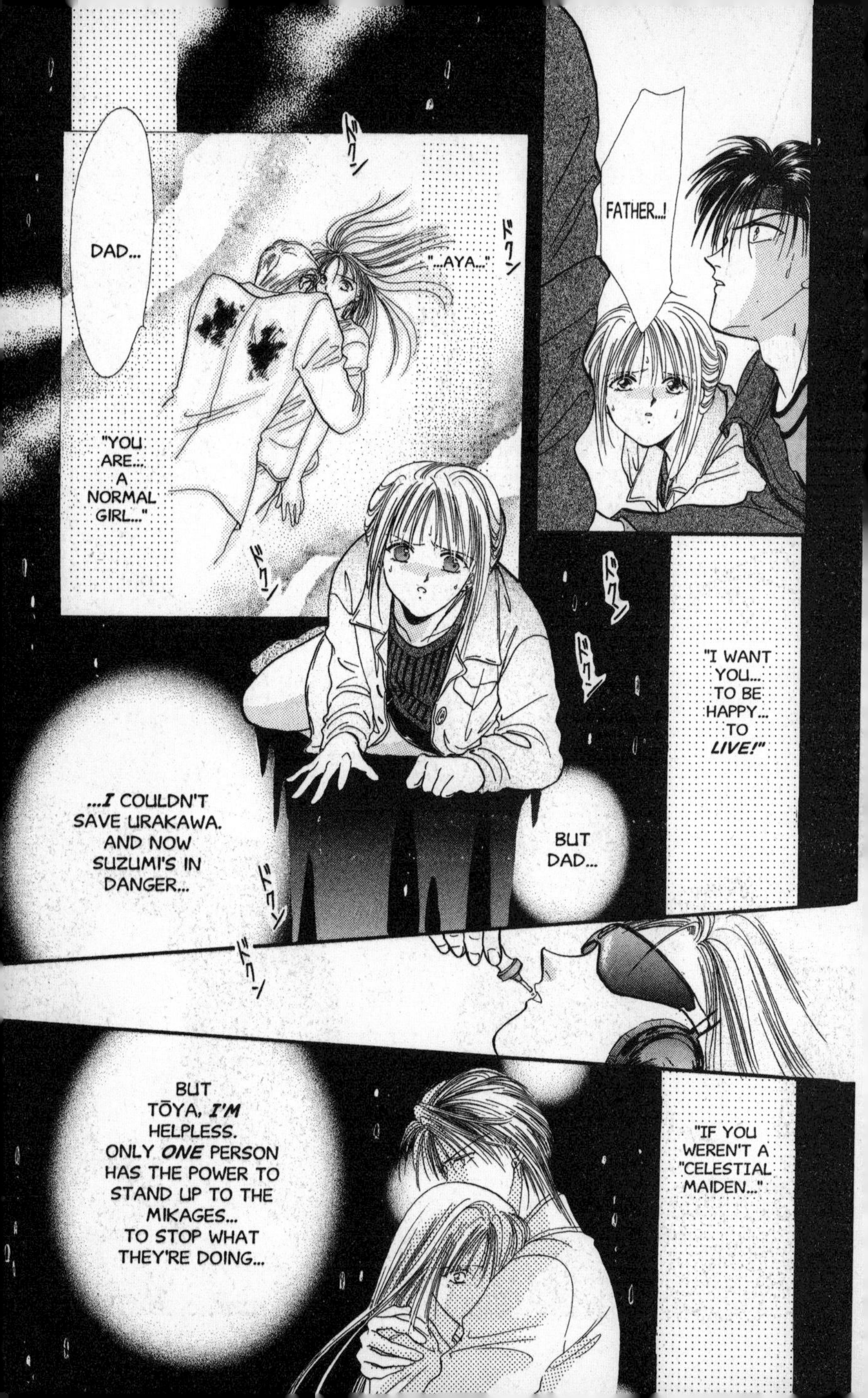
FATHER...!
DAD...
"...AYA..."
"YOU ARE... A NORMAL GIRL..."
"I WANT YOU... TO BE HAPPY... TO *LIVE!*"
BUT DAD...
...*I* COULDN'T SAVE URAKAWA. AND NOW SUZUMI'S IN DANGER...
"IF YOU WEREN'T A "CELESTIAL MAIDEN...""
BUT TŌYA, *I'M* HELPLESS. ONLY *ONE* PERSON HAS THE POWER TO STAND UP TO THE MIKAGES... TO STOP WHAT THEY'RE DOING...

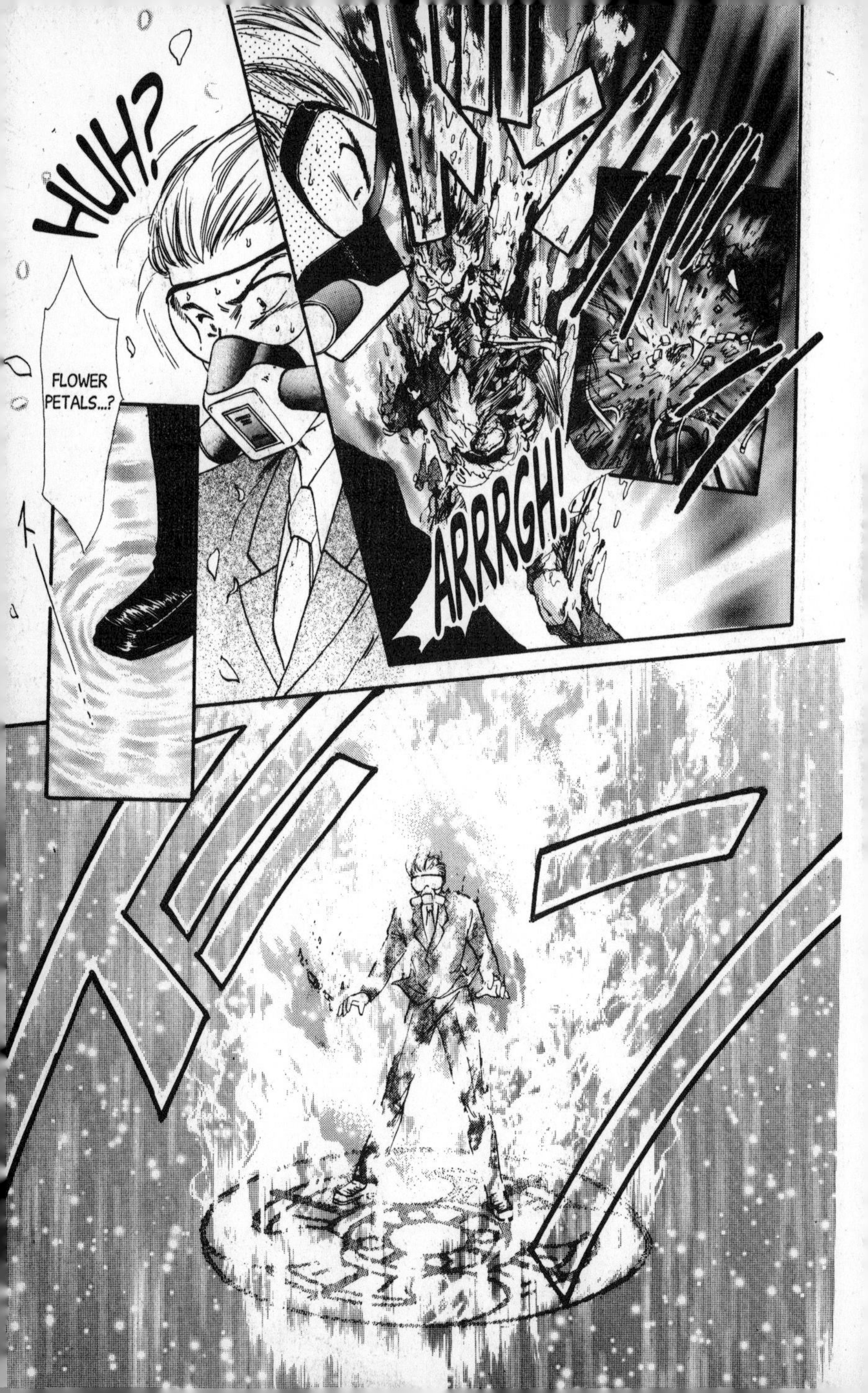
ARRRGH!
HUH?
FLOWER PETALS...?

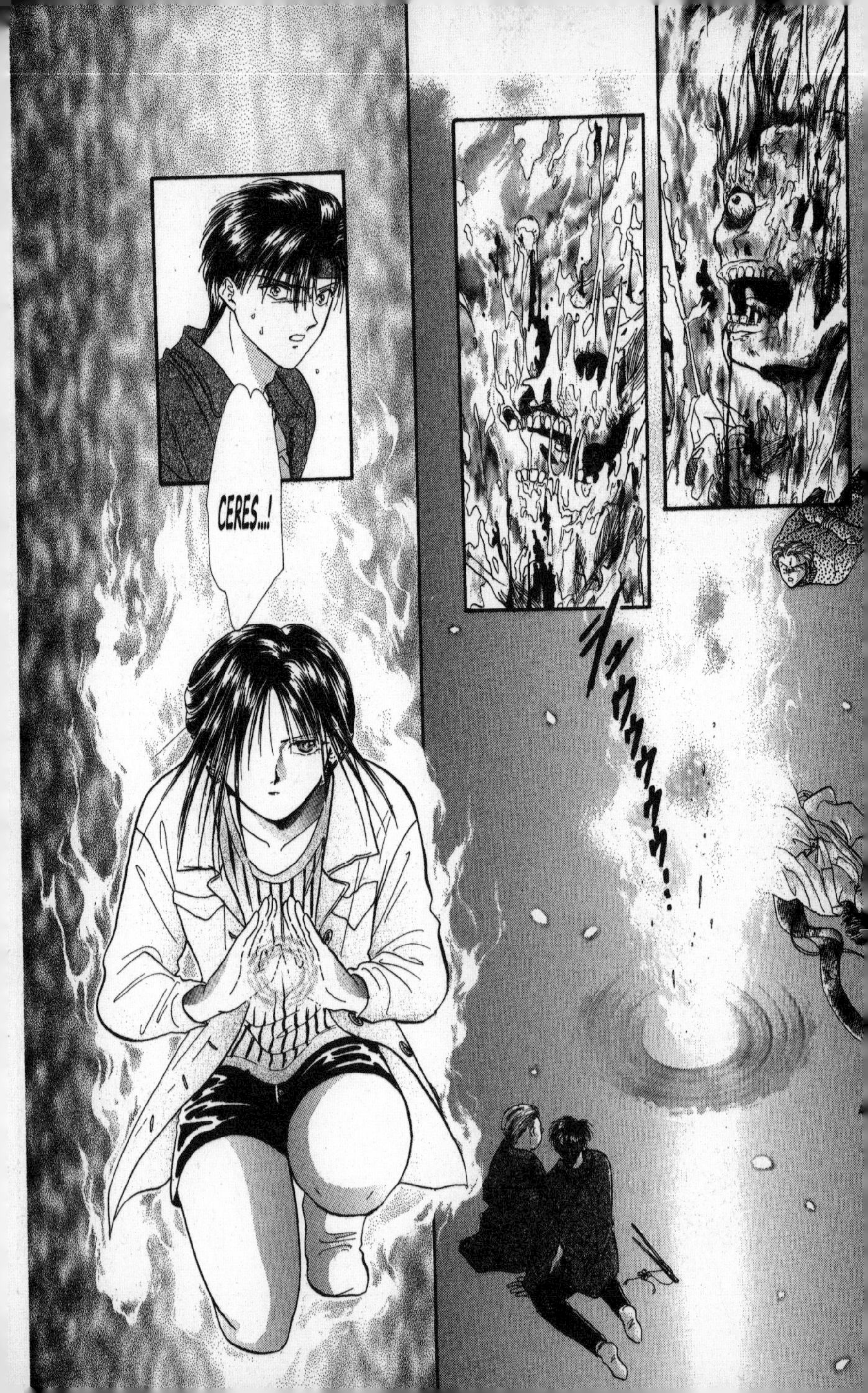
シュウウウウウウ...
CERES...!

SUZUMI...?!

ISN'T THAT RIGHT, KAZUMA?

...HE TOLD ME THAT I SHOULDN'T TAKE ANY MEDICINE...

SHE'LL NEVER COME BACK TO *REALITY*...

WE WERE TOO LATE. HER SPIRIT STILL REMAINS IN THE DREAM.

I'VE DESTROYED THE DEVICE, BUT SHE'S NOT COMING OUT OF THE HYPNOSIS.

!!

TO BE CONTINUED...

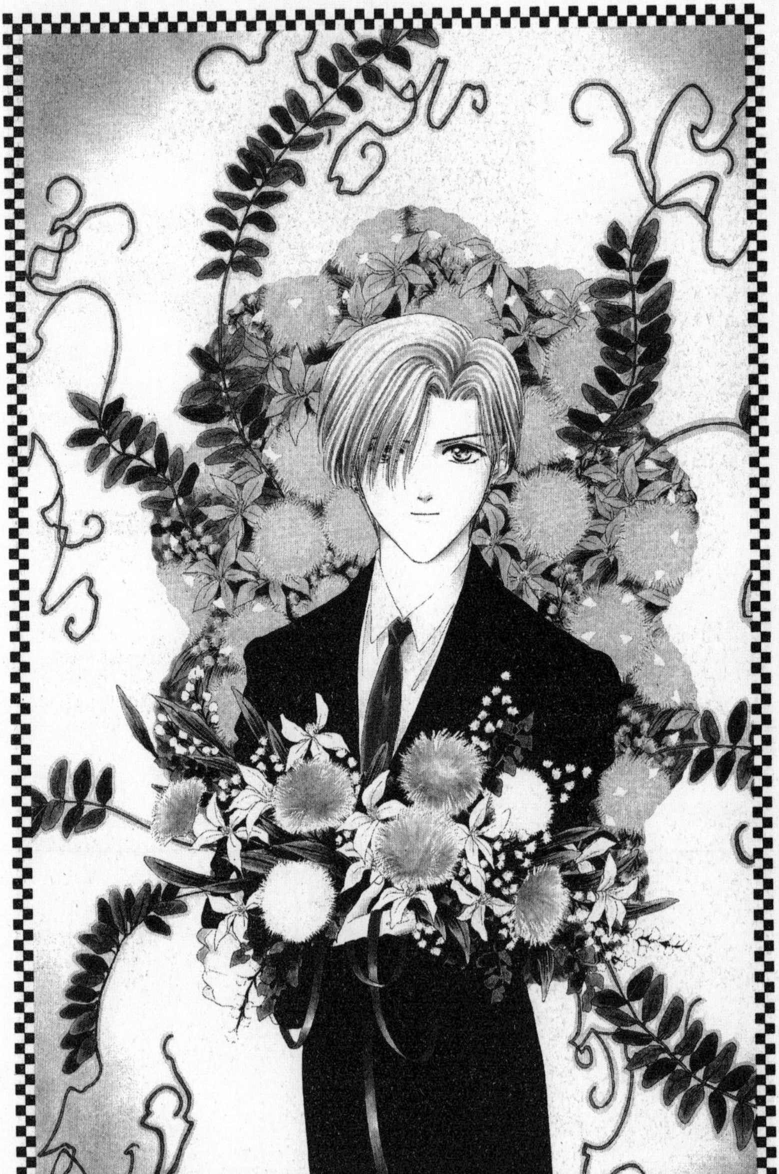

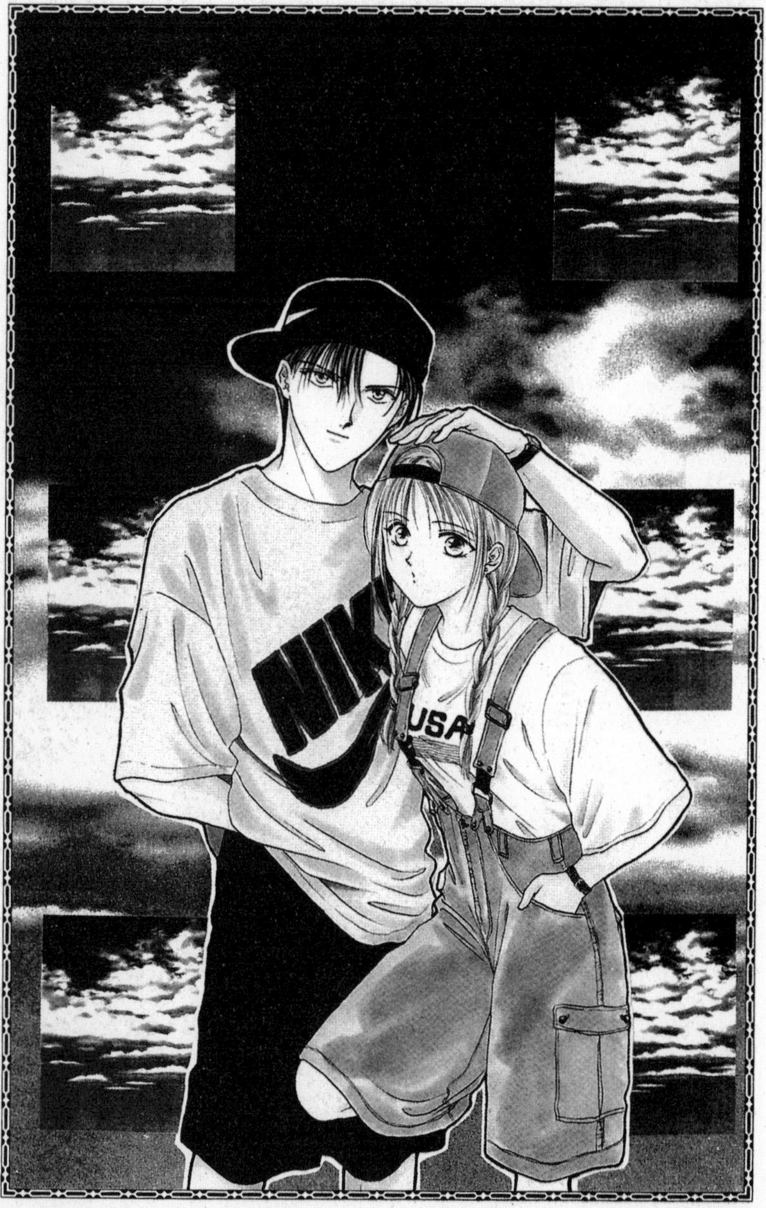
USA

The Ceres Guide to Sound Effects

We've left most of the sound effects in CERES as Yuu Watase originally created them — in Japanese.

VIZ has created this glossary to help you decipher, page-by-page and panel-by-panel, what all those foreign words and background noises mean. Use this guide to impress your friends with your new Japanese vocabulary.

The glossary lists the page number then panel. For example, 3.1 is page 3, panel 1.

20.3 FX: Pii (tweet)

22.3 FX: Za za (trup trup)
22.4 FX: Ha ha (huff huff)
22.5 FX: Fura (stagger)
22.6 FX: Don (bump)

23.1 FX: (Kya ha ha) kyaaa
23.4 FX: Zawa (rustle)

24.1 FX: Don (froomf)

25.3 FX: Kya ha ha (kyaaa)
25.4 FX: Meki meki (crackle crackle)

26.1 FX: Ga (whack)

27.4 FX: Pii poo pii poo (ambulance siren)

31.3 FX: Biku (urk)

33.1 FX: Kotsu (tup tup)

34.3 FX: Kacha (click)

35.1 FX: Uuu (arrr)

42.1 FX: Doki (ba-bump)

49.4 FX: Pasha (click)
49.5 FX: Kusu kusu kusu kusu kusu (giggle giggle giggle giggle giggle)

50.4 FX: Mu (grrr)

52.2 FX: Dokun (ba-bump)

5.2 FX: Kiin koon kaan koon (ding dong ding dong)
5.3 FX: Lin koon (ding dong)
5.4 FX: Ka (tup)
5.5 FX: Ka ka (tup tup)

6.3 FX: Ban (slam)

7.2 FX: Zuru (slump)
7.4 FX: Basa (fwap)

8.5 FX: Kyaaaa (Aaaaaa)

12.2 FX: Kaa (blush)

13.1 FX: Doki (ba-bump)
13.4 FX: Pa (fwip)

14.2 FX: Piku (twitch)
14.4 FX: Bata bata bata bata (trup trup trup trup)
14.5 FX: Gaah (gaah)

15.4 FX: Batan (slam)

16.3 FX: Ban (slam)

17.1 FX: Pa (swip)

18.2 FX: Dosa (thud)
18.4 FX: Kya ha ha (kyaaa)
18.5 FX: Kya ha ha (kyaaa)
18.6 FX: Kusu kusu (giggle)
19.4 FX: Doki (ba-bump)
19.5 FX: Mu (grr)

52.4 FX: Dokun (ba-bump)
52.5 FX: Dokun (ba-bump)

53.1 FX: Viku (flinch)
53.2 FX: Buru buru (tremble tremble)
53.3 FX: Gata gata gata (rattle rattle rattle)
53.4 FX: Piku (tup)

54.2 FX: Kata kata (rattle rattle)
54.4 FX: Kata kata (rattle rattle)
54.5 FX: Kata kata (rattle rattle)

55.1 FX: Zuka zuka (shuff shuff)
55.3 FX: Pasa (fwap)
56.2 FX: Kasa (rustle)
56.3 FX: Pasa (fwap)

57.1 FX: Dokun dokun (ba-bump ba-bump)
57.2 FX: Doku doku (ba-bump ba-bump)
57.2 FX: Jiii (sizzle)
57.3 FX: Zuzuzu (rumble)
57.3 FX: Kata kata (rattle rattle)

58.3 FX: Gyu (squeeze)

59.1 FX: Zuzu (rumble)
59.2 FX: Zuzu zu (rumble rumble)
59.2 FX: Bibi (rattle)
59.3 FX: Suu (fwish)

60.4 FX: Bo (fwoomf)

61.1 FX: Don (foomf)
61.3 FX: Dosa (thud)

63.2 FX: Ha ha (huff huff)
63.4 FX: Doon (boom)

64.5 FX: Kusu kusu (giggle)
64.5 FX: Hiso hiso (whisper)

65.1 FX: Kusu kusu (giggle)
65.1 FX: Hiso hiso (whisper whisper)
65.5 FX: Goo (roarrr)

66.2 FX: Don doon (boom kaboom)
66.3 FX: Ban (smash)
66.5 FX: Jiririri (ree ree ree)

67.1 FX: Don (bump)
67.5 FX: Goho goho (koff koff)

68.1 FX: Don (boom)
68.5 FX: Zu zu (slurp)

70.2 FX: Ba (slash)

72.2 FX: Za (slump)
72.4 FX: Goo (roarrrr)
72.6 FX: Ta (whoosh)

73.1 FX: Ba (slash)
73.5 FX: Kyu (wipe)

77.2 FX: Ta (tump)
78.3 FX: Za (shwiff)

79.2 FX: Su (shuf)

80.6 FX: Hyu (whoosh)

81.1 FX: Don (foomf)

82.1 FX: Chaki (cha-chink)
82.4 FX: Goo (roarrr)

83.1 FX: Zan (splash)
83.2 FX: Ha ha ha (huff huff huff)
83.4 FX: Zapa (spluush)
83.5 FX: Yoro yoro (stagger stagger)

84.5 FX: Boo (foomf)

85.3 FX: Dogu (thwok)
85.4 FX: Do (foom)

86.1 FX: Ba (leap)

87.3 FX: Zan (splash)

88.4 FX: Ha ha (huff huff)

89.2 FX: Ha ha ha ha (huff huff huff huff)

90.1 FX: Don (boom)
90.2 FX: Shu (fsssst)

93.5 FX: Ba (shwup)

94.1 FX: Ban (slam)
94.2 FX: Katsu katsu (tup tup)
94.3 FX: Katsu katsu katsu (trup trup trup)

96.1 FX: Pan (pop)
96.4 FX: Bikun (flinch)

97.1 FX: Bo (foom)
97.1 FX: Ha ha (huff huff)
97.2 FX: Ha ha (huff huff)
97.3 FX: Ha ha ha (huff huff huff)

98.3 FX: Zuru (slump)
98.3 FX: Fu (huff)

99.4 FX: Fu (fft)
100.1 FX: don (slam)
100.3 FX: Yoro (shudder)

102.1 FX: Bo (foomf)
102.5 FX: Zoro (slump)

105.1 FX: Piku (fft)

106.2 FX: Muku (pop)

107.5 FX: Su (shff)

108.2 FX: Gashan (clink)
108.4 FX: Koto (tuk)

109.2 FX: Gara (rattle)

112.1 FX: Gara (rattle)

113.5 FX: Pata pata (pitter patter)

116.1 FX: Dosu (stomp)
116.1 FX: Bu (pbbt)
116.3 FX: Gu (squeeze)

119.2 FX: Pata pata (pitter patter)

125.4 FX: Gatan (clunk)

126.1 FX: Koro (roll)

127.1 FX: Gyu (squeeze)

130.1 FX: Rrrrr (telephone ringing)

131.4 FX: Koto (clatter)

132.3 FX: Beshi (whap)
132.5 FX: Kashan (clatter)

133.3 FX: Gacha gacha (clink clink)
133.5 FX: Gacha gacha (clink clink)
133.6 FX: Gachi (click)

134.5 FX: Jita bata (floof flop)

135.3 FX: Batta batta (thump bump)

136.1 FX: Karari (rattle)

137.1 FX: Ha ha ha ha ha ha ha (huff huff huff huff huff huff huff)
137.3 FX: Kusha (rumple)
140.1 FX: Gyuu (pinch)
140.2 FX: Para para (shoop shoop)
140.5 FX: Bara bara (shoop shoop)
140.6 FX: Bara bara (shoop shoop)

141.3 FX: Bau (boom)
141.4 FX: Paa Pappaa (beep beeeep)

142.1 FX: Pappaa (beep beep)
142.1 FX: Goo (roarrrr)
142.2 FX: Bara bara bara bara (shoop shoop shoop shoop)
142.3 FX: Cha (chak)
142.4 FX: Bara bara bara (shoop shoop shoop)

143.1 FX: Gya (screech)

144.4 FX: Bara bara bara (shoop shoop shoop)
144.5 FX: Gya gya (screech screech)

145.4 FX: Doon (ka-wham)
145.4 FX: Gyaaa (screech)
145.6 FX: Bara bara bara (shoop shoop shoop)

146.3 FX: Sha (shwusssh)
146.5 FX: Dokun dokun (ba-bump ba-bump)

147.3 FX: Doka doka (whack whack)

148.4 FX: Goton (clunk)
148.5 FX: Poro poro (sniffle sniffle)
148.6 FX: Petan (slump)

151.2 FX: Jara (clink)
151.3 FX: Piku (sniffle)

152.2 FX: Pikun (twitch)
152.3 FX: Jaki (clinch)
152.5 FX: Kashan (clatter)

153.1 FX: Sha (shush)

155.1 FX: Putsu (click)
155.5 FX: Fu (tink)

156.1 FX: Zawa (murmur)
156.3 FX: Gara (rattle)

157.3 FX: Dosa dosa (thud thump)

159.3 FX: Kui (tilt)
159.5 FX: Shuru (swush)
159.5 FX: Rrrr (phone ringing)
160.2 FX: Bishii (whap)
160.4 FX: Rrrr rrrr (phone ringing)

161.2 FX: Rrrr (phone ringing)
161.3 FX: Gachin (snap)
161.4 FX: Rrrr (phone ringing)
161.5 FX: Rrrr (phone ringing)
161.5 FX: Rrrr (phone ringing)

162.5 FX: Kachan (clink)
162.6 FX: Dota dota dota (tromp tromp tromp)

163.1 FX: Gara (rattle)
163.2 FX: Doki doki (ba-bump ba-bump)

164.2 FX: Gara (rattle)

165.1 FX: Gara (rattle)

168.1 FX: pi pi piii (beep beep beeeep)
168.6 FX: Gyu (squeeze)

169.3 FX: Ira ira (fidget fidget)

171.1 FX: Pita (halt)

172.4 FX: Suta suta suta (shuf shuf)
172.5 FX: Karari (rattle)

173.1 FX: Pishi (snap)

174.3 FX: Bishi (shwip)
174.4 FX: Doka (fwak)

177.2 FX: Ka (fsssht)

178.1 FX: Zuru (slump)
178.6 FX: Pi pi (beep beep)
178.6 FX: Dokun (ba-bump)

180.1 FX: Pushu (bam)

181.2 FX: Dokun dokun (ba-bump ba-bump)
181.2 FX: Dokun (ba-bump)
181.3 FX: Dokun dokun (ba-bump ba-bump)
181.3 FX: Dokun dokun (ba-bump ba-bump)

182.3 FX: Ba (woomf)
183.1 FX: Ban (crash)
183.2 FX: Don (boom)
183.4 FX: Suu (flash)
183.5 FX: Zun (boom)

184.3 FX: Shuuu (fssssssh)

185.1 FX: Sara (fwish)

186.3 FX: Poto (plip)
186.4 FX: Pashi (snap)

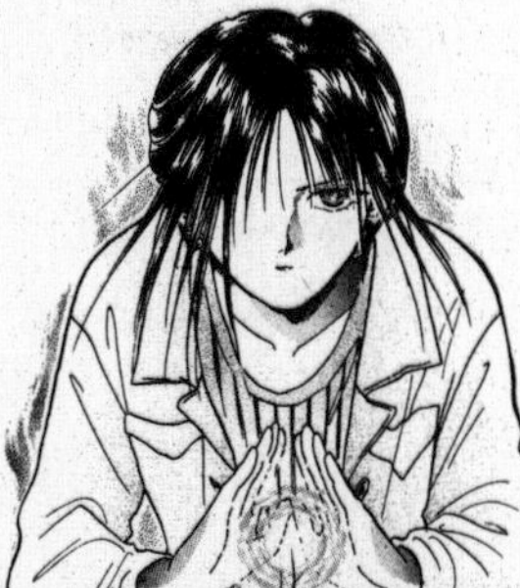

Yuu Watase was born on March 5 in a town near Osaka, Japan, and she was raised there before moving to Tokyo to follow her dream of creating manga. In the decade since her debut short story, PAJAMA DE OJAMA *(An Intrusion in Pajamas), she has produced more than 50 compiled volumes of short stories and continuing series. Her latest series,* ZETTAI KARESHI *(Absolute Boyfriend), is currently running in the anthology magazine* SHÔJO COMIC. *Watase's long-running horror/romance story* CERES: CELESTIAL LEGEND *and her most recent completed series,* ALICE 19TH, *are now available in North America published by VIZ. She loves science fiction, fantasy and comedy.*

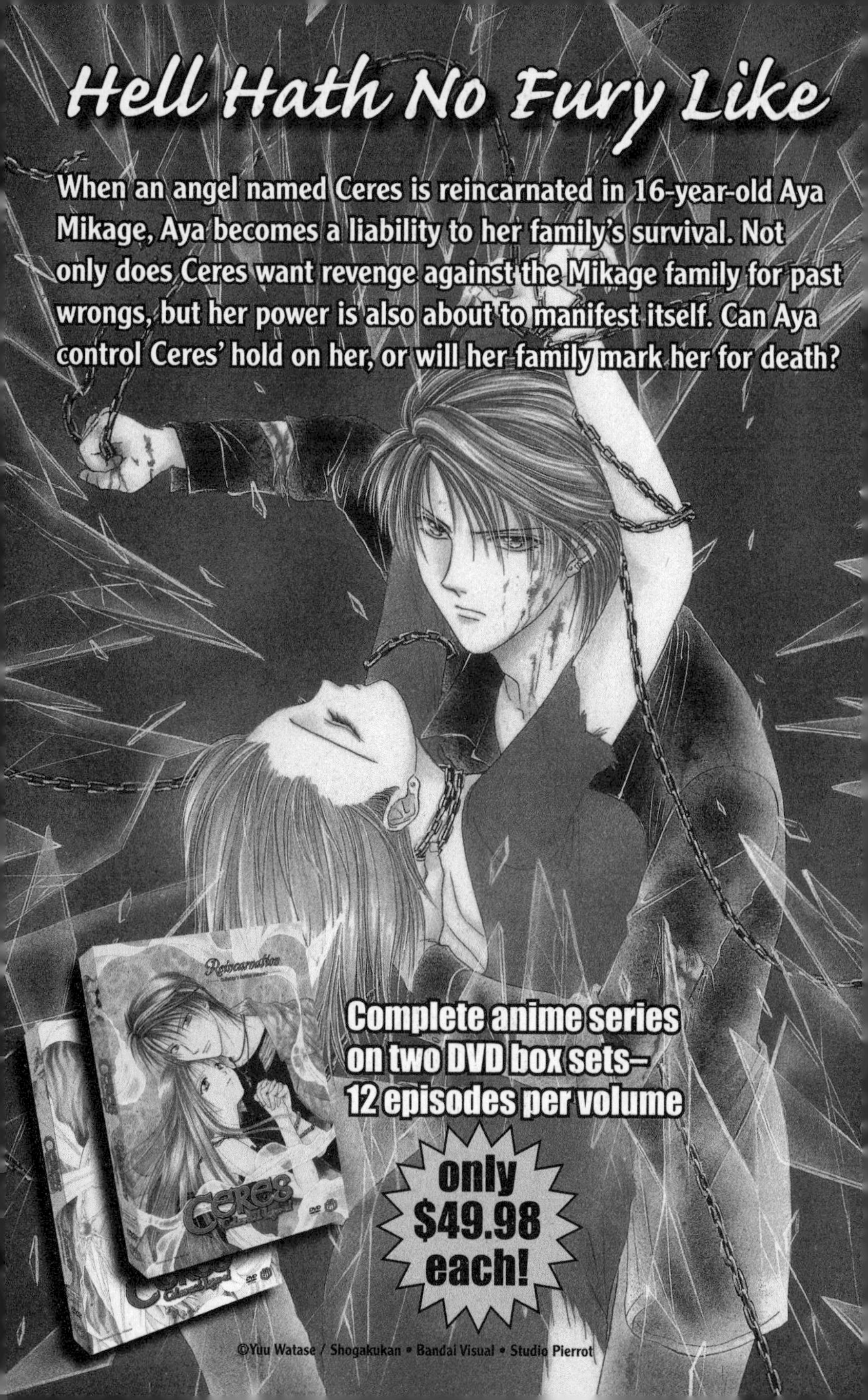
Hell Hath No Fury Like
When an angel named Ceres is reincarnated in 16-year-old Aya Mikage, Aya becomes a liability to her family's survival. Not only does Ceres want revenge against the Mikage family for past wrongs, but her power is also about to manifest itself. Can Aya control Ceres' hold on her, or will her family mark her for death?
Reincarnation
Ceres
Complete anime series on two DVD box sets– 12 episodes per volume
only $49.98 each!
©Yuu Watase / Shogakukan • Bandai Visual • Studio Pierrot

The Power of a Kiss

Soon after her first kiss, Yuri is pulled into a puddle and transported to an ancient Middle Eastern village. Surrounded by strange people speaking a language she can't understand, Yuri has no idea how to get back home and is soon embroiled in the politics and romance of the ancient Middle East. If a kiss helped get Yuri into this mess, can a kiss get her out?

Love Shojo Manga?

Let us know what you think!

Our shojo survey is now available online. Please visit **viz.com/shojosurvey**

Property of

San Mateo Public Library

Help us make the manga you love better!